RELATED APEX BOOKS

AP Calculus AB

AP Statistics

RELATED KAPLAN BOOKS

College Admissions and Financial Aid

Daystar Guide to Colleges for African American Students

Guide to the Best Colleges in the U.S.

Kaplan/Newsweek College Catalog

Parent's Guide to College Admissions

Scholarships

Yale Daily News Guide to Succeeding in College

You Can Afford College

Test Preparation

ACT

Fast Track ACT

AP Biology

SAT & PSAT

Fast Track SAT & PSAT

SAT Math Mania

SAT Math Workbook

SAT or ACT? Test Your Best

SAT II: Biology

SAT II: Chemistry

SAT II: Mathematics

SAT II: Writing

SAT Verbal Velocity

SAT Verbal Workbook

AP*
U.S. Government
& Politics

An Apex Learning Guide

Simon & Schuster

NEW YORK · LONDON · SINGAPORE · SYDNEY · TORONTO

*AP is a registered trademark of the College Entrance Examination Board, which neither sponsors nor endorses this product.

Kaplan Publishing
Published by Simon & Schuster
1230 Avenue of the Americas
New York, New York 10020

For bulk sales to schools, colleges, and universities, please contact Order Department, Simon & Schuster, 100 Front Street, Riverside, NJ 08075. Phone: (800) 223-2336. Fax: (800) 943-9831.

The material in this book is up-to-date at the time of publication. The College Entrance Examination Board may have instituted changes in the test after this book was published. Please read all materials you receive regarding the test carefully.

Editor: Ruth Baygell
Contributing Editors: Marc Bernstein, Marcy Bullmaster, and Seppy Basili
Cover Design: Cheung Tai
Interior Page Design: Laurel Douglas
Production Editor: Maude Spekes
Editorial Coordinator: Dea Alessandro
Executive Editor: Del Franz

Manufactured in the United States of America.
Published simultaneously in Canada.

May 2001
10 9 8 7 6 5 4 3 2 1

ISBN 0-7432-0191-4

Table of Contents

UNIT FIVE:
Institutions of American Government

UNIT SIX:
Civil Rights and Civil Liberties

UNIT SEVEN:
Public Policy in American Government

UNIT EIGHT:
Practice Test

APPENDIXES

UNIT ONE:

The Basics

The Basics

The AP U.S. Government & Politics Exam

So, you've decided to take the Advanced Placement U.S. Government & Politics exam. What exactly is the exam, and why should you be interested in taking it? If you have taken Advanced Placement U.S. Government & Politics in high school or have a good foundation in political science, taking the AP exam could help you earn college credit and/or placement into advanced coursework.

This book is designed to help you prepare for the AP exam. We've included information about the format of the exam, test-taking strategies, and an extensive review of essential topics. Each chapter includes review questions to help you identify your strengths and weaknesses. Also included is a practice test with answers and explanations. With Kaplan's proven test-taking strategies and the targeted political science review in this book, you'll have everything you need to ace the test.

About the AP U.S. Government & Politics Exam

What is the exam?
This exam is designed to test knowledge of one year of introductory, college-level U.S. government and politics. There are two parts to the exam:

Section I:	60 multiple-choice questions	45 minutes
Section II:	four essay questions	100 minutes

Total Length:		two hours and 25 minutes

What's covered on the exam?

The exam covers six major areas: The numbers in parentheses indicate the approximate proportion of multiple-choice questions in each area. For example, 10–20% for Political Beliefs and Behaviors indicates that there will be 6–12 questions on this subject.

1. Constitutional Underpinnings of United States Government (5–15%)

   A. Considerations that influenced the formulation and adoption of the Constitution

   B. Separation of powers

   C. Federalism

   D. Theories of democratic government

2. Political Beliefs and Behaviors (10–20%)

   A. Beliefs that citizens hold about their government and its leaders

   B. Processes by which citizens learn about politics

   C. The nature, sources, and consequences of public opinion

   D. The ways in which citizens vote and otherwise participate in political life

   E. Factors that influence citizens to differ from one another in terms of political beliefs and behaviors

3. Political Parties, Interest Groups, and Mass Media (10–20%)

   A. Political parties and elections

   B. Interest groups, including political action committees (PACs)

   C. The mass media

4. The Institutions of National Government: The Congress, the Presidency, the Bureaucracy, and the Federal Courts (35–45%)

   A. Formal and informal institutional arrangements of power

   B. Relationships among these four institutions, and varying balances of power

   C. The ties between these institutions and the following: political parties, interest groups, the media, subnational governments, and public opinion

5. Public Policy (5–15%)

   A. Policy making in a federal system

   B. The formation of policy agendas

   C. The role of institutions in the enactment of policy

   D. The role of the bureaucracy and the courts in policy implementation and interpretation

   E. Linkages between policy processes and the following:

      1. Political institutions and federalism

      2. Political parties

3. Interest groups

4. Public opinion

5. Elections

6. Policy networks

6. Civil Liberties and Civil Rights (5–15%)

A. The development of civil liberties and civil rights by judicial interpretation

B. Knowledge of substantive rights and liberties

C. The impact of the 14th Amendment on the constitutional development of rights and liberties

Anatomy of the Exam

Section I consists of 60 multiple-choice questions. There are no set categories or question types; most ask about relationships within the context of U.S. government, and a very few test your knowledge of straight facts.

Section II consists of four essay questions, called free-response questions. The questions can cover any subject in the course outline, and often will bridge two subjects, such as political institutions and public policy. Each of the four questions is equally weighted, though the nature and tasks of each will vary. You should allow about 25 minutes to prepare and write each response.

How is the exam scored?

Section I accounts for 50 percent of your overall grade, and Section II accounts for the other 50 percent. The maximum number of points you can earn is 120, with 60 points for Section I, and 60 points for Section II.

Scoring of Section I: The raw score for Section I is calculated by taking the number of questions answered correctly, and subtracting $\frac{1}{4}$ point for every incorrect response. For example, if you answered all 60 questions, 47 correctly and 13 incorrectly, your raw score would be calculated as follows:

$$\text{Raw Score} = \#\ \text{correct} - \left(\frac{1}{4}\right)(\#\ \text{incorrect})$$

$$\text{Raw Score} = \left(47 - \left(\frac{1}{4}\right)(13)\right) = 47 - 3.25 = 44.25$$

All "negative" raw scores will be rounded up to zero, so negative scores are not reported. If you did get all the multiple-choice questions wrong, you would get a score of zero.

Scoring of Section II: In this section, there are four essay questions. Each essay question may have a different point value, so there is no set maximum number of points for the raw score. However, each question—regardless of points—is given the same weight in the final AP score. So for Section II, the maximum score is 60.

Suppose that question 1 had a value of five points, questions 2 and 3 had values of six points each, and question 4 had a value of eight points. If you earned four points on question 1, four points on question 2, three points on question 3, and five points on question 4, then your score on Section II would be as follows:

$$= \left(\frac{4}{5}\right)(15) + \left(\frac{4}{6}\right)(15) + \left(\frac{3}{6}\right)(15 + \left(\frac{5}{8}\right)(15)$$

$$= (12) + (9.9) + (7.5) + (9.375)$$

$$= 38.775 \text{ points}$$

Total Composite Score: The scores from Section I and II are added to give the *total composite score*. The maximum number of points is 120.

In the hypothetical example given above, your total composite score would be: 44.25 + 38.775 = 83.025 points.

The composite scores are then converted into an AP grade from 1 to 5 (highest). The AP score uses a conversion that yields a normal distribution of grades around 3.

Composite score	AP grade	Comment
86–120	5	Extremely Well Qualified
70–85	4	Well Qualified
49–69	3	Qualified
27–48	2	Possibly Qualified
0–26	1	No Recommendation

Note: Actual scales vary from year to year. This scale applied to the 1999 exam, and should be used as an estimate only.

In the hypothetical example with a grade of 83, you would receive an AP grade of 4.

Wrong-Answer Penalty

For multiple-choice questions, there is a penalty for a wrong answer, as opposed to an answer left blank. You receive one point for a correct answer, zero points for no answer, and $-\frac{1}{4}$ point for a wrong answer. We'll talk more about what's often called the *guessing penalty* in the next section.

How Do I Get My Grade?

AP Grade Reports are sent in July to your home, high school, and any colleges designated by you. You may designate the colleges you would like to receive your grade on the answer sheet at the time of the test. You may also contact AP Services to forward your grade to other colleges after the exam or to cancel or withhold a grade.

AP Grades by Phone

AP Grades by phone are available for $13 per call beginning in early July. A touch-tone phone is needed. The toll-free number is (888) 308-0013.

Registration

To register for the exam, contact your school guidance counselor or AP Coordinator. If your school does not administer the exam, contact AP Services for a listing of schools in your area that do.

Fees

The fee for each AP Exam is $77. The College Board offers a $22 credit to qualified students with acute financial need. A portion of the exam fee may be refunded if a student does not take the test. There is a $20 late fee for late exam orders. Check with AP Services for applicable deadlines.

What You Need to Bring

- Photo I.D.
- Your secondary school code number (see your Guidance Counselor or AP Coordinator)
- Your social security number
- Several sharpened No. 2 pencils
- Eraser
- A watch, in case your exam room doesn't have a clock you can see easily.

What NOT to Bring

- Do not bring scratch paper. You will make your notes in the test booklet.
- Do not bring books, dictionaries, notes, or correction fluid.
- Do not bring beepers or cell phones, or anything that has a beeper function.
- Do not bring food or drink.

Additional Resources

For more information on the AP Program and the U.S. Government and Politics Exam, please contact AP Services at:

AP Services
P.O. Box 6671
Princeton, NJ 08541-6671
(609) 771-7300
Toll-free: (888) CALL-4-AP (888-225-5427)
Fax: (609) 530-0482
TTY: (609) 882-4118
Email: apexgrams@info.collegeboard.org
Website: www.collegeboard.org/ap/

The Basics   *Test-Taking Strategies*

Now that you've got some idea of the kind of adversary you face in the AP, it's time to start developing your strategy mindset.

The AP is a unique test: While it requires prior knowledge of facts, it goes one step further: You will be expected to draw links and analyze relationships among governmental actors and institutions, and your score will depend on your ability to do so. Nobody expects you to know off the top of your head which interest group will win in a policy battle in an agency, but you will be expected to analyze the relevant factors and relationships in such a contest. In other words, you must be able to apply the facts that you have learned in school. If you cannot, you will be at a decided disadvantage.

The goal of the AP exam is to assess your conceptual knowledge and your ability to analyze and understand relationships between governmental institutions. Try to master all the material from your AP course, with special emphasis on how the main components of government, e.g., interest groups, the judiciary, the Constitution, are related. Before test day, review the table of contents in your textbook. Or look at the *AP Course Description* (known as the "Acorn Book").

Mastery of these institutional connections is vital for success on the exam. It requires being current, so make sure you're using a textbook fewer than two years old. Try to read as much supplementary information as possible; that doesn't mean popular news magazines or the newspaper, but rather a current, college-level textbook.

You might be tempted to skip some sections from your AP course, such as civil rights or public policy. Perhaps you're short on time, or you assume you won't be tested on these topics because they haven't appeared on recent AP tests. This is a mistake: All course topics are covered in the multiple-choice portion of the test. If you lack substantive knowledge about certain topics covered in the course, your score will suffer.

1. **Read the question twice before you begin to organize your answer.**

   Be sure you're clear on what you're being asked to do: *compare*, *describe*, *explain*, *identify*, *list*, and *select* mean different things, and if your answers take this into account, your free-response answers will be stronger. Your goal is to have a clear, directed response rather than a general, undirected essay.

   If you are asked to list things, use an itemized list with numbers or with the words *first*, *second*, and *third*. This will help keep you on track as you enumerate each item, and it will clarify your list for the grader.

2. **Understand the structure of the question.**

   For the free-response portion, make sure you answer the question that is asked, rather than transform it into one you would prefer. Doing all the right work but then getting the wrong answer can be seriously depressing. So make sure you are answering the right question.

   Many questions provide a general thesis or framework in the lead sentence. In earlier years, AP questions allowed students to articulate their own theses about a general subject, though that has changed recently. Now, in order to guide you more, the Test Development Committee has redesigned the questions so that you'll be given a thesis from which to work. As you formulate your answer, don't forget to use the given thesis as background. But don't simply restate it; make sure to present a thoughtful and well-elaborated answer.

   Other questions will caution you against using certain approaches in your answer. A statement that says "Your answer should not include a discussion of presidential primary elections" is a clear prohibition. This probably indicates that the Test Development Committee felt the question would distract some students in the wrong direction, so it included this proviso.

3. **Answer free-response questions directly and explicitly.**

   You don't want to write everything you know about a subject, though you might be tempted to do this in hopes of "hitting" the target. That reasoning won't work here (and your score will suffer), so do not beat around the bush or write a vague essay with filler. The question will guide you; if you're asked to link institutional processes with public policy, write a focused essay that presents explicit links. Consider the following questions before you begin to write:

   1. What subject(s) compose the focus of the question?

   2. What tasks are you being asked to perform?

   3. What specific information is called for?

   4. What specific information about the subject do you possess?

   5. How should you structure the answer? (an outline or a sequence of material)

   6. How can you develop a clear and complete answer without being vague or writing filler?

Questions seeking a list usually want narrow, specific items. Do not list items that you would use in a general essay about the subject. If the remainder of the question asks for links, that would be the appropriate place to elaborate.

4. Factual errors may or may not be critical to your essay.

As a general rule, factual errors in an essay won't necessarily harm your essay score. In other circumstances, they can be quite fatal.

Let's say you can't remember the exact dates of Ronald Reagan's presidency (1981–1989). Your essay incorrectly says 1984–1992. That alone will not be fatal to your score unless the remainder of your essay turns on those incorrect years.

A more serious error would be one in which you began an essay with "Reagan and his National Security Advisor Henry Kissinger interacted repeatedly during of the Gulf War of 1989 to foil attempts by the secretary of defense to prosecute the war successfully." This statement contains several errors that would most certainly hurt your score. First, Kissinger was not Reagan's national security advisor. Second, Reagan was not president during the Gulf War. And third, the national security advisor during the Gulf War did not intrude on the execution of the military operations by the secretary of defense, or even interfere with the chairman of the joint chiefs or the field commander. This answer would convey that you have no grasp of facts or relationships, which could be very detrimental to your score.

5. Guess intelligently and with caution.

Random guessing will not help your score and it may very well hurt it. There is a $\frac{1}{4}$ point deduction for a wrong answer but no deduction for a blank answer. If you can rule out a few answer choices first, your odds of guessing correctly will improve.

In other words, if you know virtually nothing about a topic, and are totally stumped on a question, you're better off leaving it blank.

6. In the multiple-choice section, answer the easy questions first.

Easy questions are worth just as many points as hard questions. To maximize your score, you need to answer as many questions correctly as possible—but it doesn't matter if they are easy or hard. And if you run out of time, you'll want to be sure to have gotten to all the questions that would earn you points. So on your first pass through the multiple-choice section, answer all the easy questions. Circle the harder questions and come back to them later. Don't waste valuable time on time-consuming questions early in the exam. You're better off spending those extra few minutes answering 3 or 4 easier questions.

As a point of interest, each test question has been refined five or six times, and must pass a stringent pretest phase. Key criteria used are a) that the question is not ambiguous, b) that there is only one correct answer, and c) that the question asks about an important concept, relationship, or definition.

7. Prioritize the free-response questions according to difficulty.

Again, your goal is to score as many points in this section as possible. Read all the questions first, then decide which ones you will be able to answer most effectively. Do those essays first, and then go back to the ones that are harder for you.

8. Prepare an outline and a list of key terms.

Graders are looking for main ideas, supporting details, and key terms. Think about what you'll write, and organize the ideas into outline form before you begin writing. Make a list of key terms to include in each paragraph.

9. Mark up your test booklet.

You may be used to having teachers tell you not to write in your books. But when taking the AP exam, it is to your advantage to mark up your test booklet. Label diagrams, cross out incorrect answer choices, write down key acronyms in the margins (for example, NIMBY can help you remember the concept behind "Not in My Backyard.") But always spell out the concept the first time you use an acronym.

10. Be careful with your answer grid.

Your AP score is based on the answers you indicate on your answer grid. So even if you have aced every question, you'll get a low score if you misgrid your answers.

Be careful! Keep track of the spaces in relation to the questions—particularly if you skip around. Otherwise, you may spend valuable time erasing and regridding your answers. Also, if you do change an answer, be sure to erase your previous answer cleanly.

11. Write neatly.

Penmanship is not graded when the free-responses are read. However, a reader who must struggle to make out sentences is bound to have a harder time evaluating the essay. Write carefully, and if your handwriting tends to be hard to read, make an effort to write more legibly than usual.

If your handwriting is hard to read because you feel pressured for time, try writing fewer sentences. A concise, neater essay may be stronger than a long, messier one. Try to resist the temptation to write long answers just to fill up the page.

12. Keep track of time.

It's important to keep track of time as you work through the test. You will have to pace yourself, or else you'll run out of time.

In Section I, you'll have 45 minutes to complete 60 questions. That means about 45 seconds per question.

In Section II, you'll have 100 minutes to write four essays. Plan to spend about 25 minutes on each: 5–8 minutes planning and organizing your essay, 12–15 minutes writing, and 5 minutes to edit and proofread your work.

13. No cheating.

It is hardly necessary to indicate that such behavior is unacceptable, but you should know that cheating on AP Exams is dealt with quite severely. The effort it takes to cheat is much greater than the effort required to learn the material. Furthermore, the consequences of such behavior are very serious and long-term.

And apart from the illegal component of cheating, you would be shortchanging yourself; if you were placed in an advanced course for which you weren't fully prepared, you would find yourself at a disadvantage.

The Basics   *Stress Management*

The countdown has begun. Your date with the test is looming on the horizon. Anxiety is on the rise. The butterflies in your stomach have gone ballistic. Your thinking is getting cloudy. Maybe you think you won't be ready. Maybe you already know your stuff, but you're going into panic mode anyway. Don't freak! It's possible to tame that anxiety and stress—before and during the test.

Remember, a little stress is good. Anxiety is a motivation to study. The adrenaline that gets pumped into your bloodstream when you're stressed helps you stay alert and think more clearly. But if you feel that the tension is so great that it's preventing you from using your study time effectively, here are some things you can do to get it under control.

Take control.

Lack of control is a prime cause of stress. Research shows that if you don't have a sense of control over what's happening in your life, you can easily end up feeling helpless and hopeless. Try to identify the sources of the stress you feel. Which ones can you do something about? Can you find ways to reduce the stress you're feeling about any of these sources?

Focus on your strengths.

Make a list of areas of strength you have that will help you do well on the test. We all have strengths, and recognizing your own is like having reserves of solid gold at Fort Knox. You'll be able to draw on your reserves as you need them, helping you solve difficult questions, maintain confidence, and keep test stress and anxiety at a distance. And every time you recognize a new area of strength, solve a challenging problem, or score well on a practice test, you'll increase your reserves.

Imagine yourself succeeding.

Close your eyes and imagine yourself in a relaxing situation. Breathe easily and naturally. Now, think of a real-life situation in which you scored well on a test or did well on an assignment. Focus on this success. Now turn your thoughts to the test, and keep your thoughts and feelings in line with that successful experience. Don't make comparisons between them; just imagine yourself taking the upcoming test with the same feelings of confidence and relaxed control.

Set realistic goals.

Facing your problem areas gives you some distinct advantages. What do you want to accomplish in the time remaining? Make a list of realistic goals. You can't help feeling more confident when you know you're actively improving your chances of earning a higher test score.

Exercise your frustrations away.

Whether it's jogging, biking, pushups, or a pickup basketball game, physical exercise will stimulate your mind and body, and improve your ability to think and concentrate. A surprising number of students fall out of the habit of regular exercise, ironically because they're spending so much time prepping for exams. A little physical exertion will help to keep your mind and body in sync and sleep better at night.

Avoid drugs.

Using drugs (prescription or recreational) specifically to prepare for and take a big test is definitely self-defeating. (And if they're illegal drugs, you may end up with a bigger problem on your hands than the AP U.S. Government & Politics test.) Mild stimulants, such as coffee or cola can sometimes help as you study, since they keep you alert. On the down side, too much of these can also lead to agitation, restlessness, and insomnia. It all depends on your tolerance for caffeine.

Eat well.

Good nutrition will help you focus and think clearly. Eat plenty of fruits and vegetables, low-fat protein such as fish, skinless poultry, beans, and legumes, and whole grains such as brown rice, whole wheat bread, and pastas. Don't eat a lot of sugar and high-fat snacks, or salty foods.

Work at your own pace.

Don't be thrown if other test takers seem to be working more furiously than you during the exam. Continue to spend your time patiently thinking through your answers; it will lead to better results. Don't mistake the other people's sheer activity as signs of progress and higher scores.

Keep breathing.

Conscious attention to breathing is an excellent way to manage stress while you're taking the test. Most of the people who get into trouble during tests take shallow breaths: They breathe using only their upper chests and shoulder muscles, and may even hold their breath for long periods of time. Conversely, those test takers who breathe deeply in a slow, relaxed manner are likely to be in better control during the session.

Stretch.

If you find yourself getting spaced out or burned out as you're taking the test, stop for a brief moment and stretch. Even though you'll be pausing on the test for a moment, it's a moment well spent. Stretching will help to refresh you and refocus your thoughts.

"Managing Stress" adapted from "The Kaplan Advantage Stress Management System" by Dr. Ed Newman and Bob Verini, copyright 1996 by Kaplan, Inc.

UNIT TWO:

Foundations of American Government

Chapter 1   *The Study of American Politics*

The study of government and politics is enhanced by the use of an analytic approach with which to explain relationships and behavior. No single approach is necessarily the best or the most definitive. Nor does any single approach satisfactorily explain all aspects of U.S. government. By using an analytical approach, however, one acquires a consistent understanding of the relationships among actors and institutions, and an explanation for outcomes and policy results.

Listed below are the major categories to consider when examining U.S. government and politics. Keep in mind that these are not commensurable variables.

1. **Actors** are individuals or groups that seek to obtain goals through political activity and policy-making.

   > The value of using an analytic framework is that it provides a consistent and systematic overview of all the pieces of the puzzle.

2. **Interests** are the values that people hold. These might be economic, social or philosophical, or political values. These fuel the actions and efforts of actors in politics.

3. **Institutions** involve the formal organizations that exercise political power. Congress, the president, the courts, and the bureaucracy are all institutions that develop and implement public policy, as formally outlined in the Constitution.

   Less formal institutions also play a significant role in government and politics. These include political parties, interest groups, and the mass media. Considered to be linkage institutions rather than formal, governmental institutions, these institutions focus on the accomplishment of a goal in the political system.

The interconnected-
ness among interests,
individuals, and insti-
tutions is one of the
most important fea-
tures of politics and
government in this
country.

4. **Processes** are the steps that various actions, that is, policy proposals, must go through to approach formal public policies. This is the way the policy-making institutions formally consider policy proposals.

5. **Outcomes** are the actual results of these components. Outcomes may be in the form of an adopted formal policy, or they may be no action and a continuation of the status quo. Their impact and consequence on policy are an important feature of politics and government.

Various analytic perspectives could explain U.S. government and politics. Each may contribute to understanding, although none is a completely adequate or satisfactory perspective.

Government involves the institutions and processes by which public policies are made for a society. Politics is connected to questions of who gets what, when, and how. Politics produces an authoritative allocation of values in our society.

Elitism is based on the idea that political decisions and power are controlled by a small elite of powerful, often rich, individuals. This perspective posits that society is divided along class lines, based on wealth and tradition, and upper-class elites rule, regardless of whatever else appears to be taking place.

Pluralism posits that policy is the product of group conflict and that the public interest tends to emerge from competing individual and group claims as they bargain and compromise. No single interest can dictate the outcome; people must compromise or form coalitions in order to attain their goals.

Hyperpluralism is an extreme form of pluralism. A hyperpluralistic government is so fragmented, and pressures from competing interest groups are so diverse, that it gets very little done. The result is often gridlock.

To assess your
knowledge of a politi-
cal approach, take a
subject, e.g., interest
groups, and assess
its role in different
frameworks.

The *political system* provides a "systemic" view of relationships between individuals, interests, institutions, and policy decisions. It explains politics in terms of:

- inputs (the demands and supports from individuals or intermediate groups);
- processing of these inputs by the formal institutions of government;
- outputs (the policies set forth by the government); and
- feedback (from outputs to the actors).

Power is the ability to cause others to modify their behavior. It is a constant feature of government and politics, though power is quite unevenly distributed among actors and institutions. This perspective views actors and actions in terms of what interests possess what power, and how that power influences governmental actions.

A *political culture* underlies the behavior of Americans and the values they have within the political system. These values serve as the context in which politics takes place, and though they are not homogeneous across the country, there is a degree of uniformity that underlies most political actions and behavior.

POINTS TO REMEMBER

- The result of government and politics is policy that is desirable to at least some, if not most, citizens.

- People and interests seek favorable policies by participating in politics and government.

- The government involves formal and informal power relationships between and among actors and institutions.

- The politics of the United States is unique. Its uniqueness comes from our history, our experiences, and cultural values.

- Politics operates in the context of formal institutions of government and the interests of individuals and groups of actors.

KEY TERMS AND CONCEPTS

aristocracy

A system of government in which control is based on rule of the highest class.

capitalism

An economic system based on individual and corporate ownership of the means of production and a supply-demand market economy.

communism

A political, economic, and social theory based on the collective ownership of land and capital and in which political power lies in the hands of workers.

conservative

One who believes in and supports the typically traditional values of conservatism, and who resists change in the status quo.

democracy

A system of government placing the ultimate political authority in the people. Derived from the Greek words *demos* (the people) and *kratos* (authority).

direct democracy

A system of government in which the people, rather than elected representatives, directly make political decisions. This system is probably possible only in small political communities.

free market economy

The economic system in which the invisible hand of the market regulates prices, wages, and production.

gridlock

A situation in which government is incapable of acting on important issues often because of divided government.

indirect (or representative) democracy

A system of government that gives citizens the opportunity to vote for representatives who will work on their behalf.

liberal

A person slightly to the left of the center of the political spectrum who believes that change is good. Today's liberals tend to believe that the government has a role in preserving individual freedoms and equality, and in solving social and economic problems.

libertarian

One who favors a free market economy and no governmental interference in personal liberties.

majority rule

The central idea of governance in which only policies that have the support of a majority of voters will be made into law.

minority rights

Protections that guarantee that the minority will not be destroyed because they favor policies or actions different from the majority.

monarchy

A form of government in which power is vested in a monarch, an hereditary king and/or queen.

oligarchy

A form of government in which the right to participate is limited to those who possess wealth, social status, military position, or achievement.

personal liberty

A fundamental characteristic of democracy in the United States that protects individuals from government intrusion or interference.

political culture

Political beliefs and attitudes concerning government and political process held by a group of people, such as a community or nation.

political ideology

The collectively held ideas and beliefs concerning the nature of the ideal political system, economic order, social goals, and moral values.

politics

The method in which decisions are made, either by or for a society, to allocate resources, distribute benefits, and impose costs. Politics is a difficult term to define and has been summed up in many ways, including: "the art of the possible," the "authoritative allocation of values," "who gets what, when, and how" in a society, and "the competition among individuals and groups over the allocation of values or rewards."

popular consent

The idea that government must draw its powers from the governed or the people who are sovereign.

popular sovereignty

A principle originating in natural rights philosophy that claims political authority rests with the people and not the government. People have the right to create, change, or revolt against their government. In practice, people usually choose representatives to exercise their political authority.

republic

A government in which ultimate sovereignty belongs to the people, and the people elect officials to represent them in government decisions.

social contract

A basic tenet of liberal democracy that people are free and equal by natural right and therefore people give their consent to government. Advocated by John Locke and reflected in the Declaration of Independence.

socialism

A political philosophy that supports government control of markets and production as well as government determination of peoples' needs for social and economic benefits.

totalitarianism

A philosophy of politics that advocates unlimited power for the government so that it controls all sectors of society.

Multiple-Choice Questions

1. All of the following characteristics are features of the pluralist analytic perspective except

   I. A multiplicity of institutional access points

   II. A diverse and numerous set of actors with competing policy objectives

   III. Changing coalitions of actors

   IV. A single process for making policy outcomes

   A. I and II

   B. II and III

   C. III and IV

   D. III

   E. IV

2. Political participation is an essential element of all of the following approaches except

   A. the political system.

   B. elitism.

   C. pluralism.

   D. power.

   E. hyperpluralism.

3. The value or importance of an analytic framework in understanding politics and government is that

   A. it predicts results of the process.

   B. it explains all dimensions of politics and government.

   C. it encompasses all the variables that might account for policy outcomes.

   D. it provides a comprehensive and systematic perspective of politics.

   E. it results in the disclosure of truth.

4. Initiatives and referenda are examples of

   A. direct, popular government.

   B. Republicanism.

   C. political party control.

   D. oligarchy.

   E. indirect democracy.

5. Popular sovereignty can be defined as

A. translation of legislation into a set of government programs and policies.

B. the level of popular support that presidents enjoy from approval surveys.

C. the influence that public opinion polls have in deciding policy questions.

D. the right of the majority to govern themselves.

E. the idea that governments draw authority from the governed.

Essay Questions

1. List three variables that pluralism uses to explain politics. Then, list three variables that elitism uses in explaining politics. Compare and contrast these two approaches in terms of democratic policy making.

2. Select one approach below and identify at least three strengths and one weakness it has for studying government and politics.

- Elitism

- Pluralism

- the Political System

ANSWER KEY

Multiple-Choice Questions

1. E
2. B
3. D
4. A
5. D

Essay Questions

1. Variables that could be listed for the pluralist approach to explaining politics include:

   - Many interest groups with specialized or narrow interests
   - Competition among interests for governmental attention
   - A number of policy making institutions
   - Various processes for influencing policy making

   Elitist variables might include:

   - Powerful, concentrated policy makers, usually based on economic power
   - Members of the elite are strongly and actively engaged in politics as well as ideologically committed to their interests
   - Elite members may or may not occupy elected positions in order to control policies
   - There are interlocking connections among the members of the elite so the same actors appear in various policy making contexts

   The question does not specify the number of comparisons and contrasts required, so a general statement of comparison and contrast is probably sufficient.

   Comparisons:

   1. Both approaches provide a comprehensive perspective for explaining politics and policy results.
   2. Both approaches tie institutions to actors and to results (policies).

   Contrasts:

   1. Pluralism is a more complicated explanation for policy outcomes than is elitism: pluralism involves more actors, and both winners and losers, and they cannot be easily predicted by pluralists beforehand.
   2. Elitism is a more simplistic approach to explaining politics because everything is the result of the presence of a controlling elite.

2. This question asks you to identify three strengths and one weaknesses of one approach. Make sure that you do precisely that, or your answer will be incomplete.

Strengths	**Weaknesses**
Elitism	
Provides a consistent and uniform explanation for all political activity.	Does not account for outcomes or policies that are not in the supposed elite's interests.
Focal point of explanation, the elite, is relatively easy to uncover.	Too simplistic an approach to identify the subtleties and complexities of politics.
Requires attention to the relative power and influence of actors.	
Focuses on coordinated efforts by elite members in all areas of policy making.	
Pluralism	
Accommodates the empirical evidence that different parties and interests "win" different political battles throughout the country.	The extreme of this approach is complete chaos and conflict among interests, none with enough influence to prevail, or win, in policy contests.
Provides some explanation for the confusion that exists in explaining politics in this country.	Ignores or cannot accommodate unorganized interests who may not even get their views articulated.
Permits recognition of temporary policy coalitions.	
Encourages open government with many different access points for influence	
Political System	
Provides a comprehensive view of politics and government. All the actors, institutions, and processes "fit" somewhere in this model.	No clear specification of relationships or prediction of outcomes (policy results) using this approach.
Emphasizes the connections among pieces of the political system.	Relationships between parts of the political system are not clearly spelled out.
Requires attention to all the actors and interests that might affect policies and outcomes.	
Provides a methodical treatment of politics and government.	

Chapter 2   *Constitutional Foundations*

A constitution is an essential part of a democratic political system. Whether written, as is the U.S. Constitution, or unwritten, as is the British Constitution, this organic document outlines a structure for policymaking and governing institutions, and specifies the powers that those institutions should possess. It outlines how officials are selected and how long their terms will be; it specifies the relationship between the government and its people, both in terms of the power of institutions to act and in terms of the rights and liberties that government cannot infringe; and it specifies how constitutional changes or amendments must be made.

More specifically, a constitution does the following:

- It outlines the institutions of governance.

- It provides for the selection and tenure of those who exercise power.

- It articulates the powers as well as the limits of the institutions.

- It defines the relationship between the government(s) and individual citizens.

- It provides an explicit method(s) for amending or achieving formal changes to the organic act.

Though written over two centuries ago, the U.S. Constitution still reflects values that are central to our political culture: individual liberty; inalienable rights; limited government power and suspicion of powerful government; and participatory and representative democracy.

In the United States, the power delegated to national and state institutions has evolved a good deal since those institutions were created. In examining the U.S. Constitution, both as originally drafted and as it operates today, many questions can be raised about how well these functions are being performed.

The U.S. Constitution

The Declaration of Independence listed "life, liberty, and the pursuit of happiness" as basic human rights. The elaboration of these rights was the foundation for the U.S. Constitution:

1. People have certain inalienable rights that the government must ensure or protect, and secure. This means governing by consent of the governed.

2. Government has the ability to become all powerful, and to protect against that, government is limited to the powers delegated to it by the Constitution. One way to do this is to divide the government among institutions.

3. The people are to participate in governing themselves, either directly or through elected representatives.

4. The government is a creature of the people, so the people can dissolve the government when it no longer achieves their goals and objectives. This embodies a social contract perspective on the creation of government.

The U.S. Constitution was created to organize central power in this country and to fashion a relationship between the central government and the states. It was founded on the proposition that, since the people are sovereign and possess natural rights and independence, the government must govern with the consent of the people. Written in language that was vague and open-ended, the intention was to design a Constitution that could evolve with some flexibility, according to practice, evolution, experience, and need. And in fact today, many people attribute the Constitution's longevity and success (and failures) to that ambiguity.

Articles of Confederation

After the Revolution, the way in which the thirteen states made policy and governed themselves remained unchanged. The states remained sovereign in a true confederal system. A central government was a foreign idea that most colonists did not consider or find useful. The Continental Congress worked for some five years, until 1781, when the Articles of Confederation were written. The Articles were little more than a loose outline with no central government, but they were in essence the first constitution.

There were a variety of problems with the Articles of Confederation:

1. There was no central executive to enforce acts of Congress.

2. There was no taxing or revenue authority, so the only money the central government had was the money given it by individual states.

3. There was no military to defend the country.

4. There was no centralized power to regulate or protect against commercial warfare among the states or with other countries.

5. The amending process to change the Articles required the unanimous agreement of all thirteen states.

As a result of these difficulties, there was great civil and economic unrest, including Shay's Rebellion, forcing many prominent state leaders, including James Madison and George Washington, to press for a constitutional convention. Madison succeeded in getting most state legislatures to send delegates to a convention so that the Articles could be amended. Only Rhode Island failed to send delegates.

In 1787, delegates met with the intention of amending the Articles of Confederation. However, they quickly agreed that the Articles were unwork-able and needed to be replaced, not amended. This constitutional convention engaged in lengthy debate and "loud" argument over several constitutional issues, which were eventually resolved or finessed (left to be resolved later).

The framers of the Constitution were a collection of landed aristocratic white men who were interested in creating an effective and stable central authority. They were also interested in protecting their own economic interests. While they agreed on the importance of stability and mediated interstate conflict, they disagreed about the wisdom and reliability of the people to govern themselves. They also disagreed about various economic issues, including slavery and commercial activity. In the end, the framers developed a consti-tution that reflected a good deal of compromise among their perspectives. The issue of the "reliability" of the masses in government was resolved through the following mechanisms:

> The Constitution balanced competing interests among the framers, particularly those who advocated a stronger central government against those concerned with the loss of state independence and power. That balance is different today than it was at the time of drafting the Constitution.

1. The Connecticut Compromise or the "Great Compromise" balanced the interests of the large (populous) and small states by creating a bicameral legislature.
   - The House of Representatives would be the only directly elected legislative body, and it would be based on the population in each state. A representative's term in office would be two years.

- The Senate would be elected by state legislatures and thus represent the states' interests. Each state would have the same representation in the Senate: two senators who would serve six years each.

2. The chief executive—the president—would be elected indirectly by an electoral college, selected through popular voting in each state. The presidential term in office was set at four years, and he would be removable by impeachment or by non-reelection.

3. Judges would be appointed by the president, with the advice and consent of the senate. Federal judges would serve during good behavior and they would be removable by impeachment.

Some framers feared that a strong central government would result in a one-sided concentration of power. As a result, the separation of powers divided the power of the central government into three separate branches: legislative, executive, and judicial. Each branch would assume some role(s) in the operation of the other branches, so that no one branch could indiscriminately do as it pleased. This is known as *systemic checks and balances*. The power of the central government was also limited by the continued existence of the states, and the federal system of government.

The original drafters doubted the ability of the general population to govern and make decisions, but today, most Americans do participate in some political activity. Some are so deeply involved that they influence policy decisions. This level of participation was not built into the Constitution but it was also not prohibited.

The ratification (approval) of the Constitution between 1787 and 1789 gave rise to what were the first "political parties": the Federalists (advocates for) and the Anti-Federalists (opponents to) the Constitution. The debate over ratification in New York produced the Federalist Papers, anonymously written by (Federalists) Alexander Hamilton, John Jay, and James Madison to persuade the New York legislature to ratify the Constitution. These are the only contemporaneous commentaries on the provisions of the Constitution, and they are still used today to fashion meaning from some parts of the Constitution. In order to win Anti-Federalist support for the Constitution, the Federalists agreed to a compromise agreement, the Bill of Rights. This document related primarily to the relationship between the government and the individual, and it contained the core civil rights and liberties we enjoy today.

The election of George Washington as the first president involved the appointment or election of various proponents and opponents to the government. This meant the framers helped develop the operation of the government by participating in its implementation.

Constitutional Amendments

The Constitution has been formally amended only 27 times, though there have been hundreds of proposed amendments introduced in Congress. Formal amendments are not often used today. Rather, practice has come to be the primary determinant for constitutional adaption, including those decisions made by the Supreme Court which make changes in interpretation. For example:

1. The "advice and consent" of the senate in treaty-making now means that the Senate votes to approve or reject a treaty negotiated by the president.

2. President Washington began the practice of a two-term limit for the presidency, until Franklin Roosevelt violated that practice by running for and winning a third term in 1940. After that, the Constitution was formally amended to impose a two-term limit on presidential service (Amendment XXII) in 1951.

> The powers of modern-day political institutions have grown substantially in order to permit the kind of governance that people desired or felt was necessary.

3. Supreme Court interpretation of the Constitution and the operation of the government has allowed the Constitution to change. For example:

   - The power of judicial review was established by the Court in the case of *Marbury v. Madison* (1803). It gave the Supreme Court a major role in determining the validity of legislative acts and presidential actions.

   - The Court's interpretation of the necessary and proper clause in *McCulloch v. Maryland* (1819) added greatly to the discretionary power of the Congress when enacting legislation.

   - The Court's selective incorporation of the Bill of Rights through the Due Process Clause of the 14th Amendment has applied most of the protections of the Bill of Rights to the states. This occurred gradually throughout the 20th century.

POINTS TO REMEMBER

- The Constitution is both an historical artifact and an operational document still functioning today.

- The Constitution structures power and relationships among various contending actors in our system, and it is used to advantage (or disadvantage) by most actors in order to gain desired policy ends.

- The meaning of the provisions of the Constitution has evolved over time. This adaptation has been a major feature of the survival of the Constitution and the continued stability of the political system.

- The Constitution strikes a balance between competing values, such as freedom and order, or central/decentralized power and control.

- As they wrote the Constitution, the framers finessed two major difficulties by reaching some compromises: the status of the entire slavery issue, and the nature of the Union (whether the Union was created by the people or by the states).

KEY TERMS AND CONCEPTS

10th Amendment

The final part of the Bill of Rights that declares "the powers not delegated to the United States by the Constitution, nor prohibited by it to the states, are reserved to the states respectively, or to the people."

advice and consent

Power the Constitution (Article II, Section 2) grants the U.S. Senate to give its advice and consent to treaties and presidential appointment of federal judges, ambassadors, and cabinet members.

amendment process

The means spelled out in Article V by which formal changes in, or additions to, the Constitution are made.

anti-federalist

A person opposed to the adoption of the Constitution because of its centralist tendencies and who attacked the Constitution's framers for failing to include a Bill of Rights.

Articles of Confederation

The compact made among the 13 original states to form the basis of their government. Officially adopted in 1781.

bicameral legislature

A legislature made up of two parts. The U.S. Congress, composed of the House of Representatives and the Senate, is a bicameral legislature.

Bill of Rights

The first ten amendments to the U.S. Constitution. They contain a listing of the freedoms that a person enjoys and that cannot be infringed on by the government, such as the freedoms of speech, press, and religion.

checks and balances

A major principle of the U.S. governmental system whereby each branch of government exercises a limiting power on the actions of the others and in which powers are distributed among the three branches in a manner designed to prevent tyranny.

confederation

A political system in which states or regional governments have ultimate authority except for those powers expressly delegated to a central government. Member governments voluntarily agree to limited restraints on their actions.

delegates to ratifying conventions

Representatives from each of the 13 original states who attended their state conventions to ratify the Constitution. These delegates were chosen by special elections. Nine of the 13 states had to vote to ratify for the Constitution to become the law of the land.

Democratic-Republican

The political party founded by Thomas Jefferson in 1792. It was dissolved in 1828.

elastic clause

The final paragraph (clause 18) of Article I, section 8 of the Constitution, which grants Congress the power to choose whatever means are necessary to execute its specifically delegated powers. Officially known as the "necessary and proper" clause.

electoral college

The group of electors selected by the voters in each state and Washington, D.C. This group officially elects the president and vice president of the United States.

enumerated powers

Powers specifically granted to the national government by the Constitution. The first seventeen clauses of Article 1, Section 8, specify most of Congress' enumerated powers.

faction

A group in a legislature or party acting in pursuit of some special interest or position.

federalist

A person who supported the adoption of the new Constitution and the creation of the federal union. As a group, federalists formed the first American political party, which was led by Alexander Hamilton and John Adams.

Federalist No. 10

A Federalist Paper written by James Madison that discusses factions (or single interest groups) that seek to dominate the political process.

Federalist Papers

A group of 85 essays published in several New York newspapers in 1787 to persuade people in New York to adopt the Constitution, which had recently been drafted in Philadelphia. Alexander Hamilton, James Madison, and John Jay wrote the Federalist Papers under the name Publius.

Great Compromise

The compromise reached during the Constitutional Convention of 1787 between the New Jersey and Virginia plans, creating a bicameral government with states represented equally in the Senate and by population in the House of Representatives. Also called the Connecticut Compromise, the Great Compromise gave disproportionate influence to states with small populations by granting them equal representation in the Senate.

Hamilton, Alexander (1755–1804)

The first U.S. Secretary of the Treasury. He established the National Bank and public credit system.

implied powers

Authority possessed by the national government by inference from those powers delegated to it in the Constitution.

indirect democracy

Democracy in which people do not directly govern or directly vote for their representatives. For example, citizens vote for the electoral college, which elects the president.

interstate commerce

The buying and selling of commodities, transportation, and other commercial dealings across state lines. It also includes radio, television, telephone, and telegraphic transmissions.-

judicial review

The power of courts to judge legislative or executive acts unconstitutional. All national and state courts hold this power, though the highest state or federal court usually makes the final decision. Judicial review is not mentioned in the Constitution. The Supreme Court claimed this power in *Marbury v. Madison* (1803). Judicial review is based on the following assumptions: the Constitution is the law of the land, acts that violate the Constitution are void, and the judicial branch is best suited to protect and interpret the Constitution.

Madison, James (1751–1836)

Fourth President of the U.S. (1809–1817). A member of the Continental Congress and the Constitutional Convention, he wrote many of the Federalist Papers, including Federalist No. 10 and Federalist No. 51.

Madisonian model

The political philosophy proposed by James Madison that espoused a system of checks and balances and harmony among differing interests. Madison's assumptions were that the primary dangers of a republican government were factions and the possibility of tyranny if power became too concentrated. To counter these dangers, he argued for a powerful, three-branched national government that could hold state governments in check and prevent the national government, or its branches, from exercising too much power. The Constitution produced during the Philadelphia Convention of 1787 owes much to this model.

***Marbury v. Madison* (1803)**

This case that struck down for the first time in U.S. history an act of Congress as unconstitutional. It declared the Constitution to be the supreme law of the United States, and that it was "the duty of the justice department to say what the law is."

mischiefs of faction

Madison's reference, in Federalist No. 10, to his concern about the dangers posed by "factions," or groups, who might attempt to dominate the political process. He warned such dangers could take place if political parties misused their freedom and created conflict by pitting their interests against one another. While factions will always exist, Madison argued, a republican (or representative) system could control them.

natural rights

The doctrine that humans have certain inalienable rights in a "state of nature" and that government's role is to protect these rights. American political culture claims that all people hold these rights and a government can't infringe on them. John Locke claimed natural law was superior to human law and specified the rights of "life, liberty, and property." The writers of the Declaration of Independence changed these to "life, liberty, and the pursuit of happiness."

necessary and proper clause

The final paragraph of Article I, section 8 of the Constitution, which delegates legislative powers to the Congress. Also known as the elastic clause.

nullification

Declaring something null or void. Before the Civil War, states' rights advocates in the South claimed a state had the right to nullify a national law. They argued that ultimate power rested with the state governments.

popular sovereignty

A principle originating in natural rights philosophy that claims political authority rests with the people and not the government. People have the right to create, change, or revolt against their government. In practice, people usually choose representatives to exercise their political authority.

Publius

The name used by the three authors of the Federalist Papers: Hamilton, Madison, and Jay.

rage for paper money

Madison's reference, in Federalist No. 10, to the decision by some state governments to print currency that was not backed by gold. This meant the money was essentially worthless, yet it would allow farmers and other debtors to pay off their debts. This action was perceived as a threat by creditors and other members of the propertied class, of which Madison was one.

ratification

The formal approval, as of a law or Constitutional amendment.

separation of powers

The principle that divides American government among three branches: the executive, legislative, and judicial. The officials of each branch come into power in different ways, have different terms, operate independently from one another, have different responsibilities, and have a series of checks and balances over the other branches. The system is devised to prevent any one branch from gaining too much power and to prevent the same agents from making, enforcing, and interpreting the laws.

Shay's Rebellion

An armed revolt by farmers in Massachusetts in 1786–1787, seeking relief from debts and possible foreclosure of mortgages. It is credited with being a major factor in the demand for revision of the Articles of Confederation.

social contract perpective

A theory that posits that government is formed by the people, by means of an agreement by which all agree to give up some of their freedom and liberty in exchange for a safe environment.

state

A political community with a specific territory, organized government, and internal and external sovereignty. Sovereignty often hinges on the state's recognition by other states, which allows it to enter into international agreements. The term *state* is also used to refer to smaller subunits within a federal government system, as is the case in the United States.

super majorities

Defined voting blocks of greater than 51 percent needed to approve a proposal. For example, a two-thirds vote is required for proposing a constitutional amendment.

supremacy clause

The provision in the Constitution (Article VI) that makes the Constitution, federal government, and federal laws superior to state and local laws that contradict them. The supremacy clause does not give the federal government absolute power in all arenas and over all issues, but only on issues over which the federal government has a constitutionally granted authority.

unicameral legislature

A legislature made up of only one legislative body, as distinct from the bicameral, or two-house, legislature used by the U.S. Congress. Nebraska is the only unicameral state legislature, though many local governments use this form.

writ of habeas corpus

Habeas corpus is Latin for "you have the body." It's a court order that requires a jailer to bring a person to a court and explain the charges on which he is being held. If sufficient cause for imprisonment is not produced, the prisoner must be released. This is considered the most important guarantee of liberty because it protects citizens against arbitrary imprisonment. The right to habeas corpus is guaranteed in the Constitution, though Congress can suspend it in cases of rebellion or invasion. President Lincoln suspended the writ on his own during the Civil War, though Congress later affirmed his doing so.

writ of mandamus

An order issued by a court to compel performance of an act.

Multiple-Choice Questions

1. The presentment clause in the Constitution states that
   A. the House of Representatives must be presented with appropriations bills first.
   B. the president must be presented with bills passed by both houses of Congress for his approval or veto.
   C. the Senate must give its advice and consent to treaties negotiated by the president.
   D. each house of Congress must be presented with bills that have been approved by the other chamber.
   E. the vice president must be allowed an opportunity to break a tie vote in the Senate.

2. The Federalists and the Anti-Federalists disagreed about all of the following except:
   A. the need to have the people represented in the new government.
   B. the amount of power given the national government by the Constitution.
   C. the power of the central government versus that of the states.
   D. the absence of a Bill of Rights in the original Constitution.
   E. the need to ratify the Constitution.

3. The process of amending the Constitution can include all of the following except:
   A. a two-thirds vote by both houses of Congress to approve a proposed amendment.
   B. a vote of two-thirds of the states to call a constitutional convention.
   C. a vote of three-fourths of the states to call a constitutional convention.
   D. ratification by three-fourths of state legislatures.
   E. ratification by three-fourths of state conventions.

4. Judicial Review has which of the following characteristics?
   I. It was first announced in Marbury v. Madison.
   II. It was a point on which the framers all agreed.
   III. It applies to federal laws.
   IV. It applies to state laws.

      A. I
      B. I and II
      C. I, II and III
      D. II, III, and IV
      E. I, II, III, and IV

5. The 27th Amendment to the U.S. Constitution states that pay increases for congressmen may not go into effect until after a new Congress is elected. This amendment was first proposed and sent out for ratification in

   A. 1951.

   B. 1817.

   C. 1939.

   D. 1789.

   E. 1847.

Essay Questions

1. Compare and contrast the separation of powers with the principle of checks and balances. Use three examples, at least one from each branch of government.

2. Some constitutional experts believe the framers represented only the interests of their own economic class (property, money, and political power, i.e., an aristocracy.

   Identify and explain three provisions of the Constitution that support this thesis, and three provisions that refute this thesis.

ANSWER KEY

Multiple-Choice Questions

1. B
2. A
3. C
4. E
5. D

Essay Questions

1. This question asks you to compare and contrast the separation of powers with checks and balances, using three examples. First, you could begin with a definition of both principles. This would provide a comparison between them at the outset.

    Separation of powers focuses on the separate functions or powers of each branch. It relates to individual powers that are unique to each branch. Checks and balances are more numerous, relating to the cooperation necessary and the overlap between the branches.

    How you structure your examples is a matter of judgment, but be sure that they illustrate the similarities and differences between the two principles.

Separation of Powers	Checks and Balances
Legislation must be initiated and approved by Congress.	Senate approves treaties developed by the president.
The chief executive enforces enacted laws.	The House and Senate must approve identical bills before it can be signed into law by the president.
Courts settle legal disputes that arise under the laws: statutes and the Constitution.	The president must rely on Congress to appropriate and authorize the expenditure of money to carry out laws.
Each branch derives its authority from different constituents.	The courts rely on the parties and other branches of government to enforce its decisions.
The occupants serve for different lengths of time.	Congress can alter the federal courts' jurisdiction.
Presidents can pardon convicted persons.	The president has veto power over legislation.
Congress can impeach the president.	Courts can rule a statute unconstitutional.
Congress can override a presidential veto.	Presidents appoint justices with the advice and consent of the Senate.

2.   The thesis that the framers represented only the interests of the aristocracy originated with historian Charles Beard. Whether it is a correct thesis is not the question. Rather, you are being asked to identify and explain three constitutional provisions that support the theory, and three provisions that refute the theory.

Support the Thesis

Indirect election of president and senators: This illustrates the doubt the historian had about the wisdom of the populace and their choices.

Lack of a bill of rights or set of civil rights and liberties: This reflects a strong preference for a central government that could maintain order.

The power to regulate commerce among the states: This reflects the desire for stable economic relations and regulation and control of interstate commercial activities.

The Due Process Clauses protect property as well as life and liberty. Neither of these, in the 5th and 14th Amendments, were written by the framers but were added later. So these are probably not as strong as the provisions of the original Constitution as support for the thesis.

The Supremacy Clause: This made the U.S. Constitution, the statutes, and treaties the supreme law of the land.

Any provision of the Constitution that could be argued as protecting property: The slavery provisions, protection from export tariffs, and so forth. These suggest that the goal of the Constitution was to protect the economic interests of the would-be elite.

Refute the Thesis

Direct election of U.S. Representatives: This could reflect the framers' interest in opening the process to ordinary citizens.

The origination of appropriations bills in the House: This could indicate a belief that the taxpayers (the people) should have control over the initiation of government revenues.

No grant of policy power to the central government in the Constitution: This indicates the desire to let states protect the health, welfare, and safety of the people.

Regarding the Bill of Rights, the tremendous boost of the first eight amendments to personal freedom and liberties counters the thesis.

Chapter 3   *The Federal Framework*

Federalism is a division of governmental authority between at least two levels of government. In the United States, those two levels are state and federal (national). This arrangement differs from a unitary government, in which all governmental power is lodged in a central government, or from a confederal government, which involves a league of sovereign states joining together for limited purposes.

The value of a federal system is that it provides some limitations on both levels of government, and it ensures that the policies enacted address local, regional (state), and national interests. The two levels of government act directly on the people within a jurisdiction, so the people of New York and California, for example, are subject to both the same federal policies and different state policies. Local government in the United States is considered a creature of state government rather than an independent (third) level of government.

While federal-state relations have always been a central feature of American government, this relationship has evolved over time. And since the relationship is not specified in the Constitution or in judicial decisions, the evolution is sure to continue.

Various factors affect the actual relationship between the two levels of government, the two greatest being the U.S. Constitution and money. The Constitution has established a foundation for the federal relationship. However, with expanding federal policymaking and Supreme Court decisions, the federal-state relationship has changed federalism over time. Taxing, or revenues/expenditures by each level of government, has affected the relationship as well, because money allows governments to control people. This is called *fiscal federalism*. Fiscal federalism is based on the flow of money and the consequent control the government has over lower levels of government. As new federal policies are adopted, and as they provide state and local governments with financial incentives and regulations, federalism changes.

Central vs. Peripheral Power

The system of supreme control at one level of government in this country has evolved over the years. Originally, under the Articles of Confederation, the states possessed ultimate authority. But with the writing of the Constitution in 1787, the federal-state relationship changed: The national government gained significant power, and that reduced the power of the states.

Moreover, two events in our nation's history changed that relationship even more. First, the Civil War settled, though by force, the nature of the Union. States could not secede from the Union or interpose themselves between the central government and the people. That meant that the U.S. Constitution was not a creation of the states, but rather a creation of the sovereign people. Second, the Civil Rights Amendments (the 13th, 14th, and 15th Amendments) gave a significant amount of new and unique power to the federal government, vis-à-vis the states.

Today, some of the more important features of federalism in the United States are:

- The federal government has had increased independence since it began collecting more revenue (federal taxes) and spending it for the defense and general welfare of the nation.

- The federal government has the power to regulate, and to police, interstate commerce. This power has been expanded greatly through Supreme Court interpretation.

- The *Necessary and Proper Clause* (the elastic clause), which delegates legislative powers to the Congress, provides the federal government with choices for determining how (i.e., selecting the means by which) it achieves policies.

- The *Supremacy Clause* (Art. VI, Paragraph 2) specifies that the U.S. Constitution and the law and treaties made under it are the supreme law of the land. This general principle establishes federal supremacy if there is a conflict with any state law.

- Some powers are explicitly denied to the national government and those are listed in Art. I Section 9. These include, for example, no titles of nobility, spending requires prior appropriation, and no tax can be imposed on exports from any state.

- The 10th Amendment articulated the principle that the powers of the federal government were those itemized in the Constitution. It left the residual powers to the people or to the states.

- Each state has, in its constitution, some indication that the people grant it general police powers. In other words, the states have the power to enact laws that promote the welfare of the people, by protecting their "health, safety, welfare, and morals." The U.S. Constitution does not contain such a general grant of police power to the federal government.

- The Constitution does ensure some aspects of state power. First, in order to amend the Constitution, three-fourths of the states must concur. Second, state legislatures originally elected U.S. senators so that state interests could be directly represented in the national legislature. Third, states must agree to any changes in their physical boundaries. And fourth, states are prohibited from some powers. For example, states cannot enter into treaties, coin money, or impair the obligation of contracts. Art. I, Section 10 contains a list of these.

The Constitutional Division of Power

There are different kinds of constitutional power. *Enumerated powers* are those powers that the Constitution explicitly assigns to the federal government. An example is the power to regulate interstate commerce. *Implied powers* are those powers that can be inferred from the explicit powers. These might include the power to create the Federal Reserve Banking System to "regulate the value of money." *Inherent powers* are those powers that are not expressly granted to the federal government, but are nevertheless required in order to ensure the nation's survival. An example of this would be the power to make war and negotiate terms of peace. *Reserved or residual powers* are those powers not identified in the Constitution, and so are reserved to the people or to the states. *Concurrent powers* are joint powers that both the state and federal governments posses, such as the power to tax and spend.

The state/federal relationship will always be in flux. This relationship depends on "the times" or circumstances. It depends on money and politics. It also depends on the Supreme Court acceptance of some idiosyncratic statutes that protect only parochial (state or local) interests. This creates tension with the national government's desire to ensure uniform, central laws. There are several dimensions to this tension:

1. How strong should the central government be?

2. How independent and strong should the state governments be?

3. For a period in the late 19th and early 20th centuries, the Supreme Court's doctrine of dual federalism left some areas of power beyond the reach of both levels of government. That doctrine was replaced by Court interpretations since the 1930s. However, recent Supreme Court decisions in *United States v. Lopez* (1994) and *Printz v. United States* (1997) indicate that some members of the court have once again adapted that perspective (that is, a view that the states and the national government have coequal sovereign powers).

4. It is "the people" who created both the state and the federal constitutions. However, many people think that the states are necessary to protect individuals from the power of the federal government.

Federal Supremacy

Federalism has evolved largely through its focus on the Constitution and the Supreme Court's interpretation of relevant provisions. Some of the most significant court decisions have included:

1. *McCulloch v. Maryland* (1819)

   The Supreme Court held that the Necessary and Proper Clause permitted Congress to create the National Bank, even though there is no explicit grant of such power in the Constitution. It further held that a state could not tax an instrumentality of the central or national government because that unit was a creation of all the people.

2. *Gibbons v. Ogden* (1824)

   The Court held that Congress' power to regulate interstate commerce should involve an expansive and general reach to include commerce in general.

3. *N.L.R.B. v. Jones & Laughlin Steel* (1937)

   The Supreme Court held that Congress could regulate labor-management relations in a factory because of the effect it had on interstate commerce.

4. *Heart of Atlanta Motel v. U.S.* and *McClung v. Katzenbach* (1964)

   The Court upheld the Civil Rights Act of 1964, which prohibited racial discrimination in places of public accommodation because (1) of the effect discrimination had on people travelling in interstate commerce and (2) of the negative effect on the flow of articles in commerce that result in racial discrimination.

5. *South Dakota v. Dole* (1987)

   The Court held that the federal government could condition the receipt of federal money for highways in states that adopted a federal drinking age of 21 years.

6. *Printz v. United States* (1997)

   In this recent case, the Court held that the federal government could not require state and local law enforcement officials to enforce a federal law without providing federal money and state acceptance of that federal support.

The Dynamics of Federalism

Because most federal programs involve the expenditure of great amounts of money, often by state and local government recipients, fiscal federalism has gradually become quite significant. While most government revenues (taxes) are generated at the national level, the state, local, and single-purpose districts are often allocated federal money to administer.

All levels of government are involved in fiscal federalism, that is, national, state, local (general purpose), and single-purpose governments. Some taxing and revenue powers are shared among these levels. However, most government revenue is generated at the national level. Tax revenues may come in the form of taxing property (real or personal); sales/transactions; or income. The federal government focuses primarily on taxing income, though there also are some federal sales taxes, e.g., on tires and gasoline, and property taxes, e.g., on luxuries. Money raised from income taxes has lead to increasing amounts of federal revenue—and expenditures—for federal programs.

State governments, on the other hand, rely more heavily on sales taxes, and local governments rely most on property taxes. And because local governments have few other sources of incomes, the revenue received from those property taxes is not very great. As a result, some states end up with very low revenues and thus low expenditures and few public programs. Local governments have even lower levels of revenues to fund local programs. These levels of government rely heavily on federal monies for revenue.

With regard to spending, the different levels of government have both similar and different powers. The federal government often restricts how federal monies are spent by state or local governments. Federal programs involve a variety of expenditure arrangements, and these all have limitations that recipient governments (state, local, or special districts) must comply with in order to receive the money. General units of government like a state government may spend for the general welfare of the people. However, a state government may spend federal funds only for the purposes or the policy specified by federal law. Special units of government, such as school districts or water districts, can spend for those single purposes.

> Revenue is crucial to governmental policies. Without it, the government could not adopt programs that require spending or the distribution of goods and services. As the source of government revenue, taxes are a source of widespread complaint, but without them, the government could not respond to the needs of people.

Federal programs include various spending mechanisms and limitations. The programs include:

- *Grants-in-Aid* or *Categorical Grants* are narrow and specifically focused on a particular policy of the federal government. These programs limit spending to the discretion and flexibility of the recipient government. Specific types of categorical grants are:

    1. *Formula Grants*, distributed according to a formula that specifies which governmental recipients are eligible and how much they're eligible to receive.

    2. *Project Grants*, based on competitive applications. These require competition by the recipient governments and some do not received these funds because they have lost to a competitor. For these grants, matching is often required. The recipient government must provide sources of its own money to match the federal money it receives. The interstate highway system, for example, required a 10% state match to receive 90% of federal funds to build the interstate highways.

- *Block Grants* are more general than Categorical Grants, in that they treat large segments of policy, i.e., community development, law enforcement, or education. For these, recipient governments have more flexibility in determining how to spend the federal funds.

For economic and political reasons, a state government may limit local government's taxing and spending. Home-rule would give the local government independent authority to tax and spend, but few states have given any of their cities or towns such unilateral power. States generally do not trust these localities with this kind of independence.

In order to offset the legal and economic limits on revenue and spending that local and state governments face, they often seek federal money. This makes the recipient government dependent on federal money. It also means the federal government exerts control over employment, spending, and policy practices of the recipient government.

Taxpayers can most easily oppose increased taxes at the local or special-district level, because they can reject special tax levies and bonding efforts in local elections. And, at this level, opposition to state taxation tends to be more visible than at the federal level. Most often, voters reject spending choices and bond issues at a state level of government where they may have some control through the voting process. But local voters have no say over federal spending or the regulations and limits that come with federal money.

Federalism will continue to evolve with issues, policies, and the preferences of the people. Things to look out for in the future:

- The federal government may continue to enact laws that federalize criminal acts—even though it has no police power.
- For policies like health care and welfare, a continued shift of responsibility from the federal government to individual state governments (called *devolution*).
- Increased cost burdens on state and local governments for unfunded mandates. These are federal requirements for state or local programs that receive no federal funds.

POINTS TO REMEMBER

- The federal/state balance of power written into the Constitution has changed drastically over the years. It is a continuing rebalancing of power, responsibility, and money. This continual change involves the courts, the federal government, and state rights advocates.

- Federal money may not be sufficient for various programs. As a result, severe limits are imposed on recipient governments—in terms of policy choices and spending decisions.

- The necessary and proper clause, the commerce clause, and the spending clauses of the U.S. Constitution have all contributed to the growth of federal power in the federal/state relationship. That is because federal revenues have grown with an expanding economy and because the federal government's role in making policy has increased greatly since the 1930s.

- Recently, because of the slight Republican majority in the Congress, and a somewhat conservative view of federalism on the Supreme Court, shifts have taken place that favor state power and independence from the federal government.

KEY TERMS AND CONCEPTS

block grant

Federal funding to state and local governments for general functional areas, such as criminal justice or mental-health programs, rather than for specific programs.

categorical grant-in-aid

Federal funding for states or local governments that is for very specific programs or projects.

Civil War

The war between the southern and northern states, the Union and the Confederacy, from 1861 to 1865.

commerce clause

The section of the Constitution giving Congress the power to regulate trade among the states, with foreign countries, and with the Native American tribes.

concurrent powers

Authority held jointly by the national and state governments.

confederal system of government

A system of government consisting of a league of independent states, each having sovereign powers. The central government created by such a league has only limited and delegated powers over the states.

cooperative federalism

The theory that the states and the national government cooperate in solving problems.

devolution

The return of responsibility for various policies to state and local governments.

direct regulation

Government regulation targeted at a specific firm or industry, as opposed to a regulation that's not targeted at a specific firm or industry but affects them anyway, as is the case with some environmental regulations.

division of power (horizontal and vertical)

Granting some powers to one government and some to another. A horizontal division of power separates power between executive, legislative, and judicial branches. A vertical division of power separates power between national and state governments (federalism).

dual federalism

A system of government in which the states and the national government have coequal sovereign powers. Under dual federalism, acts of states within their reserved powers could be legitimate limitations on the powers of the national government.

elastic clause

The final paragraph (clause 18) of Article I, section 8 of the Constitution, which grants Congress the power to choose whatever means are necessary to execute its specifically delegated powers. Officially known as the "necessary and proper" clause.

enumerated powers

Powers specifically granted to the national government by the Constitution. The first seventeen clauses of Article 1, Section 8, specify most of Congress' enumerated powers.

expressed powers

Presidential powers expressly written into the Constitution or congressional statute.

federal mandate

Federal rules requiring compliance by states and municipalities in order to obtain federal grant money, or rules requiring states to pay for specific nationally defined programs.

federal system of government

A system of government that divides power between a central government and divisional or regional governments. Each level must have some domain in which its policies are dominant and some genuine political or constitutional guarantee of its authority.

federalism

A system of government in which power is divided between a central government and regional or subdivisional governments.

framers

The authors of the Constitution.

full faith and credit clause

A section of the Constitution (Article IV, Section 1) requiring states to recognize the laws and court decisions of other states. Due to this clause, deeds, wills, contracts, and other civil matters in one state must be honored by all states.

Gibbons v. Ogden

This case determined that Congressional control over interstate commerce includes navigation of waters. The result was to broaden the definition of interstate commerce to include all commercial exchanges.

horizontal federalism

Relationships among states that are either constitutionally mandated or voluntary. The phrase distinguishes state-state relations from state-federal relations. The Constitution imposes the following requirements on states: to give "full faith and credit" to other states' public acts, records, and judicial activities; to allow the citizens of other states to enjoy the same privileges and immunities that citizens of their own state enjoy; and to return fugitives from justice.

implied powers

Authority possessed by the national government by inference from those powers delegated to it in the Constitution.

indirect regulation

Regulation that's not written to target a specific firm or industry but affects them anyway.

interstate commerce

The buying and selling of commodities, transportation, and other commercial dealings across state lines. It also includes radio, television, telephone, and telegraphic transmissions.

interstate compact

Agreement between two or more states. The Constitution requires that these agreements receive Congressional consent, but in actuality only those that increase the power of the contracting states relative to other states or the national government are considered for Congressional consent. Agreements on minor matters go without Congressional consent. Today's interstate compacts mainly aid in solving regional problems.

intrastate commerce

The buying and selling of commodities, transportation, and other commercial dealings entirely within a single state.

laboratories of democracy

A concept that advocates allowing states the freedom to approach and try to solve problems in whatever way seems right to them. Each state then acts as one of 50 "experiments," and all the rest of the states, as well as the federal government, are able to learn from the resulting mistakes and good ideas.

matching funds

An agreement between two levels of government in which each level agrees to contribute funds to a specific project. These agreements can be between federal and state governments, federal and local governments, or state and local governments. The "match" usually isn't dollar for dollar. In some cases the smaller government contributes as little as 10 percent.

McCulloch v. Maryland

A case in which the Court upheld the power of the national government to establish a bank and denied the state of Maryland the power to tax a branch of that bank.

necessary and proper clause

The final paragraph of Article I, section 8 of the Constitution, which delegates legislative powers to the Congress. Also known as the elastic clause.

New Deal

The programs and policies introduced during the 1930s by President Franklin D. Roosevelt, designed to promote economic recovery and social reform.

new federalism

A plan designed to limit the federal government's regulatory power by returning power to state governments. It gives states greater ability to decide for themselves how government revenues should be spent.

NLRB v. Jones and Laughlin Steel Corp.

The case that upheld the National Labor Relations Act of 1935, which guarantees labor the right to organize and bargain collectively and established the NLRB to regulate labor-management relations.

nullification

Declaring something null or void. Before the Civil War, states' rights advocates in the South claimed a state had the right to nullify a national law. They argued that ultimate power rested with the state governments.

police power

The power and authority to promote and safeguard the people's health, morals, safety, and welfare. In the United States, the federal government does not have police power. This is reserved for the states. Police power is the most vital power granted to the states by the Constitution, and broadly increases their power over individuals.

Multiple-Choice Questions

1. Federal–state relations are best characterized currently as
   A. cooperative.
   B. marble cake.
   C. picket fence.
   D. dual.
   E. uncooperative.

2. Which of the following are not concurring powers; that is, not shared by both the federal and the state governments?
   I. The power to tax
   II. The power to borrow money
   III. The power to set the manner, place, and time of elections
   IV. The power to declare war
   V. The power to charter banks and corporations

   A. I and II
   B. II and III
   C. III and IV
   D. IV and V
   E. II, IV, and V

3. The meaning of devolution in the federal context is
   A. the government's effort to stop the spread of communism.
   B. the return of spending authority to state and local governments.
   C. the removal of government rules and authority that once controlled industry.
   D. the legal doctrine that local governments are creatures of the state.
   E. the return of governmental responsibility to state and local governments.

4. Dual federalism is
   A. a view that holds power is divided into executive and legislative.
   B. a theory that all levels of government can work together to solve common problems.
   C. a view that holds the Constitution is a compact among sovereign states so that powers of the national government are fixed and limited.
   D. a doctrine holding that states have the authority to declare acts of Congress unconstitutional.
   E. a view of federalism that holds the national government must share monetary resources with state and local governments.

5. Sales tax is an example of a(n):

    A. regressive tax.

    B. progressive tax.

    C. fiscal tax.

    D. monetary tax.

    E. in-kind subsidy.

6. Selective incorporation of provisions of the Bill of Rights and their application to the states by means of the 14th Amendment's Due Process Clause is an example of

    A. a centralization of the federal system.

    B. the carrots and sticks of federal programs.

    C. dual federalism.

    D. marble-cake federalism.

    E. preemption of state laws.

Essay Questions

1. Explain the theoretical or constitutional differences between federalism and the separation of powers. Use three different provisions of the Constitution to illustrate these differences.

2. Describe two ways in which the "necessary and proper clause" of the Constitution could be defined or interpreted. Which of these two interpretations did Chief Justice Marshall adopt in his opinion in *McCulloch v. Maryland* (1819)? Explain what that view or interpretation of power has meant to our federal system since then.

ANSWER KEY

Multiple-Choice Questions

1. A
2. C
3. E
4. C
5. A
6. A

Essay Questiions

1. This question calls for differentiating between federalism and the separation of powers in theoretical or constitutional terms. The second part of the question asks for examples (or illustrations) of the difference between the two terms.

    The explanation of the difference between the two concepts is really just definitional, but essential to responding to the question. The separation of powers involves the division of powers among different branches or institutions of government within one level (the federal level) of government. On the other hand, federalism involves the division, distribution, and sharing of powers between two separate levels of government (state and federal).

    The question then asks for three constitutional provisions that illustrate these differences, but it is unclear from the question how specific or general they should be. Select constitutional provisions that relate to federalism and others that relate to the separation of powers, or select three provisions that focus on *both* federalism and the separation of powers.

Federalism	Separation of Powers
The Supremacy Clause	Division of Legislative, Executive, and Judicial Power into three branches. This is the essential and very general core of the separation of powers.
Coinage of money and the prohibition of states coining money.	Any example that illustrates the sharing or overlap of power between two of the branches, e.g., the president and the Senate and treaties or appointments; the president as Commander-in-Chief and Congress's power to declare war.
Really any provision of Art. I Section 8 or Section 9 that limits the powers of the federal and state governments, respectively.	

2.   The necessary and proper clause could mean that Congress can select any method or means to achieve one of the powers enumerated in the Constitution, as long as the means was not prohibited and as long as it was related to the constitutional objective. "Necessary and proper" could also mean, however, that only those means that are absolutely and narrowly necessary can be used by Congress to achieve its enumerated objectives. This does not allow Congress to expansively create elaborate methods or institutions for achieving these powers.

Clearly, Marshall adopted the former of these two definitions and that has continued to prevail through today. The significance of this interpretation is that any policy choices made by Congress in this context are constitutional (and necessary and proper) as long as the Supreme Court can be persuaded that (1) the method chosen is likely to achieve the policy objective, (2) the method is not specifically prohibited by the Constitution, and (3) the policy objective is granted to Congress by the Constitution. There have been very few examples of the Supreme Court ever denying Congress' choice of what is necessary and proper in the course of legislating.

UNIT THREE:

Political Beliefs and Attitudes

Chapter 4   *Political Culture*

Culture is a very broad concept. As a segment of that broad social setting, political culture focuses on the background in which U.S. politics operates: It is a collection of attitudes, beliefs, and values about the government, and it binds a community together. Probably the most important feature of political culture in this country is that even though we hold a variety of beliefs and values, there is some consensus of views.

Most Americans hold strong and fundamental beliefs in liberal democracy based on a somewhat capitalist economic system. These core beliefs include:

1. natural rights
2. individual liberty
3. the pursuit of happiness
   (numbers 2 and 3 together might be called *competitive individualism*)
4. equality under the law
5. government by consent of the governed
6. limited government

These values and beliefs evolve through the process of socialization, which begins at an early age in school and at home. In the United States, this all takes place in an environment of multiculturalism, which presents two competing values: distinct cultures and ethnic identity versus a melting pot of assimilation.

Political socialization, the learning of cultural and political values, significantly affects a country's political culture. The success of such socialization will largely determine the strength or failure of the legitimacy of the political system.

The traditional liberal political philosophy of 17th century Europe is often the core set of values that people advocate in modern-day America.

The socializing process varies greatly among people and groups. These variations also are important for the cultural values that are passed on to generations. Reflecting a breakdown of traditional socializing agents such as families and schools, the media has become a socializing agent for some.

The ideological spectrum in this country ranges from liberal to conservative, including left and right extremism. Many Americans are not ideologues or true believers, but they do hold some ideological perspective.

The Political Spectrum in the United States

In the United States, people's cultural beliefs (ideologies) tend to change slowly over the course of their lives. Their opinions (i.e., public opinion), on the other hand, are often more malleable. In other words, people's fundamental beliefs may not change much over time, but as their economic and social circumstances change during their lifetimes, their policy preferences are more likely to change as well.

In actuality, the political spectrum that exists in this country covers only the middle range of positions. The liberal to conservative portion of the spectrum includes a large segment of people who believe themselves to be moderates—"middle of the road." As you can see from the diagram below, Democrats and Republicans overlap to some degree. Most legislators consider themselves to be more liberal or more conservative than the average American.

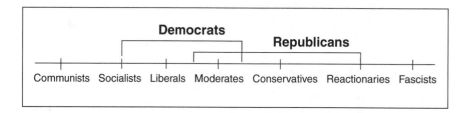

Some people have values that are often in conflict with and inconsistent with each other. For example, many individuals believe in *both* social equality and individual liberty. There are also specific differences in what different generations believe, given their life experiences and all levels of "success."

Political Culture in a Social and Political Context

The political culture of a country is the social and political belief system with which people live, act, and make policy and candidate choices. The primary characteristics of the U.S. population are its:

1. ethnic diversity
2. economic disparities
3. social and ethnic heterogeneity
4. dispersion of political values and preferences

These characteristics reflect a true sense of diversity, and this diversity has political consequences. First, it requires people to compromise or else get nothing out of the political system. Individuals will always have disagreements about policy problems, priorities, and solutions, and at some point, these differences must be resolved or else nothing will be done. Second, some people become socially, politically, and economically isolated as they continually "lose" in policy contests. This may lead the "have nots" to adopt unconventional political tactics, while the "haves" tend to defend the status quo and view challenges as attacks on their fundamental rights.

> While the American population has its origins in immigration over the past two centuries, most people have adopted, since their arrival, significant features of a uniform political culture.

Shared and Differing Values

In our political culture, there are some widely accepted principles or values: Individualism and freedom are two examples. Some observers would say that intolerance is yet another. Free-market entrepreneurialism is a value that many hold and others aspire to achieve. This is based on the belief in the equality of economic opportunity rather than in economic equality.

Another widely shared value is limited and responsive government. This includes a variety of components:

1. majority rule

2. minority rights

3. the loyal opposition

4. popular sovereignty

> Most Americans share, and take for granted, some core values.

While there are some areas of agreement with respect to beliefs, there are other areas of fundamental disagreement. For example:

Though it appears as if most policies reflect the narrow, specialized interests of policy advocates, many in fact reflect a widespread unity of beliefs about the proper role and scope of government.

- *Is government the problem or the solution?*
  To what degree should government intrude on market activities, individual privacy, and proactive policy making?

- *The issues surrounding rich versus poor*
  Some believe in assisting economically disadvantaged people and nations, while others do not.

- *Civility and tolerance*
  Some support a "take no prisoners" approach to political conflicts. Others believe that the "loyal opposition" must include tolerance of different opinions.

- *Conflicts arise between different generations of Americans*
  For example, older Americans feel entitled to financial support by younger Americans. This requires intergenerational redistribution of wealth from younger productive members of society to older, less productive members. Clearly this can lead to intergenerational conflict.

It is important to note that the cultural features listed here are constantly changing, albeit gradually. At some point these features may even reverse direction. This occurs as people age, or as they attain economic success and their values change. So the degree to which Americans agree or disagree varies with time and with the issue at hand.

POINTS TO REMEMBER

- The population of the United States is ethnically, economically, and politically heterogeneous.

- The distribution of people on the political spectrum in this country concentrates around the middle of the spectrum. Although few people support extreme values and ideas (either liberal or conservative), some policy makers adopt extreme views and tactics in order to achieve their desired goals.

- Immigration of ethnically identifiable groups always presents challenges or threats for those populations. Historically, the result has been ethnic isolation, violence, or subjugation, followed usually by gradual assimilation.

KEY TERMS AND CONCEPTS

agents of socialization

Institutions through which people learn the core values of their society and political culture. They include family, educational institutions, peers, media, gender, and religion.

communism

A political, economic, and social theory based on the collective ownership of land and capital and in which political power lies in the hands of workers.

conservative

One who believes in and supports the typically traditional values of conservatism, and who resists change in the status quo.

conservatism

A term for a set of beliefs that includes a limited role for the national government in helping individuals, support for traditional values and lifestyles, and a cautious response to change.

fascism

A political system of the extreme right, which incorporates the principles of a dictatorial leader, one-party state, totalitarian regimentation of economic and social activity, and arbitrary exercise of absolute power by the regime.

gender gap

A phrase frequently used to describe the different voting patterns of men and women. It was widely used to explain the different percentage of votes received by candidates in the 1980 presidential election.

generational effect

The effect that events have on the political opinions, thoughts, and preferences of people from a single generation.

ideology

A person or group's political or economic beliefs, ideas, values, concerns, and goals. People use ideology to justify the way their institutions and nation are set up and run, or to present a vision of how institutions and nations should be set up and run.

inalienable rights

Rights that the writers of the Declaration of Independence and Constitution thought all people held as a consequence of natural law. These rights didn't come from the government, and the government could not infringe upon them. The Declaration of Independence listed these rights as "life, liberty, and the pursuit of happiness." Though the writers claimed all people held these rights, in fact they were withheld from groups such as women, African Americans, Native Americans, and non–property owners.

individualism

The political, economic, and social concept that places primary emphasis on the worth, freedom, and well-being of the individual rather than on the group, society, or nation.

liberal

A person slightly to the left of the center of the political spectrum who believes change is both progress and good. Today's liberals tend to believe that the government has a role to play in preserving person freedoms and equality and in solving social and economic problems.

liberal democracy

The democratic model, which accepts the basic principles of democracy, such as representation, majority rule, and the rule of law as the means by which the system functions.

liberalism

The belief that people are rational beings who can use their intelligence to create a better world, overcoming social and natural obstacles. Liberalism developed in the eighteenth and nineteenth centuries as influential thinkers said that people could reach their full potential if freed from the restrictions of government.

liberty

The right and power to act, believe, or express oneself in a manner of one's own choosing.

moderate

Opposed to extreme or radical views or measures.

opinion leader

A person who can influence other people's opinions through position, experience, knowledge, sheer force of personality, or some combination of these. Opinion leaders help to form public opinion.

peer group

A group whose members share common relevant social characteristics. These groups play an important part in the socialization process, helping to shape attitudes and beliefs.

political culture

Political beliefs and attitudes concerning government and political process held by a group of people, such as a community or nation.

political ideology

The collectively held ideas and beliefs concerning the nature of the ideal political system, economic order, social goals, and moral values.

political socialization

The method through which people learn and develop their political attitudes and opinions. Socializing forces within American culture include the family, schools, media, religious organizations, friends, organizations, and institutions. Most people learn and adopt a set of social and political beliefs when they're young and keep them throughout their life, but change is possible.

political spectrum

The range of political ideas and beliefs.

popular sovereignty

A principle originating in natural rights philosophy that claims political authority rests with the people and not the government. People have the right to create, change, or revolt against their government. In practice, people usually choose representatives to exercise their political authority.

radical left

Extremist political groups who advocate substantial or fundamental political, social, and economic changes. They often have a Marxist or socialist orientation. On the radical right, are ultraconservative groups.

reactionary

A person who advocates substantial political, social or economic changes, favoring a return to an earlier, more conservative system.

socialism

A political and economic theory based on a mixed government and private control of economic activity and the means of production.

tyranny of the majority

Abuse of the minority by the majority through excessive use of power. Fear of tyranny of the majority led to the incorporation of certain basic principles in the Constitution, such as separation of powers, checks and balances, federalism, and the rule of law.

universal suffrage

The right of all people to vote.

Multiple-Choice Questions

1. In the United States, the term "political culture" refers to

   A. the environmental influences that shape a person's political party affiliation.

   B. a person's interest group and association memberships.

   C. societal consensus around the values of democracy, liberty, and equality.

   D. the full spectrum of political ideologies, from extreme left to extreme right.

   E. the trend towards negative campaigning and political mudslinging.

2. The definition of political culture is

   A. beliefs and attitudes about government and the political process.

   B. a set of beliefs and attitudes about the proper purpose and scope of government.

   C. the substantive content of public learned opinion.

   D. concerts, operas, and art displays designed to gain support for the regime.

   E. beliefs and values learned by youngsters before they attend school.

3. The term "gender gap" generally refers to

   A. the greater proportion of men to women in Congress than in the population as a whole.

   B. the greater support of female candidates by women and of male candidates by men.

   C. the difference in the percentages of men and women who participate in politics.

   D. the difference between Democrats and Republicans in defining women's rights.

   E. the difference in the percentage of women versus the percentage of men supporting a particular candidate or issue.

4. The preamble to the Constitution asserts that "We the People of the United States" possess the political authority upon which our constitutional system of government is based. This asserts

   A. limited government.

   B. inalienable rights.

   C. popular sovereignty.

   D. pluralism.

   E. liberalism.

5. The generational effect refers to

    A. the dramatic changes in political preferences that individuals go through at various stages in their adult life in response to world events.

    B. the long-term effect the events of a particular period have on the political preferences of those coming of political age at that time.

    C. the tendency for individuals of the same generation to have opinions opposite the prior generation.

    D. the effect friends of a similar age will have on an individual's opinions.

    E. the tendency of individuals to become more conservative as they age.

Essay Questions

1. Select three of the following and explain how each of these components of U.S. political culture manifests itself in the operation of Congress. Use an example to illustrate each of the three items you select.

   - Individualism
   - Liberty and Freedom
   - Economic Freedom
   - Majority Rule/Minority Rights
   - Citizen Responsibility

2. Explain how the "technological revolution" of the Internet will affect the socialization of children in the next generation. Identify three components of what young people will learn from the Internet and compare those with the values from previous generations.

ANSWER KEY

Multiple Choice Questions

1. C
2. A
3. E
4. C
5. B

Essay Questions

1. *Individualism*: There is widespread belief in individual freedom and independence of action. This can be recognized in both the independent actions of a representative and in his actions representing constituent interests.

   Liberty and Freedom: Protection of freedom and liberty is evident in repeated claims that government should not intrude on individual privacy and free action, though there are countervailing pressures on individuals to conform to majority views, e.g., flag burning and proposed protections of the flag.

   Economic Freedom: This feature of our political culture is manifested in lip-service and policies enacted to encourage or require individual economic independence. Advocates propose less or no governmental regulation of small business so that these entrepreneurs can succeed on their own.

   Majority Rule/Minority Rights: There is a strong current that requires the majority party in a chamber to respect and listen to the minority party. This does not mean minorities prevail or win, but that their views are heard respectfully.

   Citizen Responsibility: There is a strong belief in an individual's rights and responsibilities. This is reflected in policy advocates that demand limitations on government intrusion on individual freedoms.

2. Children who are widely engaged in using the Internet may well adopt views displayed on any of the accessible Websites. These might include politically acceptable cultural views, or extremist or conspiratorial views held by small but active segments of society. Presented in this form, views may be very unrepresentative of political culture in this country.

   First, Web information is not screened or filtered by parents or other leaders whom earlier generations respected. In other words, unknown, unreliable, and certainly unconventional socializing agents will convey their views to children.

Second, children have no idea about the reliability of Internet sources. The new generation may learn little or nothing about how to evaluate news sources or about how to develop a critical eye toward information.

Third, without an intermediary or filter such as parents or teachers, young people may feel cross-pressure from so many Internet sites. That may force them to choose views based their own best guess. Students may become so confused that they disengage from such discourse and withdraw from the political system.

Chapter 5   *Public Opinion in America*

Public opinion is a major part of the American political landscape today, though in earlier times it was not so visible or important. In a representative democracy or republican form of government, policy makers must consider the preferences of the people. Yet since 1789, the framers and most public officials have had no formal or agreed upon way of determining or responding to public opinion.

> Public opinion is the substantive basis upon which people act in political settings.

Within any given political system, individuals have opinions about government, public policy, society, and culture. These opinions, known collectively as *public opinion*, affect the way public officials behave and make decisions. Public opinion may be based on facts about problems and solutions. It may be based on emotion and crises. It may be based on beliefs that people adopt through the process of political socialization. Above all, it reflects the way the people would like the government to act.

Public opinion can be measured in different ways, and the accuracy of the opinion depends on that measurement. Carefully conducted random sample polls can accurately indicate a population's preferences, whether it be the entire country or a specific segment. Informal polls can be very imprecise in determining pubic opinion. Some informal polls question only friends of the official(s) in question, or interpret a few responses as reflective of the population.

Policy makers often seek the public's approval for their votes, and they use public opinion to support their actions in office. People's opinions are determined by a great many variables, and the strength of those opinions is also affected by various things.

1. Public opinion can be visible or latent (invisible like a "mood") in society. When representatives actively pursue the preferences of their constituents, it is quite visible. And when they choose to passively filter constituent preferences in the decisionmaking process, it is far less discernable in society.

2. Public opinion as a whole can be quite stable and nearly permanent; that is, it doesn't change much or quickly. It can also be quite temporary. In the case of a controversial cabinet nominee, for example, public opinion would be fleeting. People would either support the nominee, or not support him. After the public matter is resolved (in this example, after the cabinet nominee is confirmed or rejected by the Senate), the public's view—and opinion—will disappear.

3. Some individuals have mixed—and conflicting—beliefs, which may cause them a good deal of cognitive dissonance. For example, if an individual supports a right-wing conservative cabinet nominee, but also supports a woman's "right to choose," he will likely have inner turmoil about how to resolve those two conflicting beliefs.

4. Some people don't have a coherent ideology, but rather have independent and isolated views on particular issues.

5. Opinions need not be based on precise, factual information. Often, they are based on emotional reactions and psychological world views, and as a result, are internally inconsistent.

Sources of Public Opinion

There are many processes and influences that help people form political opinions. The most important of these is political socialization—the process by which individuals form their beliefs and values about public issues as a result of influences from home, schools, communities, peers, and the media. Socialization does not affect all people equally; some are deeply socialized with belief systems from a young age, while others get mixed signals that leave them without deeply held beliefs.

Public opinion varies according to
* The population holding the opinions
* The times or the circumstances that exist
* The socioeconomic and political characteristics of the opinion holders

- **The family**

  This is the single most important socializing agent for most Americans.

- **The media**

  The media is a unique and modern socializing agent because it mixes information with values: It provides news with entertainment and issues of public concern.

- **Education**

  Education provides some people with information and perhaps beliefs. In general, the more education one receives, the more tolerant and open-minded one seems to be.

- **Economic interests**

  Some people adopt opinions that coincide with their economic interests, i.e., labor unions with worker's interests, business people with governmental protection and deregulation.

Measuring Public Opinion

Measuring public opinion is problematic, though modern-day polling tends to be moderately accurate. Most often, polling organizations such as Gallup or Roper conduct random polls that are designed to be representative of a certain population. They use extensive telephone surveys and sampling techniques to accomplish this task.

Though quite costly, random polls are considered far more accurate and representative than nonrandom polls. However, even random polls are based on only a sample of randomly selected responses. Questions used in these polls are neither biased nor designed to give respondents a clue about what answer to provide.

Random sample polls apply a sampling error (say +/− 3%). Assuming the U.S. adult population is the statistical population involved, the sample size used is generally between 1,200 and 1,500 respondents.

Nonrandom polls, which quite literally means "not randomly selected individuals," are not reliable representations of people's true opinions. However:

1. Many candidates rely on nonrandom polls hastily conducted by their party.

2. U.S. senators and representatives often rely on letters, phone calls, e-mails, and telegrams to indicate public opinion on some issues. This is clearly *not* representative of the population. It represents simply the views of those people motivated enough to contact their legislator. Interest groups may mobilize their members to engage in these kinds of activities so that the legislators have a skewed and unrepresentative perception of public opinion.

3. The way in which questions are worded can significantly influence the opinions reflected. "Slanting" the questions can get policy makers the kinds of answers they want.

4. Exit polls are used by the media to find out how people say they voted, and why they voted in a particular way. These are not random and not representative, but if a large enough proportion of voters is polled, the responses can form the basis for some generalizations.

The influence of public opinion is unclear. It depends on:
- The issue
- The target
- The policymaker and his or her sensitivity to public opinion

The Distribution of Public Opinion

Some public opinion is skewed toward one particular view. For example, most Americans favor a capitalist economic system. Other public opinion can be bimodal, divided nearly equally between two extreme positions. For example, most people either support a woman's right to choose an abortion, or they do not. There's generally little middle ground on this issue.

Most people in this county would characterize themselves as moderates (in the middle of the political spectrum). More specifically, they think of themselves as slightly liberal or slightly conservative. Few people think of themselves as extremely liberal or extremely conservative.

There are various elements that go into determining an individual's opinion.

- *Education*

  In general, the higher one's education, the higher one's awareness and understanding of politics and issues.

- *Income*

  Income divides people on their opinions: The higher one's income, the more he is apt to value freedom and less government control.

- *Region in which one lives*

  People who live in the mountain states or the midwest are generally more conservative than people who live on either coast. People living in the southern states generally are more conservative on civil rights than are northerners.

- *Ethnicity*

  African Americans in particular tend to be more liberal on various social issues than are whites.

- *Religion*

  Generally, Jews are more liberal than Catholics, and Catholics are more liberal than Protestants.

- *Gender*

  Women favor government programs promoting equality more than do men. But there are no set generalizations that can be made about gender. Rather, the differences between men and women are issue specific.

Some officials believe in closely following public opinion, and with respect to making policy decisions, may even use it to set the limits within which they exercise their own discretion and preferences. Other officials don't trust public opinion, because it can change, quickly and dramatically. In short, how closely public opinion is followed or heeded by policy makers is uncertain.

POINTS TO REMEMBER

- Public opinion is often a take-off point for media inquiry about public officials. It can be based on any form of polling, whether it is an accurate or inaccurate method.

- Legislators often pay close attention to the opinions and issues of their constituents. Two key issues for legislators are the personal economic welfare of their consituents and the commercial interests of their districts.

- Policy makers often feel that they have more latitude to disregard opinion about foreign affairs/world issues than about domestic issues or policies directly related to economic interests.

KEY TERMS AND CONCEPTS

aggregate opinion

Opinion shared by group of people.

census

The counting, every ten years, of the population of the United States, conducted by the Bureau of the Census.

cognitive dissonance

A psychological condition where an individual is presented with conflicting or inconsistent beliefs, and in order to resolve this conflict, must either ignore the inconsistencies, develop irrational explanations for them, or reject some beliefs.

congressional reapportionment

The reallocation of legislative seats, based on population.

consensus

General agreement on an issue.

demographics

The characteristics of human populations and population segments.

fluidity

The changing of public opinion as time passes.

intensity

The strength with which one feels for or against a public policy or issue. Intensity is often very important in generating public actions, and intensely held minority views often defeat less intensely held views held by majorities.

latency

The degree to which an opinion is held but not expressed.

latent public opinion

Political opinions that citizens hold but don't express or act on. These latent opinions have the potential to become widely expressed and acted on within the political arena.

opinion poll

Questioning a selected sample of people that are considered representative of a population (the entire United States or a smaller group, for example) on a given topic or topics. Politicians, government officials, businesses, scholars, and the public use or study these polls to find information about populations. Advances in polling techniques over the years have led many to believe that data from polls is reasonably accurate.

policy agenda

Issues arising from the aggregate public opinion that politicians have decided to pay attention to and respond to. Items on the policy agenda have a good chance of becoming law.

political agenda

A list of issues on which a variety of political agents, such as interest groups, political parties, social movements, and elected officials, want to see the government take action. An item can be on the political agenda and not on the policy agenda.

polls

Places where votes are cast and registered.

public opinion

The collected attitudes and beliefs of some groups of individuals. There is no single "public opinion," since the U.S. is made up of many people with different beliefs. In a democracy, one key issue is how responsive legislators should be to public opinion.

random sample

A sampling method in which each member of the population being surveyed has an equal chance of being selected for the sample.

relevance

The degree of importance that an issue is considered to have at a particular time. Issues become relevant when the public believes they're a direct or important concern. The media plays a large role in the public's perception of an issue's relevance.

sampling error

The estimated difference between the results of a poll using a sample of the population and the true results that would have been found if the entire population had been polled.

stability

A gauge for determining the consistency of public opinion on a certain issue over time. If public opinion stays very consistent on an issue over time, stability is high. If public opinion changes frequently or widely, stability is low.

stereotype

A standardized notion held in common about members of a group. It typically represents an oversimplified opinion, prejudiced attitude, or uncritical judgment.

Multiple-Choice Questions

1 The most significant agent of political socialization is
   A. religion.
   B. education.
   C. the media.
   D. race and ethnicity
   E. the family.

2. Inconsistent public opinion can result from which of the following:
   I. A lack of accurate knowledge about public affairs
   II. Misleading statements by officials
   III. Insufficient knowledge about public affairs

   A. I only
   B. II only
   C. II and III
   D. I and II
   E. I and III

3. Polling techniques that produce the most reliable or accurate results are
   A. random samples.
   B. skewed samples.
   C. two-staged least squares samples.
   D. exit poll samples.
   E. survey samples.

4. Which of the following statements about the stability of public opinion is correct?
   A. Public opinion is unstable in the face of media coverage, but tends to be more stable for issues the media ignores.
   B. Public opinion is frequently stable for periods of many years.
   C. The opinions of women tend to be more stable than those of men.
   D. Public opinion has been generally stable in the northeastern states, but remarkably unstable in the south.
   E. Public opinion is always unstable.

5. Which of the following is true about the expression of public opinion?

   A. New communication technologies, such as the Internet, have not introduced new opportunities to express public opinion.

   B. Interest groups don't express public opinion, they only express the opinions of interests.

   C. News media, activism, lobbying, polls, and elections all provide some expression of public opinion.

   D. Political activism is an important part of a democratic society, but not as an expression of public opinion.

   E. The single most important form of public opinion in a democratic society is response to polls.

Essay Questions

1. List a systematic but quick process or framework for a legislator to follow in assessing the public opinion and preferences of her constituents on an issue of economic concern. This process should contain three features or steps. Explain why you are recommending each feature that you outline.

2. Which of these two models of democracy—pluralist or elitist—is correct in its assumptions about public opinion? Outline the assumptions each makes about public opinion and indicate how each view would consider or weigh opinion in the course of making policy.

ANSWER KEY

Multiple-Choice Questions

1. E

2. E

3. A

4. B

5. C

Essay Questions

1. The goal of a legislator is to represent the views of voters at home. A framework might begin with the legislator considering only the views of her constituents since nonconstituents are nonvoters. Second, she may heed the views of those who are known supporters and who have made campaign contributions. Third, the legislator might consider the general economic impact of the policy or the interests in the district, though this would require accommodating additional (conflicting) views, and may introduce too broad a perspective.

2. Elitism would consider public opinion to be unimportant since the general population does not control any decision making in government. At most, elitists would pay lip service to opinion, in order to give the impression that public opinion mattered in making policy. Pluralism would suggest just the opposite—that public opinion is essential and reflective of preferences and likely policy outcomes. For pluralists, public opinion would explain preferences, actions, and results in the policy making process.

    Both views could be considered correct. On some issues, elitism might be the more relevant and compelling view, while for others, pluralism is the more sound perspective. So, an "it depends" response might be best, as long as you itemize the relevant variables. When many interests and policy advocates contend over proposals, pluralism appears the most compelling. When a few powerful interests seem to prevail, elitism might be a strong explanation. On medical care or a patient's bill of rights, the elitist view of powerful interests might prevail, regardless of any counterarguments raised by various patient interests.

UNIT FOUR:

Political Parties, Elections, Interest Groups, and the Media

Chapter 6   *Political Parties*

Two major political parties dominate the political landscape of the United States—Democratic and Republican. It is has been difficult for third parties to gain effective control of government or to win seats in legislatures. Unless all the seats in an institution are contested by party candidates, government control is very difficult to achieve. Tradition, the separation of powers, and single-seat, winner-take-all districts have all prevented this from happening. Recently some third-party presidential candidates have made some headway in the primaries and even in the general election, but they have failed to win the election. Major party candidates continue to win the majority of the electoral college vote.

The primary goal of a political party is to mobilize voters and their funds in an effort to win office. In the United States, political parties are not recognized in the Constitution, though some of their functions might be considered essential to the operation of the political system.

1. First and foremost, a party seeks to win control by means of gaining public office and making policy. One way it does this is to provide voters with signals or "directions" about how to make voting choices on election day.

2. Parties adopt policy positions that are favored by certain segments of the population. They may combine various positions into one policy agenda in an attempt to attract supporters (voters and candidates) who share common views.

3. Once a party wins a majority of the seats in an institution, it has the power to organize that institution. That is, the majority party in each institution elects its leaders and controls that body.

Political parties are organized largely by state law. While there is a national-level organization for both major parties, state election laws largely determine how a political party must structure. Since most elections are local or statewide (rather than national), the parties must be focused at those levels. Organized from the bottom up to mobilize or influence voters, state law defines:

Party success in local and state elections can be uncertain. While the two major parties can field competitive and viable presidential and vice-presidential candidates, they may be unable to field a complete slate of candidates for local elections. They may also be unable to win a majority of a state legislature or governorship.

- The offices to be elected
- The terms of office (and whether there are term limits)
- How and when the elections will take place
- How parties can select their candidates (primary elections, caucuses, or state-wide conventions)
- The majority or plurality rules for winning an election
- The precinct, county, and state party organization

Political party organization is uneven across states or within a state due to law, or because party strength (funds, voters, and candidates) differs in various places. In certain regions, non-compete situations have been established, with one party dominating that region—sometimes for decades—simply because the other party suffers from poor organization and limited funds, or even from an inability to contest an office (that is, to find a candidate to run for that office).

Party Membership

In its broadest sense, a political party can be defined as a group of voters that supports certain candidates in the general election. That is called the party in the electorate. More narrowly, a party can be defined as a group of people that works for a party during a campaign. These party members include:

- Volunteers who answer telephones and stuff envelopes

- Individuals who contribute campaign funds to local or state party organizations rather than to individual candidates

- Elected party precinct committee members who are formally responsible for identifying and mobilizing party supporters in each precinct

- County party organizers, including elected precinct committee members and an elected county chair

- State party members, including the county chairs and the elected state chair, who participate in fundraising, in party campaign decisions, and in identifying party candidates

- National delegates from each state's party organization, headed by a national party chair

History of Political Parties

The framers of the Constitution did not anticipate the need for political parties or for their "inevitability." In the late 18th century, no political parties existed—either in the Americas or in the rest of the world. Madison's Federalist No. 10 discusses factions, but those most closely parallel interest groups, not political parties.

> The functions parties perform may be essential to the operation of the American political system.

The first parties focused around the ratification of the U.S. Constitution in 1787. The Federalists, led by the New England framers, supported the new constitution, while the Anti-Federalists (Democratic Republicans), led by Thomas Jefferson, opposed it. The Federalists were largely disbanded after the election of 1800 because they failed to win seats in congress, they lost the presidency, and they had a narrow geographic base (New England).

With the demise of the Federalists in 1800, the Democratic-Republicans became the predominant political organization for the next quarter century. It focused on commercial development and organizing the national government. Some consider this to have been the first party system. But the system splintered in the presidential election of 1824: Andrew Jackson won the popular vote and led in the electoral vote as well, but John Quincy Adams won the presidency. Adams's supporters had struck a deal with Henry Clay, the Speaker of the House of Representatives, when the election went to the House for resolution.

Adams was the last vestige of the old Federalist Party which was dead by 1824. Jackson represented the emerging popular Democratic-Republicans, and Henry Clay was not really a member of any party. During this time, there were no organized parties. Eventually the Jacksonians were successful in developing the Democratic Party of the Pre–Civil War era, but that took some time—20 to 30 years.

Andrew Jackson won the election of 1832, and that began a new era of party politics: one of populism and the expansion of the franchise and the mobilization of more and more voters. Jacksonian Democracy focused on economics, slavery, and the nature of the union—the power of the federal government as opposed to the power of state governments—and won elections against a variety of narrow-issue parties. The Republican Party emerged in the 1850s and advocated a strong national government and union, while the Democrats, with substantial support in the south, advocated states' rights and slavery. Eventually, the predominantly Democratic Party moved to secede from the Union and form the Confederacy with the election of the Republican, Abraham Lincoln.

Since the Civil War, the major parties have remained the Democrats and the Republicans, though their coalitions of supporters and policies have changed a good deal. The Reconstruction Era saw Republican dominance throughout the Industrial Revolution until 1932. The Democrats were more than a regional (southern) party because they advocated populist policies that favored the lower classes. As a result of the Depression and the election of Franklin Roosevelt in 1932, the Democrats gained control of government, and developed a long-term coalition of voter support through much of the country.

Presently, at the national level, neither of the two major parties has clear dominance or control of policy-making institutions. One or the other party does control major portions of state and local institutions, however, because of uneven party organization and strength. However, neither party seems to have a long-term hold on any policy-making body.

Third Parties

While the two party system predominates in this country, various minor parties do exist. Some flourish for a time and then disappear, while others may have longer lives. Such parties may retain their viability at the local or even the state level with local support but they are unlikely to present a competitive slate of candidates at the national level. Historically, some of the more prominent third parties have been:

- Ideological parties, such as the Libertarian Party, which believes that one consistent ideology is the solution to all problems in society.

- Single-issue parties that promote one principle about government, rather than a general philosophical position. An example would be the Prohibition Party.

- Bolter parties, which are usually factions of a major party that disagree with its position on an issue. The Dixiecrat Party in 1948 split from the Democrats over the issue of civil rights. The American Independent Party led by George Wallace in 1964 left the Democratic Party over "states rights," which really meant civil rights. The Bull Moose party split from the Republican Party in 1912 under the leadership of Theodore Roosevelt.

Third parties are generally not organized at the grassroots level, so they are usually only in a position to field a presidential candidate, or perhaps a state gubernatorial or senatorial candidate. And since third parties often lack widespread electoral support (voters) at the polls, major parties will commonly adopt third party "issues" as their own in order to garner votes. Stealing third party issues and supporters has added to the strength and success of the two major parties.

Third party candidates rarely win elections. However, the issues they raise often have great impact on policy debates in this country.

There are institutional hurdles to third parties as well. First, in many states it is difficult for a third party with no electoral record to gain ballot access. In other words, if a third party has had no votes or candidates in previous elections, it will not be listed on the ballot. Second, funding is difficult, though the Federal Election Commission will allocate some money to a party that has won five percent of the popular vote in the previous presidential election. Third, the single-member, winner-take-all district means that even if a third party wins a significant proportion of the popular vote, it will not get its candidate elected unless that candidate wins a plurality or an absolute majority (50% + 1). This is virtually impossible to achieve.

Party-Voter Connections

The two major parties have distinctly different ideological positions, yet for the purpose of securing votes, their candidates usually take middle-of-the-road positions. Their goal is to attract weak party identifiers or independent voters who, in the middle of the liberal to conservative political spectrum, hold the key to many elections. Even if these candidates initially adopt a strong "party line" in order to get the party's nomination, they eventually settle into more moderate positions.

Once in government, a party may try to organize a legislative body into partisan leaderships (the majority party) and committees. This partisan organizing principle does not carry over to every vote on all issues in a legislative body: In the end, constituent interests (and the need to be reelected) come first, and so some legislators may vote with the "other side of the aisle" on some issues. However, the majority party in a legislative chamber uses its power over committees and resources to reward loyalists.

As for the voters themselves, the Democrats and the Republicans can be described as:

- A loose collections of voters, some of whom may switch sides in particular elections. For example, the Reagan Democrats in 1980 and 1984

- A heterogeneous collection of partisans who disagree with each other on some issues, and may split from the party over these issues once they are formulated in the party platform

> Party discipline is a difficult feature to establish in the U.S. Parties are eclectic and broadly based, with little ideological foundation. And, since candidates can get campaign support from constituents, PACs, and interest groups, they can win elections with nothing more than a party nomination.

Responsible Party Model

The responsible party model provides a dramatic contrast to the American party system in place, and as such, is frequently used in political analysis. The responsible party model forces a very strong—even absolute—party discipline upon all members. That is, they must follow the voting and advocacy directions of the party leadership. This model is based on several principles:

1. The party presents a clear, distinct, and understandable set of programs to voters.

2. Voters choose candidates on the basis of the party's platform.

3. The party that wins the majority of seats in the legislature adopts its policy platform.

4. In the following election, voters must hold the majority party responsible for the success or failure of its policy agenda.

The functions that parties have long served include the selection of candidates to compete for public office. This selection has become more open and democratic over the years. Currently, rank-and-file party members are often permitted to select candidates through party primary elections.

Clearly, parties in this country are not like this. Rather, U.S. parties are heterogeneous collections of office holders and leaders, so it may be impossible for them to generate clear policy platforms. Parties are not ideologically consistent on policies positions. Furthermore, there is so little party discipline in legislatures that the majority party is often unable to get its members to support (vote for) its policy proposals or to carry out its policy agenda.

During a campaign, U.S. voters cannot always tell whether a candidate is promising to support a party's program. Nor can they determine if a policy has been successful, or whether to blame the incumbent if it has not. Voters also pay little attention to policy proposals or platforms, and lack information for making such choices at the polls. As a result, while political parties can make explicit campaign pledges and deliver on them if elected to a majority, that does not happen in this country. Here, political parties have neither the discipline nor the ideologically committed members or candidates to be held responsible for policy consequences.

The Rise and Fall of Parties

Many people wonder whether political parties are disappearing, or at least losing their essential role in American politics. Some believe that political parties are in decline because they have lost control over most of their candidates. Primary elections give candidate selection to voters, and candidates will campaign with little regard to party platforms. Though they have been in many ways unsuccessful, the functions that political parties play are integral to the political system.

POINTS TO REMEMBER

- The functions of political parties may or may not be changing but the ways in which parties *perform* those functions is changing.

- The strength and organization of the two major political parties varies greatly throughout the United States.

- To succeed in the long term, parties must be continual; must compete for all elected offices with a slate of candidates; and must address voters' preferences with attractive policy preferences.

KEY TERMS AND CONCEPTS

Australian ballot

A secret ballot prepared, distributed, and tabulated by government officials at public expense. First used in 1888, all states now use the Australian ballot rather than an open, public ballot.

congressional campaign committee

Committee of members of the House and Senate that organize and help finance election campaigns.

critical election

An election that establishes the dominance of a particular political party that lasts for a period of time.

Democratic party (Democrats)

A major American political party that evolved from the Democratic-Republican group supporting Thomas Jefferson.

divided government

In American government, a system in which presidential administrations of one party are opposed by Congressional majorities of the opposing party. The term is used to describe the persistence of such election results over time, with either party controlling the presidency.

franchise

The right to vote.

independent

Voter or candidate not affiliated with a political party.

linkage institutions

Institutions, such as political parties, that provide a link between citizens and the government.

multimember electoral districts

Electoral districts in which voters choose multiple officials to represent them, instead of just one.

national committee

A national political party's standing committee that directs and coordinates the party's activities during the period between national party conventions.

national convention

The meeting held every four years by each major party to select presidential and vice presidential candidates, to write a platform, to choose a national committee, and to conduct party business. In theory, the national convention is at the top of a hierarchy of party conventions (the local and state conventions are below it) that consider candidates and issues. Parties have selected presidential candidates in every election since 1832. The delegates are selected in one of several ways: presidential primaries, party conventions, or party committees. Delegates are apportioned on the basis of state representation; bonuses are given to states that showed a voting majority for that party in the previous election.

New Deal coalition

A collection of groups who joined together to support Franklin D. Roosevelt and his New Deal, including Catholics, Jews, union members, Southerners, people of lower income, middle-class urban liberals, and African Americans.

party dealignment

The term refers to a time characterized by the absence of a dominant political party.

party identification

The practice of aligning oneself with one political party, including their beliefs, values, and agenda.

party organization

A political party's structure and leadership. It includes election committees; executives at local, state, and national levels; and staff.

party platform

A document prepared by a political party, outlining its policies and objectives and used to win voter support during a political campaign. Candidates do not feel obligated to fulfill the items laid out in a platform if elected to office.

party-in-electorate

Citizens who identify with a specific political party or have a preference for one party over another.

party-in-government

All the elected and appointed political officials who identify with a particular political party.

patronage

Appointing government jobs and contracts to faithful party workers as a reward for their contributions. Unrestricted patronage came about with Andrew Jackson's spoils system and began to lose influence with the Civil Service Act of 1883.

platform

A statement of principles and objectives held by a party or candidate. It's used during a campaign to win support from voters.

political party

A group of people who hold similar political beliefs and goals and organize to win political elections, set political policy, and take power over the machinery of government. There are many political parties in the United States. The two main parties are, and have long been, the Democrats and the Republicans. There is no formal membership requirement to participate in either of these parties.

political ward

The division of a city for purposes of electing members to the city council.

precinct

The basic unit in the United States in the election process and for party organization. Cities and counties are divided into precinct polling districts.

proportional representation

An electoral system in which parties receive a share of seats in a legislature proportional to the popular vote they win in elections. The United States does not have a proportional system of representation.

Reagan coalition

A coalition that came together to elect Ronald Reagan president in 1980 and 1984. It included people from middle-class suburbs, social and religious conservatives, white Southerners, business people and professionals, and blue-collar workers who had once been Democrats. George Bush was elected president with many of the "Reagan Coalition" votes in 1988, but the coalition fell apart by 1992.

realignment

The shifting of public sentiment that puts one party ahead of a previously dominant other party.

Republican party (Republicans)

One of the two major American political parties at the moment, along with the Democrats. The Republican party emerged in the 1850s as a party opposed to slavery. It succeeded two former parties, the Federalists and the Whigs. Presently the Republican party is generally conservative in nature. Voter support for Republicans tends to increase with higher levels of income, education, and property ownership.

Republican Revolution

Refers to the 1994 Congressional election in which Republicans turned around the 1992 Democratic gains, gaining 52 seats in the House and 8 seats in the Senate.

single-issue party

Political parties that focus on one issue, such as today's Right to Life party.

single-member district

An electoral district from which a single legislator is chose, usually by a plurality vote, in contrast to proportional representation or at-large systems.

spin-off party

A new party created when a faction within an earlier party becomes dissatisfied with that party and forms their own. Theodore Roosevelt's Bull Moose party, which spun off from the Republican party, is an example.

splinter party

A party composed largely of people who have broken away from one of the major parties. Also called a third, or secessionist, party.

sustaining election

An election in which voters reaffirm their support for the party in power and its policies.

third party

A political party other than the two main parties in a two-party system. Third parties are usually made up of independent voters and dissatisfied members of one or both major parties. They are larger, have more influence, and have more effect on election results than minor parties. Third parties in American history include the 1856 Republican party, which took power from the Whigs, Theodore Roosevelt's Bull Moose party, which split the Republican vote, the 1948 Dixiecrat party, which had little influence outside the deep south, John Anderson's 1980 campaign, and Ross Perot's 1992 campaign.

ticket splitting

Voting for a candidate from one party for one office and a candidate (or candidates) from another party for another office(s).

two-party system

A political system with only two parties that have realistic chances of winning. While other parties exist, their political power is small.

Whig party (Whigs)

One of most influential and important U.S. political organizations during the first half of the 19th century. The Whig party was formed in 1836 and was dominated by the forces opposed to Andrew Jackson (the same forces that organized the National Republican faction of the Democratic (Jeffersonian) Republicans). The Whigs fell apart as a party in the early 1850s because they were not as effective at capturing antislavery sentiments as the Republicans were.

Multiple-Choice Questions

1. Which of the following does not explain why U.S. politics has been predominately a two-party system?

    A. The first strong parties that developed were Federalist and Anti-Federalist, and historical experience has sustained this two-party tradition.

    B. The two-party system perpetuates itself because of the way families socialize their children to identify with the major parties.

    C. The U.S. system of proportional representation dictates that a candidate who finishes second may hold office.

    D. U.S. political culture is fairly consensual, and the parties' appeal fairly broad.

    E. Election laws require minor party candidates to go to much greater lengths to get on the ballot than the two major parties.

2. When asked about party affiliation, the number of Americans who identify themselves as "Independents"

    A. has steadily declined since 1940.

    B. has held steady since 1940

    C. is at an all-time low.

    D. has steadily increased since 1940.

    E. currently exceeds the number of Americans who identify themselves as Democrats or Republicans combined.

3. The closest feature of recent American politics that reflects a responsible party model of government is

    A. the Contract with America.

    B. Newt Gingrich as Speaker of the House of Representatives after the 1994 election.

    C. the impeachment of President Clinton in 1999.

    D. the failure of Congress to adopt a prescription drug provision for the Medicare Program.

    E. the cooperation between President Clinton and the Congress to adopt the 2000 Budget.

4. Which of the following is not considered a function of a political party?

    A. recruiting electoral candidates

    B. uniting a broad coalition of voters to support a set of public policies

    C. taking responsibility for operating the government after its members are elected to office

    D. registering new voters to participate in elections

    E. regulating interest group participation in the political system

5. Voter dissatisfaction with the two major political parties has

   A. helped Democrats to maintain control of Congress.

   B. declined steadily since 1972.

   C. enabled third party presidential candidates to win record numbers of electoral votes in the last three elections.

   D. resulted in higher levels of ticket-splitting over the past 50 years.

   E. had no apparent effect on rates of voter turnout in presidential elections.

6. Obstacles to the third-party success in the American political system include

   I. the winner-take-all electoral system.

   II. restrictive state ballot access laws.

   III. the tendency of most voters to consider themselves moderates.

   IV. the historical tradition of having a two-party system.

     A. I only

     B. II and III only

     C. III and IV only

     D. I and IV only

     E. I, II, III, and IV

Essay Questions

1. Some observers indicate that political parties are essential to the operation and functioning of government in the United States. Others see parties as historical artifacts which are unnecessary.

   Write a tightly reasoned essay in which you identify one of these two positions, and develop three different reasons for the position you adopt. Use actual data or examples to support your thesis.

2. Identify three institutional and three political reasons that third or minor parties have not persisted in United States politics. Explain how each of these factors has contributed to the demise of such political factions.

ANSWER KEY

Multiple-Choice Questions

1. C
2. D
3. A
4. E
5. D
6. E

Essay Questions

1. *Parties are necessary.*

   Political parties perform core functions in our political system: (1) they select candidates to compete for elected office; (2) they mobilize voters, thereby increasing voter engagement in politics and policy making; and (3) they organize legislative and executive bodies.

   No other intermediate institution can perform these functions that are essential to the operation of our political system. The media could not possibly perform any of these essential functions. Interest groups might be a possibility, but these do not aggregate interests; they represent narrow and single interests. PACs might be another possibility; they may be able to bundle money for campaigns, but they would be unable to present a full slate of candidates on any local, state, or national ballot. Furthermore, with thousands of PACs, and thousands of candidates across the nation, the selection process (voting) would become virtually impossible.

   Parties are unnecessary.

   This side of the position is virtually impossible to argue if you recognize the crucial functions that parties perform. The only "decline" you could argue would be that voters are losing interest in politics, and that can be blamed, in part, on parties. But lower voter interest does not indicate that parties do not perform essential political functions. The argument that fewer people are identifying with political parties is simply not true, so the "rise of the independent voter" is not a viable argument against parties.

2. Reasons that third parties have not persisted over the long run include:

   Institutional Reasons:

   • Single-member, winner-take-all plurality elections greatly reduce the chances that a third-party candidate will win office at all, let alone continue to win re-election.

   • Third parties have difficulty gaining ballot access and then remaining on the ballot from one election to the next.

- Third parties have had repeated difficulty in fielding a full slate of candidates. At most, a third party could compete for control of one office.

Political Reasons:

- It is very difficult to mobilize voters for third parties. Most third party efforts are candidate specific or issue specific. In fact, their candidates may not run for election a second or third time, and issues are resolved or disappear from the public's agenda after a few elections.

- Party identification is deeply embedded with the two major parties. Changing that level of support for the Democratic and Republican parties would be largely impossible. Such a change would be essential in order to develop a persistent third party.

- Since third parties are often narrowly ideological, they can attract only a small proportion of the voter support needed to win office. If a third party is linked closely to a particular individual, then party support generally dries up when that individual disappears from public life. In other words, party support is not transferred to the institutional third party.

Apex Learning

Chapter 7   *Campaigns and Elections*

Campaigns and elections are the primary ways in which people voice their political preferences. Elections are essential for a representative democracy to function, since this system of government requires that policy makers be selected by the people (the political sovereigns). Without the mandate of being elected to office, these policy makers would have no legitimacy and no authority. There are a number of electoral systems that could be used to select representatives, but in this country, the direct election of officials in a winner-take-all, single-member district framework is the predominant method.

Campaigns are designed to mobilize supporters for a candidate; whether to reinforce their preferences, or to persuade undecided voters. The methods and the costs of campaigning have changed rapidly. These changes place a very heavy premium on raising and spending large sums of money. In fact, some potential candidates are now precluded from running for office because of the costs of campaigning.

Methods of Political Participation

Individuals participate in politics in various ways. Participation requires positive action on the part of the individual, and people do it at various levels of involvement.

Voting is not the only form of participation in the United States, though it is the most common. Conventional (traditional) participation includes voting or contacting public officials.

Voting is the primary way in which most Americans participate in politics.

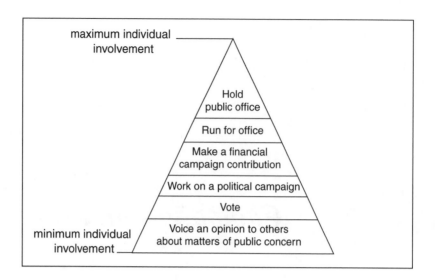

This "pyramid" indicates the varying degrees in which citizens conventionally engage in political activity. It also indicates something of the descending proportion of the population that engages in each form of participation.

More unconventional modes of political participation include demonstrations, protests, civil disobedience, or even violence. These are intended more to gain public attention—and policy change—for a particular issue than to contribute to the conduct of public affairs. These types of demonstrations may generate support and visibility for a given issue, but their concrete effects are uncertain.

The effect of participation is not always clear and direct. Voting produces a winner—an elected office holder—though it may not be the voter's choice. Demonstrating or lobbying may generate support or visibility for an issue, but that effect is uncertain.

Campaign contributors may be given "access" to the office holder. That means the contributor will be able to discuss policy proposals with the recipient after the election, if the issues requires agenda attention.

Voting

Voting turnout in the U.S. varies greatly but is relatively low compared to other countries.

Voting is the most essential feature of a representative democracy. Without it, there would be no selection of public officials to exercise policy making. There would be no one to govern.

Voting allows the public to select public officials, as well as to pass (or not) proposals for initiatives or referenda. In some states, ballots include these issues, and in those cases, the public directly votes to adopt constitutional amendments or proposed laws.

In the common form of voting, voters select between two or more candidates. There are different methods for determining the winner, the most common of which are:

1. An absolute majority of the votes.

2. A plurality of votes.

3. A plurality with a run-off election between the top two voter getters.

When an individual votes, he has to make two essential decisions:

First, he has to decide whether to vote or to abstain. Low voter turnout has been a continuing feature of American politics. It causes many observers to doubt the legitimacy of those elected, and it is a source of criticism for those committed citizens who believe voting is a civic duty. Some may not vote in order to boycott the selection process. The reasons for not voting are numerous:

- *Formal or institutional restrictions on voting*

   These are usually constitutional and legal restrictions, many of which are imposed by individual states.

   a. Age

   b. Residency

   c. Registration requirements, though the Motor Voter law facilitates some voter registration. Some states have same-day registration and voting.

   d. Scheduled election day. Absentee ballots and mail-in procedures may encourage some voting.

   e. Incarcerated adults are excluded from voting, as are convicted felons.

- *Individual, ideological, and personal reasons*

   a. People may feel ineffective. Thinking that their vote "won't make a difference," these people don't vote.

   b. The more competitive the election appears, the higher the turnout.

   c. Young people—those under 25 years of age—vote in relatively low proportion. Those above 65 years of age have a very high proportion voting.

   d. Those eligible voters with fewer than eight years of education vote at a very low rate. The more education one has had, the more likely he will vote. Polls show that nearly 75 percent of those with at least a college degree will vote.

   e. Members of racial and ethnic minorities tend to turn out less than do Caucasian voters, though here the difference is not as great as for age and education.

   f. Income levels significantly affect voter turnout. The higher one's income, the more likely he will vote.

Second, if an individual chooses to vote, he must decide for *whom* to vote. The following are some of the factors that typically influence voters:

- Party label (the most important and influential factor)
- A candidate's image or attractiveness (important in some elections)
- A candidate's position on policy issues (generally difficult to determine in many campaigns)
- Demographic and socioeconomic factors
  a. *Education level*

  College-educated voters tend to vote Republican. Less education tends to be reflected in voting for Democratic candidates.

  b. *Income and socioeconomic status (SES)*

  Professional occupations, white-collar workers, and businesspersons tend to vote Republican. Blue-collar or union workers vote more Democratic. Higher income earners vote more Republican than do lower income earners.

  c. *Religion*

  Protestants are predominantly Republican voters, while Catholics and Jews vote Democratic.

  d. *Ethnic and racial background*

  The Irish traditionally support Democratic candidates, as have Latinos, Slavs, Poles, and Italians. African Americans have generally voted for Democrats since the New Deal of the 1930s. Anglo-Saxons and northern European ethnic groups tend to vote Republican.

  e. *Gender*

  Differences in voting by gender have not been clear or consistent. Recently, women have supported Democratic presidential candidates more heavily than have male voters.

  f. *Age*

  There is some indication that younger voters tend to support Democrats, while older voters support Republicans, but this relationship is fluid and does not always occur.

  g. *Geographic region*

  Traditionally the South has been heavily Democratic but that has changed in the past 20 to 30 years. Now many southern voters support Republicans. Democrats do still draw much of their support from the large, northern states and east coast (industrial) states. Republicans win much of the electoral support in rural areas of the country, and in western (and the Mountain) states.

Running for Office

What motivates a candidate to run for office? Typically, a candidate will have both selfish and altruistic objectives, ranging from "exercising political power" to "helping people improve their lives." But there are other factors as well: how extensive are his resources—advisers, expertise, money and "backing," and prior public/private experience? What are his "perceived" chances of winning? Is his opponent an incumbent seeking re-election?

The first step in running for office is to receive a political party's nomination. This is done through either a party convention or a primary election, depending on the office and the state laws.

Presidential nominations are done by various state-wide means; the most prevalent method is through *direct party primary elections.*

- Closed primary elections prevent nonparty members from voting. Voters must declare their loyalty to a party to vote in this kind of primary. About 50 percent of the states use this kind of primary.

- Open primary elections allow individuals to vote for a party's nominee, regardless of their party membership. About 40 percent of the states use this system.

- About 10 percent of the states use some other form, including the recently invalidated blanket primary system.

Some presidential primaries (in some states) are *preference polls.* The names of the presidential candidates appear separately from the names of the party convention delegates names, so those votes for candidates require only the voter's preferences.

Other primaries involve *mandatory preference polls,* which link a slate of delegates to specific candidates. If those delegates are elected in the primary, they're pledged to that candidate at the party's national convention.

In the early stages of the presidential primary period (before the national conventions), there is great pressure to be "first" in the race. Winning early on is important for a candidate's image as his party's presidential nominee. The New Hampshire primary is important for that purpose. Other states have adopted early primaries in order to have more influence over presidential nominations.

- "Super Tuesday," adopted in 1988, was established to schedule several southern state primaries on the same day. It was believed that this would increase the influence of the south in the selection of party nominees, though it has not been particularly successful.

Many voters are less informed about issues and more interested in candidate images. As a result, candidates may be able to manipulate images by "kissing babies" or making statements that "take the high ground." So as not to alienate any possible voters, candidates tend to take middle-of-the-road positions on issues.

Election campaigns may result in four things: First, a voter may be "turned off" by a campaign and so be deterred from voting. Second, a voter's choices may be reinforced. Third, a voter may be mobilized to choose a candidate and vote for him or her. Fourth, a voter may be persuaded to change his vote.

- In 1968, 15 states (30 percent) held presidential primary elections. In 2000, over three-fourths of the states (more than 37) held primary elections.

- The media focuses on the early races in Iowa (the "Iowa Caucus") and the New Hampshire Primary in order to convey the front runners for the nomination.

- By the time the Iowa Caucus and the New Hampshire Primary are over, many presidential hopefuls are finished—both out of money and out of the limelight.

Primary election voters are usually party members, and since they are often activists within their party, the candidate who wins the nomination may reflect their preferences.

Candidates for offices besides the presidency may be nominated as well in the primary election, or in state party conventions. In some states or in some local elections, a weak party organization may mean that the party cannot even put forward one candidate for nomination to some offices or for the general election. An open congressional seat, i.e., without an incumbent seeking re-election, may produce several candidates who wish to be nominated for the vacant seat.

Factors in Campaigns for Office

There are many variables that affect the success or failure of a campaign. Some relate directly to the candidate herself, others to her resources and skills, and still others to the constituency. The position of the media and/or the time of the election must also be considered. Key elements of a successful campaign are:

- *Raising money to fund the campaign*

- *Mobilizing supporters and any "undecided" voters*

- *Getting the campaign message across to voters*

  State party organizations may provide assistance, or even professional consultants to some candidates. The Senate and House caucuses each have campaign funds for party incumbents, or for challengers with a good chance of winning an open seat. Local party organizations (county) may provide door-to-door workers and precinct officers. Organized labor may provide free campaign workers to candidates whom the interest supports. Few campaign workers are paid, but if there are any, they will be professional consultants or pollsters.

- *Optimizing free "air time"*

  This involves politicians using public relations efforts, like staging events that will be "covered" by the local media, as if they're "news."

- *Running successful paid advertising campaigns*

  Of course, this depends on the availability of money, and the cost of advertising. Media "blitzes" may generate name recognition or a favorable impression, but rarely are they used to present a candidate's position on policy issues.

Campaign Funding

Campaign funding is a serious issue when considering a run for office. The cost of campaigning depends on the office sought, the size of the constituency, and the campaign strategy of the candidate.

Presidential candidates may receive matching public funds, if they wish them and if they qualify. This money comes from the check-off section that appears on the federal income tax returns, and is distributed by the Federal Elections Commission on a matching fund basis (up to a limit). If a presidential candidates accepts matching federal funds, spending limits will be imposed.

All candidates raise funds directly, mostly from supporter contributions. Friendly PACs will contribute large sums of money in order to get like-minded candidates elected. Other contributors may just seek access to the winner, so they will donate funds to both candidates.

Winning the campaign may depend on a candidate's image as well as on the issues. Candidates generally try to attract people who are affected by a specific issue, so that they can 'promise' improvement. These issues include:

1. The economy (for small business people)

2. Health care (for the ill and the elderly)

3. Social security (for the retired and elderly)

While incumbents can run on their "record" and emphasize their accomplishments, their opponents will seek to emphasize how bad "things" are under the current situation. It is commonplace these days for candidates to make negative attacks on one another, particularly on personal character.

> There are two kinds of campaign advertising. Paid advertising allows the candidate or the sponsor to write the script, produce the ad, and then have it published. Unpaid advertisements are media coverage in which the candidate gets air time or "column inches." Paid advertising may be more effective because its content can be manipulated. The value of unpaid advertising is that it is of little cost to the campaign.

Elections Outcomes

Elections often reflect general trends as well as specific candidate preferences. A *realigning election* would generate a fundamental, semipermanent change in the support one party receives so that it becomes the majority or minority party in the country. These kinds of elections occur rarely, and some political scientists believe that realignment does not occur at all. A *dealigning election* would be one in which a prevailing coalition of partisan voters dissolves and is not replaced by another such coalition.

> Elections are the ultimate form of democracy in our system since it is a representative democracy.

These kinds of elections might appear to be more prevalent and widespread in current American politics. That is, few elections display the characteristics of a permanent and stable coalition of voter support.

Third parties and minor parties have become more visible and active in recent decades. Their efforts rarely produce elected office holders, yet they do often force the major parties to address the precise issues that prompted the voters to develop a third party.

Sometimes third parties are lead by prominent individuals (personalities) seeking the presidency—George Wallace and the American Independent Party, Ross Perot and the Reform Party, or Ralph Nader and the Green Party—making these groups more visible. Other third parties are ideological and based on a comprehensive belief system, i.e., the Socialist Workers Party or the Libertarian Party.

Some single-issue parties coalesce around a position on a particular policy issue. These tend to fade once the issue has been handled by the existing system or when advocates cannot mobilize sufficient support for their position.

POINTS TO REMEMBER

- Most Americans do not engage in political activity regularly, and after a general election, lose interest in policies and candidates. Yet some individuals participate more extensively by working on election campaigns or even running for office themselves.

- Running for elected office is very costly, and it has increasingly required more and more workers with extensive expertise.

- Rarely does the election of an individual candidate result in the adoption of an entire policy agenda. That is because political parties do not have control over their members in government to get their consistent support for a developed policy agenda.

- Winning an election is usually seen as giving the winning candidate a "mandate." This may mean drastic change, retaining the same policy direction, or something in between. Newly elected office holders usually treat their mandates as ratifications of their campaign stances. This can be risky, though, if:

  ◆ The winner barely obtained a plurality of voters

  ◆ The winner's policy messages were inconsistent, indefinite, or very indirect

  ◆ Voters voted for the winner because of dislike for the opponent

---

KEY TERMS AND CONCEPTS

15th Amendment

The amendment (1870) that forbids a state to deny a person the right to vote because of race, color, or previous condition of servitude.

19th Amendment

The amendment (1920) that forbids a state to deny a person the right to vote because of their sex.

24th Amendment

The amendment (1964) that forbids the levying of a poll tax in primary and general elections for national officials.

26th Amendment

The amendment (1971) that lowers the legal voting age to 18 for all national, state, and local elections.

Australian ballot

A secret ballot prepared, distributed, and tabulated by government officials at public expense. First used in 1888, all states now use the Australian ballot rather than an open, public ballot.

"beauty contest"

A presidential primary in which candidates compete for popular votes, but the results have little or no effect on the selection of delegates to the national convention, which is made by the party elite.

blanket primary

A primary election system in which each voter receives a single ballot listing each party's candidates for each nomination and the voter can vote for candidates for either party for any office. The United States Supreme Court declared this method of candidate selection unconstitutional in *California Democratic Party v. Jones* (2000).

bundling

The practice of adding together maximum individual campaign contributions to increase their effect.

caucus

A closed meeting of party leaders or members to select party candidates or to decide on policy.

closed primary

The selection of party candidates in an election limited to party members.

coattail effect

The influence of a popular or unpopular candidate or elected official on the electoral success or failure of candidates on the same party ticket.

credentials committee

A committee used by political parties at their national conventions. The committee inspects the claim of each prospective delegate to determine whether he or she is a legitimate representative of his or her state and can participate in the convention.

crossover voting

The ability to cast a vote in a primary for a candidate from any party. Voters can do this in open primary states.

dealigning election

A general election in which a widely established coalition of voters committed to consistent support for the candidates of one party dissolves and disappears from the electoral horizon.

elector

A person on the partisan slate, selected according to state laws and the applicable political party apparatus, who casts ballots for president and vice president. The number of electors in each state is equal to that state's number of representatives in both houses of Congress. The 23rd Amendment to the Constitution permits Washington, D.C., to have as many electors as a state of comparable population. Electors are selected early in the presidential election year.

electoral college

The group of electors selected by the voters in each state and Washington, D.C. This group officially elects the president and vice president of the United States.

eligible voter

A voter who meets the legal requirements for the right to vote.

expanding electorate

A factor contributing to low voter turnout. Since voter turnout rates are based on statistics counting all potential or eligible voters, rather than registered voters, an expanding electorate negatively impacts the overall voter turnout rate.

expansion of the franchise

Granting of voting rights to more and more members of society.

Federal Election Campaign Act

An act passed in 1972 that controls the raising and spending of funds for political campaigns. A second act passed in 1974 imposed additional reforms, including creation of the Federal Election Commission; providing public financing for presidential primaries and general elections; limiting presidential campaign spending; limiting contributions by citizens and groups; and requiring disclosure of contributions.

focus group

A small group of people in a moderator-led discussion that gathers feelings, opinions, and responses to specific candidates and political or economic issues.

front-loading

The practice of scheduling presidential primary elections during early parts of election campaign to increase the amount of influence that certain states or regions exert on the nomination.

front runner

The presidential candidate considered to have the lead at any given time in an election.

gender gap

A phrase frequently used to describe the different voting patterns of men and women. It was widely used to explain the different percentage of votes received by candidates in the 1980 presidential election.

general election

A statewide election usually held shortly after a primary election to fill state and national offices.

gerrymandering

The practice of drawing legislative district boundaries with an eye toward creating a political advantage for a particular party or faction. The shape of a gerrymandered district has been manipulated by the state legislature's dominant party to increase their electoral strength.

Hatch Act (Political Activities Act) (1939)

A law that limits contributions to political parties and spending by political parties. Most important, it made it illegal for individuals and companies under contract with the federal government to contribute to political candidates or to political parties. This came after federal employees were threatened with losing their jobs or promotions if they didn't donate to political campaigns.

independent candidate

Candidate not affiliated with a political party.

indirect election

An election in which voters do not vote to fill the office but vote for the people who will cast the votes to fill the office. For example, citizens vote for the electoral college, which then elects the president.

initiative

A procedure by which voters can propose to change state or local laws. This process may include changes in the state constitution. The process is begun by obtaining a sufficient number of signatures on petitions, so that the proposal can be submitted to the state legislature or directly to the people. The availability of this procedure depends on state law.

Iowa caucus

The first caucus of the presidential campaign season, which is closely watched and strongly contested.

issue voting

Casting a vote for a candidate primarily due to his or her stand on a particular issue of importance to the voter.

legitimacy

The acceptance of a government's right to rule by the people the government rules. It rises from a shared belief that the government is operating as it should, that is, making decisions by following correct decision-making policies and using power appropriately within a justly defined Constitutional role. By granting legitimacy to a government, people regard the government as valuable, its decisions and actions as valid and binding, and worthy of a certain level of obedience and compliance.

low voter turnout

A situation in which only a small percentage of eligible voters actually cast their votes in an election. This is seen as a problem in the American political system.

majority method (majority rule)

A principle of democracy asserting that a simple majority, defined as 50 percent plus one in most cases, should select public officials and determine the policies and actions of their government. In certain cases special majorities are needed, such as the two-thirds majority within the Senate that the Constitution requires to approve a treaty. See *super majorities*.

Motor Voter Law (1993)

A law that requires state to make voter registration procedures easier and more accessible to citizens. Two means of doing this are to offer voter registration at state driver's license offices and registration by mail.

national party convention

The meeting held every four years by each major party to select presidential and vice presidential candidates, to write a platform, to choose a national committee, and to conduct party business. In theory, the national convention is at the top of a hierarchy of party conventions (local and state conventions are below it) that consider candidates and issues. Parties have selected presidential candidates in every election since 1832. The delegates are selected in a few ways: presidential primaries, party conventions, or party committees. Delegates are apportioned on the basis of state representation; bonuses are given to states that showed a voting majority for that party in the previous election.

New Hampshire primary

The first primary of the presidential election season. It is watched closely and contested strongly.

open primary

A voting system that permits voters to choose the party primary of their choice without disclosing party affiliation.

platform plank

One of the articles, or statements, in a party platform.

plurality

More votes than any other candidate but less than fifty percent. It's possible to win an election with a plurality (and not a majority) of votes in most national, state, and local elections.

plurality method

A method of determining the winner in nearly all elections in the United States, in which the candidate who receives more votes (a plurality) than any other candidate wins. A plurality is not necessarily a majority, so a candidate can win an election even if more than 50 percent of the voters vote against that candidate.

plurality runoff method

A method used in some Southern states. If no candidate receives a majority vote, a second, runoff election is held between the two highest vote getters.

political consultant

A paid professional whom a political candidate, party, or campaign hires to develop a campaign strategy and manage the campaign's activities and efforts. The political consultant's primary concern is the image of the politician, party, or campaign.

presidential debate

Series of televised debates generally held once the two major parties (or sometimes three, as has happened recently) select their candidates for president.

presidential primary

A statewide election in which a party votes for delegates to their national convention as part of the process of determining a presidential nominee. The delegates may be pledged to a particular candidate or they may be unpledged.

primary election

A preliminary election in which voters narrow the field of candidates for specific offices.

proportional voting system (proportional representation)

An electoral system that allocates seats in the legislature to each party or group approximately equal to its popular voting strength.

realigning election

A general election in which a new coalition of electoral support (voters) coalesces around a party's candidates on their agenda to form a semipermanent electoral coalition. These are also labeled "critical elections." The last such election in America might have been the 1932 election of Franklin Roosevelt and the New Deal Majority in Congress, by a coalition of voters from organized labor, ethnic (particularly black) groups, and urban residents.

reapportionment

The reallocation of seats in the House of Representatives. Reapportionment can take place only after a census, though if there are no significant population changes, it may not. For reallocation to occur, population changes within states must be significant enough to justify the change. This is determined through a mathematical formula that considers the nation's total population and the 435 seats the Constitution allows the House. After the seats are reapportioned between states, the affected states redraw their district boundaries to match their new allotment of representatives. This is done by the majority party of the state legislature and often leads to gerrymandering, the drawing of districts intended to increase the party's political power.

referendum

A process in which legislative or constitutional proposals are presented to the voters for their approval.

registered voter

An eligible voter who has signed up to vote.

registration

Listing the names of eligible voters. Registration helps determine that people meet certain legal requirements before voting, such as age, citizenship, and residency.

registration requirements

Legal barriers enforced on all potential voters. See *registration*.

single-member district

An electoral district from which a single legislator is chosen, usually by a plurality vote, in contrast to proportional representation or at-large systems.

socioeconomic status

A group of people within a society who share similar income levels and similar types of employment.

soft money

Campaign contributions that get around laws setting maximum campaign contributions because they're given to political parties and party committees to fund general party activities, instead of to a specific candidate. The party can then use this money in a way that helps its candidates.

Super Tuesday

A Tuesday in March in which a large number of presidential primaries, including those of most southern states, are held. The number of primaries held on Super Tuesday can change with each election.

super-delegate

A party leader or election official who's granted the right to vote at a party's national convention due to the leader's political position, not due to an election at state level.

swing voters

The term refers to those voters who are uncommitted to a particular party or candidate up until election time. Political advertising is often used to try and capture the allegiances of these undecided voters.

telescoping effect

The occurrence, in a winner-take-all system, of a presidential candidate winning in a state by just a few popular votes yet receiving all of that state's electoral college votes. His or her opponent may have almost as many popular votes, yet will receive none of the state's electoral college votes.

third party

A political party other than the two main parties in a two-party system. Third parties are usually made up of independent voters and dissatisfied members of one or both major parties. They are larger, have more influence, and have more effect on election results than minor parties. Third parties in American history include the 1856 Republican party, which took power from the Whigs, Theodore Roosevelt's Bull Moose party, which split the Republican vote, the 1948 Dixiecrat party, which had little influence outside the deep south, John Anderson's 1980 campaign, and Ross Perot's 1992 campaign.

tracking poll

A poll taken on a nearly daily basis for a candidate as election day nears.

voter turnout

The percentage of citizens who participate in an election by casting votes.

Voting Rights Act (1965)

The act that eliminated restrictions on voting that had been used to discriminate against African Americans and other minority groups.

winner take all

A voting system in which the candidate who receives a plurality of the votes wins. Only one candidate can win each election.

Multiple-Choice Questions

1. In presidential elections since 1964, members of labor union families have
   A. mostly supported Republican candidates.
   B. mostly supported Democratic candidates.
   C. generally divided their votes evenly between Republican and Democratic candidates.
   D. generally voted the same way as a majority of Protestant voters.
   E. generally voted the same way as a majority of Midwestern voters.

2. Minor or third parties
   A. have their own caucus in the House of Representatives, but not in the more traditional Senate.
   B. were more common in the late 19th century than at any other time in U.S. history.
   C. rarely win elections but have an effect on American politics by forcing the major parties to recognize new issues or trends.
   D. are infrequently able to win elections in the United States and are consequently unimportant in the scheme of American politics.
   E. are given the same support and access to the ballot as the major parties, but Americans just won't waste their votes on them.

3. Since 1964, members of labor unions have been most likely to vote for which type of presidential candidates?
   A. Republicans
   B. Democrats
   C. Independents
   D. Socialists
   E. Conservatives

4. All of the following statements are true about the electoral college except
   A. it is possible for a candidate to become president without obtaining a majority of popular votes.
   B. most states award their electoral votes on a proportional basis, as opposed to a winner-take-all basis.
   C. 270 electoral votes are necessary in order to be elected president.
   D. the electoral college meets approximately one month after the general election.
   E. if no candidate receives a majority of electoral votes, the winner is decided by the House of Representatives.

5. Political parties are organized around the following principles:
   I. electoral precincts
   II. the national committee
   III. state party conventions
   IV. state electoral law

   A. I and II
   B. II and III
   C. II and IV
   D. III and IV
   E. I and IV

Essay Questions

1. Although most states use some form of primary election system to select party candidates, the major political parties were initially opposed to the adoption of this process. Why would this be the case? In addition, specifically indicate why the Democratic Party of California opposed that state's blanket primary system.

2. Explain why a presidential candidate for the nomination of the Democratic or the Republican Party has to take more extreme policy positions (Democrat more liberal and Republican more conservative) to get the party's nomination than he would take in the general election campaign.

ANSWER KEY

Multiple-Choice Questions

1. B

2. C

3. B

4. B

5. E

Essay Questions

1. Party leaders were initially opposed to a primary election system because of their concern that ordinary people, and not party leaders, would select party candidates. This type of opening of the candidate selection process was seen by political leaders to be a direct challenge to their power and to the strength of the party. They feared that candidate selection by rank-and-file party members who had no experience and knowledge would not result in selecting the strongest candidate. Primary elections let any one who wishes to claim party membership vote on the selection of candidates.

    The blanket primary, in particular, lets a voter switch parties and vote for any candidate without regard to party membership or commitment. Party regulars view this as very detrimental to party organization. Whether the blanket primary is detrimental to party control over selection of its candidates is unclear, but recently, it was seen as a direct threat to the Democratic Party in California. The Supreme Court held that this kind of primary election violated the party's 1st Amendment rights to association.

2. National party convention delegates are selected by various methods in the states: primary elections, caucuses, and state conventions. The selectors in each of these methods tend to be committed and ideological members of the party. That makes them more extreme and purely partisan than the average vote. To win sufficient convention delegate support, that is, the bulk of party activists who seek selection to the national convention, presidential candidates must appear fairly extreme or ideological.

    Once nominated by the convention, candidates must appeal to the large, middle portion of the political spectrum. This segment of the voting population is not ideological, and generally has weak, if any, partisan views. Taking advantage of this fact, candidates "move" to the center of the political spectrum in order to attract these essential voters. While candidates cannot ignore the party regulars and extreme segments of the voting spectrum, they would not be able to win the general election appealing only to those extreme groups.

Chapter 8   *Interest Groups*

The role of the interest group in U.S. politics is to influence policy at the federal, state, and local levels. More specifically, an interest group tries to influence the decisions made by legislators, bureaucrats, and even judges. Interest groups are not explicitly treated in the Constitution, but both freedom of speech and the right to petition government are guaranteed by the 1st Amendment.

Though they often have various political objectives, most interest groups tend to focus their efforts on one single issue. Oftentimes, this is an economic interest in which the members have a clear stake. A few groups may try to push a wide set of policy positions because of a broader philosophical focus such as children's advocacy.

There are various ways in which an interest group can achieve its goal.

1. It may attempt to get specific candidates elected, through campaign contributions (PACs) or electioneering.

2. It may lobby before Congress for a favorable outcome on a specific policy.

3. It may maintain constant contact with those agencies responsible for administering policies that affect its members.

4. It may litigate test cases or act as a supportive third party—*amicus curiae*—in court to obtain rulings, injunctions, or interpretations of laws that favor its interests.

5. It may attempt to persuade the mass media or public opinion to favor its particular interests.

In all, Madison's view of "factions" in *Federalist No. 10* may well illustrate a great deal about modern-day interest groups and their relations with governmental institutions. In that document, he discussed the danger that factions present to the political system, and how they can be controlled.

Kinds of Interest Groups

There are several kinds of interest groups. While they all operate differently, they all face a collective action problem, or the problem of free-riders. What this means is that, if an interest group wins a favorable policy, it cannot exclude nonmembers from receiving that benefit if they qualify. So individuals might well get a "free ride" from a group to which they do not belong or contribute. To the extent that benefits can be isolated and controlled (selective benefits), the free-rider problem can be minimized; however, many public policies produce public goods that have no ownership.

Interest groups are considered to be a universal feature of U.S. politics. Yet some interests, such as the homeless and food stamp recipients, are not represented at all. Other interests, such as U.S. swimming, are not very active, since their interests are not directly affected by policies.

- *Economic* interest groups are the most numerous, and they may be the most successful in achieving their policy objectives. These include trade associations (the U.S. Chamber of Commerce, National Association for the Self-Employed); businesses (IBM, United Airlines); labor organizations (the Teamsters Union, Communications Workers of America); and professional associations (the American Medical Association, the American Bankers Association).

- *Ideological, single-issue* interest groups tend to be composed of true believers who are actively focused on one issue, e.g., Operation Rescue and the National Rifle Association.

- *Public* interest groups, who advocate policies that would achieve a broad public interest, i.e., Common Cause or the American Cancer Society.

- *Foreign* policy interest groups, concerned with matters of foreign policy, e.g., the Counsel of Foreign Relations, the American-Israel Political Action Committee, and the National Association of Arab Americans.

- *Government* interest groups, which are governments that engage in interest group activity in order to achieve favorable policies, e.g., the National Governors' Association, the National League of Cities, and the City of New York.

- *Other* interests groups include ethnic, religious, civil rights, and environmental organizations, who advocate political, economic, or social change for a large segment of Americans.

Interest Groups in Action

How well an interest group succeeds in its policy efforts depends largely on its resources. The extent of resources will determine what strategies it can choose, and what institutions it targets. The most significant resource is *money*. Some interest groups have substantive amounts while others have little. The National Association of Manufacturers, a business-oriented group, will have significantly more money than will the Society of Welfare.

Another resource is *policy expertise*, something most groups possess. With specific objectives in mind, their leaderships are likely to know a good deal about the policies that affect them. Some groups also hire paid lobbyists who have significant contacts in Washington. These lobbyists are important for communicating group preferences, whether to contacts in the bureaucracy or on Capitol Hill. They are also policy experts.

Most groups also have various *communications* mechanisms in place: they conduct mobilization campaigns with their rank-and-file members, and public relations campaigns that seek to "educate" the public about their position.

Interest groups also may have "in their control" *technical information* and expertise that would help policy makers as they formulate public policy. Many agencies lack the resources—time, money, or even expertise—to generate the essential knowledge they need to develop policies or achieve policy objectives.

A second feature of this relationship is that many interest groups have significant control over their own compliance with government policies. The possibility of cooperative compliance is a great influence in a bureaucratic policy because such compliance is cheap for groups and agencies. Reducing compliance costs is important. Interest groups may be willing to obey agency rules when they are to the group's liking, but may not be so willing when the rules hinder their goals.

- Interest groups might seek to obtain financial benefits, such as price supports or subsidies for a particular group of people. An interest group might seek agricultural price supports on behalf of a targeted group of farmers.

- Interest groups might work to attain a public good, such as strong national defense policies. Since no one owns a public good like national defense, the entire population will benefit from the efforts of a select few. Perhaps the interest group is composed of defense contractors who will receive government contracts to build weapons.

- Interest groups might have achieved a desired policy position, and so try to protect the status quo. Other groups might seek change. Those working to maintain the status quo have a decided political advantage over those who seek change: That is because there is inertia in the political system and because changing the status quo is far more difficult than maintaining it.

Some interest group activity is designed largely to inform the public. At most, that type of activity indirectly influences policy making. "Going public" may be designed to shape public opinion, change the climate in which government deals with an issue, or educate people about an issue.

The boundaries separating interest groups are not always clear cut. Some interests may be served by outsiders in the system; for example, poor people with limited financial resources for lobbying and limited expertise about policymaking might be represented by other policy advocates who support their interests. Children, too, are frequently represented by advocates with strong beliefs in children's rights.

When interests overlap, interest groups commonly form temporary coalitions with each other. On the other hand, some groups have been known to refuse to compromise or associate with other groups, even when it would help their cause.

Characteristics of Interest Groups

Groups differ widely from one another in goals, resources, characteristics, and success. Among the important characteristics of groups, the following should be considered.

Although this country is fundamentally individualistic in nature, individual actors frequently engage in collective action. Their goal is to obtain and sustain policies that are favorable to individuals. This may appear inconsistent, but such collective action does magnify individual interests and demands on government.

- *Size or Membership*

  Some groups have hundreds of thousands of members with diverse interests, e.g., the American Association of Retired Persons, scattered throughout the country. Other groups have a few hundred members concentrated in one geographic region, with a narrow specialized interest.

- *Organizational Features*

  Tightly organized groups have phone trees and electronic connections that allow them to mobilize their membership nationwide for letter writing campaigns or grassroots lobbying efforts. Loosely organized groups might have only a quarterly newsletter. How well a group is organized will clearly affect how well its members can mobilize in times of need.

- *Leadership*

  Some groups are run by members—largely amateurs who choose to engage deeply in the organization's efforts and well-being. Other groups hire administrators such as full-time executive directors who have professional skills and a permanent position of advocacy with the group.

Interest Group Factors

Interest groups achieve their goals in different ways. They may use:

- *Direct and/or Indirect Lobbying Techniques*

  Direct efforts involve overt attempts to influence policy choices. Indirect techniques involve influencing a third party or the general public to adopt the group's position. An interest group might conduct a media campaign to persuade the public—rather than policy makers directly—of the importance of an issue.

- *Grass Roots Efforts or "Washington Insiders" Efforts*

  Grass roots efforts involve mobilizing rank-and-file members to write or call their representatives. Washington lobbying is often carried out by hired professionals rather than the rank-and-file membership. These professionals are known inside Washington, and have established contacts with the targeted policy makers.

- *Campaign Contributions*

  If they have the financial resources, some interest groups donate money to election. This is usually done through Political Action Committees (PACs), which collect small sums of money from individuals, "bundle" them into a larger pool of funds, and then donate them to the candidates who support their policy position. Most PAC contributions are given to incumbent officials who occupy positions of influence, such as committee chairs in Congress.

- *Lobbying in the Halls of Congress*

  Though most often done by professional lobbyists, this technique may mean using ordinary group members to create a public relations display on the grounds of the capital, or to visit their congressmen to convince them of the importance of their position.

- *Litigating in Court*

  If they have the expertise, some interests groups may litigate test cases before courts in order to obtain favorable public policies. These test cases give courts the chance to decide issues in ways that favor the group, and most test cases are carefully presented in the most favorable way. And in cases that are litigated by other parties, some groups present courts with *amicus curiae* (friend of the court) supporting material.

- *Bargaining with the Relevant Administrative Agency*

  In this capacity, a group will try to bargain or influence the actual policy that is to be administered. There is a two-way relationship between an administrative agency and an interest group: The agency administers the policy, but the interest groups provide expertise and voluntary compliance. And in exchange for providing this expertise and compliance, an interest group may be able to negotiate with the agency officials about the substance of the rule.

Interest groups use different strategies in order to achieve their goals: lobbying, electioneering, litigating, or public relations. The success of these efforts depends on the issue involved, the credibility of organized interests, the resources an interest group may possess, and the public impression or climate.

In some policy areas, iron triangles exist. These involve: (1) relevant interest groups, (2) the related subcommittees in Congress, and (3) the administrators of the policy. These three entities form a closely knit, mutually dependent relationship that can effectively control a policy. This phenomenon also leads to career "revolving doors" for participants who can move between the public and private portions of such a triangle.

An issue network is a larger, loosely knit set of players (officials, experts, and the public) all concerned about or affected by policy, such as national transportation or communications.

Patterns of Success

Over the years, interest groups have had different levels of access and success in the political arena.

- Interests representing organized labor are generally powerful because of their numbers and because of the money and workers they can provide to legislative candidates who support their interests. These interests are spread throughout the country, in all states and congressional districts.

- Organized business interests are also fairly successful because of the financial resources they can offer campaigns and the technical expertise they can provide to policy makers.

- Some interest groups lack money and numbers, but still effectively represent their positions. They may use their expertise, perhaps in litigation strategies, as have the NAACP and Jehovah's Witnesses.

- Other interest groups may not be organized or may have fewer channels by which to voice their needs, and so gain little attention in the policymaking arena. Policies that may address their interests are formulated without their direct participation or representation: poor people or welfare recipients; children; and even consumers, who are difficult to organize because all Americans are consumers yet their consumer beliefs differ. The Consumer's Union, or even individual representatives like Ralph Nader (long considered the "voice" of consumers) are unorganized, albeit loud.

As technology develops and organizational strategies take hold, more and more interest groups will likely enter the political arena. And as they do, they will test the idea of a true representative democracy: Congress and the executive must try to balance all of their interests, many of which are mutually exclusive. Insofar as each group seeks its own narrow goal rather than a broad public interest, that will be a significant task.

POINTS TO REMEMBER

- Computer technology can facilitate the success of an interest group, in how well it mobilizes members, raises money, and develops public relations campaigns.

- For some Americans, an interest group can bridge the gap between individual citizens and policy makers. That is, an interest group may allow a person to magnify his preferences and voice.

- Interest groups face little legal control by government. They are limited and regulated in how and when they can contribute to campaigns, and they are, as are we all, prohibited from bribing public officials. Beyond that, they enjoy the same 1st Amendment rights that we all enjoy.

KEY TERMS AND CONCEPTS

amicus curiae brief

A brief is a document filed with a court containing a legal argument supporting a desired outcome in a particular case. An *amicus curiae* brief is filed by a party not directly involved in the litigation but with an interest in the outcome of the case. *Amicus curiae* is Latin for "friend of the court."

collective good

Something enjoyed by all members of a society or community, such as clean air.

direct technique

Direct interaction with government officials that is used by interest groups to further their goals.

economic interest group

Interest groups that work to gain economic benefits for their members. Examples include the National Association of Manufacturers (NAM) and the American Federation of Labor-Congress of Industrial Organizations (AFL-CIO).

Federal Election Campaign Act

An act passed in 1972 that controls the raising and spending of funds for political campaigns. A second act passed in 1974 imposed additional reforms, including creation of the Federal Election Commission; providing public financing for presidential primaries and general elections; limiting presidential campaign spending; limiting contributions by citizens and groups; and requiring disclosure of contributions.

Federal Regulation of Lobbying Act (1946)

An act that sought to regulate the lobbying activities of pressure groups.

free-rider problem

The problem that interest groups face when people can benefit from their activities without actually joining or participating in the interest group.

gridlock

A complete lack of movement or progress in the passage of legislation, typically resulting from conflicts between political parties or between the Congress and president.

incumbent

A person who holds an office or an official position.

indirect technique

The use by interest groups of third parties to influence government officials and their decisions.

interest group

A group of organized individuals who share common goals and try to influence government decision makers on issues that directly or indirectly affect the members of the group. Interest groups may differ in goals, financial power, size, and political power and influence, but their methods are generally the same: lobbying and producing and disseminating propaganda. They are also called a pressure group or lobby.

iron triangle

A three-way alliance between political organizations or agents. It's generally thought that iron triangles hinder the political process by putting their own interests ahead of national interests. A well-known iron triangle involves the Pentagon, defense contractors, and the Congressional committees in charge of defense spending.

labor movement

Generally speaking, the concerns and expressions of the working class regarding the economy and politics. In a political sense, the organization of working-class groups to further their economic and political interests. Unions are the interest groups formed to address the concerns of these laborers.

lobbying

Efforts by individuals or organizations to pass, defeat, change, or influence the crafting of laws and the decisions, policies, and actions of the government.

material incentive

An economic motivation for doing something.

political action committee (PAC)

An interest group that gives money collected from members to political candidates or parties. The Committee on Political Education from the 1940s began the movement toward PACs. The Federal Election Campaign Act of 1974 authorized PACs for interest groups, corporations, labor unions, and others. Under the 1974 law, PACs could give as much as $5,000 dollars to as many as five candidates in a federal election, as long as the money was freely donated by at least fifty donors. PACs have revolutionized campaign finance.

pressure system

A theory of American politics in which organized special interest groups dominate government. It tends to have a business or upper-class bias.

private interest group

An interest group working in the interests of a small group of people, as opposed to a public interest group.

professional interest group

Type of private interest group that represents the interests of professionals. Examples include the American Bar Association (for lawyers) and the American Medical Association (for doctors).

public employee interest group

A type of private interest group that works to further the interests of government employees.

public interest

To the benefit of the members of an entire community. Generally, this is in contrast to a private interest, or something that is of benefit to an individual or group.

public interest group

A type of interest group that work on issues affecting broad segments of the population. Public interest groups often form as social movements mature.

purposive incentive

A motivation that is dependent on ethical beliefs, values, or ideological principles.

selective incentive

Material benefits available to members of an interest group. These are given to avoid the "free-rider" problem.

single-issue group

Interest group concerned with a single issue, such as the National Rifle Association.

social movement

Activation of a segment of the public for political, economic, or social change.

soft money

Campaign contributions that get around laws setting maximum campaign contributions because they're given to political parties and party committees to fund general party activities, instead of to a specific candidate. The party can then use this money in a way that helps its candidates.

solidary incentive

Motivation based on shared associations, hobbies, or interests.

subsidy

Financial aid that the government provides to individuals, groups, businesses, or other levels of government.

Multiple-Choice Questions

1. Which of the following is not true of the American Association of Retired Persons (AARP)?

    A. It is the nation's largest interest group.

    B. It is one of the most powerful interest groups in Washington.

    C. It provides selective incentives for its members.

    D. Its members tend to be poor and in need of special protective legislation.

    E. It is a strong supporter of the social security system.

2. A public good is all of the following except

    A. it is a good owned by the public in general.

    B. it includes national defense.

    C. it is a good you can enjoy without contributing.

    D. it is a collective good.

    E. it involves problems with enforcement of property rights.

3. Which of the following is an example of an indirect interest group technique?

    I. meeting privately with public officials to persuade them to vote on behalf of the group's interests

    II. testifying at congressional hearings about proposed legislation

    III. providing members of Congress or bureaucratic agencies with drafts of proposed legislation or administrative rules

    IV. taking out advertisements in a national publication in support of a specific position

        A. I and II

        B. II and III

        C. I, II, and III

        D. II, III, and IV

        E. I, II, III, and IV

4. Which statement is not true about lobbyists and lobbying?

    A. Lobbyists frequently provide needed information to public officials.

    B. Lobbyists sometimes invite legislators to social occasions such as cocktail parties.

    C. Lobbyists sometimes write or help write pieces of legislation.

    D. Lobbyists can exert influence when they testify before executive rule-making agencies.

    E. Foreign lobbyists do not have the same rights of access to government officials as do domestic lobbyists.

5. Interest groups

    A. offer potential members incentives to join.

    B. rely solely on lobbying to influence the political process.

    C. are allowed to contribute as much money as they want to candidates for Congress.

    D. only represent corporations and other business interests.

    E. run candidates for political office.

Essay Questions

1. Select and define three of the following interest group resources. Define each selection and explain how it affects interest group success on influencing policy.

   - Technical expertise
   - Money
   - Membership
   - Narrow or single issue policy interest
   - Professional, paid lobbyists

2. Some interests in this country are virtually silent in terms of interest group politics. Why is that? Explain three characteristics of these interests or segments of the population that make their organization difficult.

ANSWER KEY

Multiple-Choice Questions

1. D
2. A
3. E
4. E
5. A

Essay Questions

1. *Technical expertise* is the expert knowledge an interest group has about the policy area or interests that concern it. Expertise may clearly indicate what kinds of policies are most likely to succeed, and how to formulate successful policies.

   Money is a self-explanatory resource since it facilitates a great many methods by which a group might wish to influence policy. Money is required to fund a group's organization, communication with its membership, and influence on public policy as the interest would like.

   Membership as a resource means that the more members in a group, the stronger the group will be. This means more voters, more experts, and more contributors of money and energy to lobbying or electoral politics. How easily or well an organization can mobilize its rank-and-file membership to vote, lobbying, or campaign is an open question, but without significant membership, an organization will be hard pressed to influence policy.

   Single issue relates to the narrowness of a group's focus. The narrower the interest, the more focused the group can be in achieving its policy goals. Broad interest groups have a harder time getting members to focus on narrow issues or to coalesce around a specific policy proposal. Narrow interests can remain focused.

   Professional, paid lobbyists provide crucial and reliable contacts between members and relevant legislators and policy administrators. Amateur lobbying by members can influence legislators since these are voters who can at least threaten not to vote for the incumbent's re-election. Professionals have credibility and experience with lobbying, and that makes them very effective in getting the group's viewpoint across.

2. Silent interest groups are generally those that lack resources or that have characteristics which limit their ability to organize. That includes knowledge about how to advocate and influence policy making. Many organized groups are visible, at least on those occasions when their essential interest is threatened.

    Following are characteristics that will significantly limit the group's strength.

    - No organization or means of communicating

    - No articulate (or visible) leader

    - Few resources like money or knowledge about the policy making process

    - A lack of knowledge about the policy issues that will affect the interest

    - A lack of a focused, clear position on an issue of policy concern

Chapter 9   *The Media*

In the United States, the mass media has roles that are both related and unrelated to politics and governing. One fundamental feature of the media in this country is that it is privately owned and is commercial. That means media outlets must be profitable to their owners or else they will not continue. And since they do not rely on the government for funding, it also means that for the most part, they function independently. The free press prides itself on independence, accuracy in reporting, objectivity, and currency, and while there are exceptions, most would recognize these as important features of the U.S. media.

As an "information and opinion" provider, the media provides a major conduit between government and the citizenry of this country. Some media broadcasters make an effort to present objective facts and news, but others actually advocate positions or seek to persuade. And since the media's market penetration is uneven throughout the country, its impact on the American public is uneven. Moreover, not everyone reads newspapers, has cable TV, or has access to the Internet. The result is a disparity of sources and information for many Americans.

> Electronic media has superseded print media for most Americans. Instantaneous news and expected immediate responses leave little time to think or reflect. Thus, "cooler heads" are less likely to prevail in times of crisis or deadline.

The Dynamics of the American Media

Media broadcasters play a significant role in this country. They are the primary channels through which social, political, and factual information is transmitted from the "system" to the population. Conversely, the media may convey demands and concerns

Broadcast reporters tend to rely on sources they develop over time. These sources are often government officials who can provide information, perhaps without attribution, that allow individual broadcasters to "scoop" their competitors. At the same time, these same sources may use the media to float trial balloons about new policy proposals. This provides useful information for the media, and useful feedback to the government sources.

back to policymakers. Media broadcasters also fulfill a watchdog function, by scrutinizing the actions and decisions of government.

Yet the broadcast media is by nature entertaining, and that is largely at odds with its political function. After all, broadcasters want to attract as many paying viewers or readers as possible, and as a result, Americans today seem to expect that reporting—even political reporting—has entertainment value. Ironically, though, many people question the value of media coverage: it is not necessarily comprehensive, systematic, or analytic, and may be biased. In fact, whether or not it is biased, the media is often perceived to be so. But regardless of this fact, many people continue to rely on only one media source for their news.

Representatives of the People

The process by which the media affects the political process, and vice versa, is a bidirectional one. That is, policymakers use the media to communicate their plans and impressions to the public, and the public uses the media to communicate back its preferences for governmental policy. The primary characteristics of this relationship are:

1. The media is the watchdog of government.

2. The media is the primary way that information about actors and events is conveyed.

3. The media informs voters of electoral choices at the same time that it informs political candidates of voter preferences.

Politics and Policy Making

The relationship between media broadcasters and political candidates is a mutually dependent one: Broadcasters can be closely linked to campaigns and election results, and they rely on candidates to provide interesting news for broadcast. Broadcasters also allow candidates to relay their platforms, and "trial balloons," of their policy issues. Candidates, on the other hand, use the media to campaign and convey their platform, whether through paid or unpaid (free) air time. The interdependent nature of their relationship has resulted in "horse-race" journalism. That is, the media reports more on who is ahead, and less on who is trailing in the polls.

Given the strength of the media in society, politicians and institutions wage a constant war in trying to limit media access to information or to manipulate the way the media portrays information. Naturally, certain officials, such as the president, have more access to the media than do others. In fact, press organizations very much rely on the president's press secretary and the White House press corps for news. How much access the media is given depends on how much public relations ability an official has. On the other hand, what kind of interest the media takes in an official depends on the office and its visibility, and the level of controversy.

Agenda Setting

The media's role in agenda setting is a visible one, for both public and institutional agendas. It communicates issues that appear to demand governmental attention. In this context, the "media" is plural and multiple, and does not act with one sole purpose or speak with one voice. Having said that, media outlets, particularly electronic ones, all need to attract audiences, and with no incentive to explore unique material, tend to be homogenous in their coverage. The print media, on the other hand, is more diversified in its perspective and coverage because its readers are more fractionated or divided.

Socialization

The media, particularly the electronic media, serves as a socializing agent for many people. It presents audiences with beliefs and impressions of officials and governmental institutions. Children watch a good deal of TV, and are naturally affected by these impressions, whether good or bad. Some adults are impressionable as well. How effective this unintended function is in shaping values is an unsettled issue. However, for many people, the media teaches political values.

> The effect of media on public opinion is not at all automatic or direct. It depends on conditions and the climate, as well as the issue and individuals involved. If people are strongly predisposed to certain positions, they will be less likely to react to media information.

Government Regulation of the Media

Although media outlets are largely independent in this country, they do have some regulations. The government controls the allocation of most of the electromagnetic spectrum; that is, the airwaves. Though the spectrum technically belongs to the people, its limited capacity has forced government to take on this task. Some people advocate the sale and ownership of the spectrum, claiming private ownership would ensure its optimal use. But because the spectrum is so scarce, the non-broadcast media (Internet, e-mail, etc.) may well replace it in the future.

The 1st Amendment, freedom of the press, ensures the media of significant freedom from government control. This protects journalists from having to disclose their sources. It is common to see an "anonymous governmental official" sourced. This allows the media to gain more information and thus appear to be doing a good job of "covering" government and politics.

In that broadcasters may be biased by editorial or headline considerations, they inevitably influence how people perceive government. The choices that a television station makes about what stories will lead and what stories will not even air communicate certain values to the public. And since this is done imperceptibly, many Americans are unaware that there is a bias in their news coverage. For those individuals who are not "skeptical" or cautious viewers, these biases take on even more significance. Quite likely these viewers will make incorrect or incomplete assessments about what they have seen.

In an effort to sell newspapers, the media tends to position campaigns as "political races," where one individual is seen as ahead of the rest. As a result, little or no media attention is paid to third-party candidates or to policy proposals that are not mainline. The net result is that the American public unknowingly receives limited information about candidates and issues.

Another slant in the American media is that broadcast coverage tends to focus on problems rather than successes. Some issues are entirely ignored; perhaps because they are too complicated to convey in a brief timeslot or column. Perhaps they are omitted from broadcast because they affect only a small number of people, or an insignificant amount of money.

The media is not completely uncontrolled or unlimited by government and by law. There are libel and slander laws against certain kinds of publications that protect people from invasions of their privacy. However, the courts have given the press more freedom with regard to reporting on public figures than on private citizens. Since the public figures have chosen to enter public life, whether it be in politics or in entertainment, they must expect criticism and some intrusion into their lives by the press. As a result, it is difficult for public officials to use libel laws to restrain the press.

In the same way that the media transmits information *to* the public, it also conveys impressions and preferences *from* the public back to policymakers. In an attempt to "speak for the people," the media communicates impressions—many of them critical—back to the government. It is important to note, however, that while the media sometimes uses accurate polling to gauge public impressions, it frequently does not. As such, the media has great leverage in how it shapes and colors the public interest, but has little accurate or empirical basis for the content of its coverage.

Trends in the Media

Given the costs of publication and the shrinking size of readership pools, the "mass" dimension of the media may spell the downfall of print journalism in the United States. Because of its convenience and speed, electronic media is more emphasized than print. In fact, C-SPAN television was designed to provide the public with an "unvarnished," objective glimpse into how the different branches govern, though it only reaches cable subscribers. Electronic and print media each have different audiences: audience size and wealth differ. As a result, their audience expectations differ.

- The growth of electronic media specialization, such as 24-hour news channels, will have a significant continuing affect on the information people have. The fractionation of the audience occurs for cable viewers (about $\frac{2}{3}$ of the television audience has access to cable). This "narrowcasting" will increase as audiences become more able to sift through the programming to select specialized coverage.

- Newspaper readership is significantly declining in this country given the cost and speed of alternative sources. In its place is the Internet, which is an exploding political phenomenon. As it continues to expand, the Internet will segregate the population according to availability, access to technology, and wealth. This phenomenon will no doubt affect the kinds of information available, and more important, the accuracy of that information.

- The nature of television programming has become quite controversial, particularly in connection with programs containing sex and violence. Many argue that this kind of programming has desensitized viewers—particularly children and younger people—to the sanctity of human life and the importance of tolerance and civility. This controversy spills over into politics when a public official is suspected of indiscretions or criminal activity. The lack of government control (censorship), and the broadcast industry's need for a profit have been identified as major reasons for increased criminal activity and violence.

- With the Internet, people now have access to a multiplicity of information sources. While there are advantages to this, it also puts more strain on their ability to assess the accuracy and usefulness of these sources. This open access also permits transient and unidentified sources to "blast" an official or policy proposal, and then disappear when questions about veracity appear.

- Many schools now depend on computers and the Internet for instructional material, and how this will affect student learning is unknown today. Many concerns have been raised about this kind of instruction:

  1. Technology breaks down.

  2. Technology is accessible only to those who can afford it.

  3. In a school setting, technology can individualize information, thereby reducing contact between the student and teachers (and even other students).

  4. Students have access to an indiscriminate source of materials, and if they lack discriminating analytic skills, may be unable to distinguish fact from fiction, or bias from objectivity.

- Individual privacy, now protected by the Constitution, has been recognized by many in society as a fundamental right. Yet given the media's right to investigate and inform the public, individual privacy rights and the freedom of the press often clash. Lurid celebrity headlines, accusations unsupported by fact, and "doctored" photographs make it nearly impossible for public figures to enjoy personal privacy, or to sue the media for libel—even when grounded in fact.

Media Accuracy

The accuracy of the media can be problematic, though that is beyond the reach or control of government. The print media regularly prints corrections or apologies, which may or may not be satisfactory. The electronic media is instantaneous or "hot," meaning it moves quickly from subject to subject. By jumping from issue to issue without elaboration, or a permanent record of what information has been conveyed, mistakes are less easily spotted or corrected.

Concern over foreign "cyber-attacks" has recently increased. Some countries with less significant traditional military establishments may invest developing money in computer viruses. Given the number of "civilian" virus attacks on computers worldwide, it is conceivable that an adversary could disable the U.S. military, banking, and/or government operation systems.

Media Coverage

There are wide disparities in the coverage of local issues, by local media, and of national or international issues, by both local and national media. Wire services, such as AP, UPI, *The New York Times*, or *Gannett*, provide subscribers with standard, useable stories about national or international events. Continual news institutions such as CNN and MSNBC bypass local media entirely. Local coverage depends greatly on either homogenous wire service stories about national and international events, or local idiosyncratic treatment of local issues.

Public officials commonly try to control media access, and to manipulate or slant the information that broadcasters convey on the air. With their public persona at stake, officials go to great lengths to position themselves in the best light: they use spin control and consult spin doctors, they stage media events, and they use media consultants.

At odds with these officials is a media that, in order to attract audiences and exhibit a "government watchdog" role, does its best to convey controversial and visible information. As new technologies develop, the role of media in politics will change. The media will continue to grow in political importance because of its control over the distribution of information. The role of the media in politics will change as new technologies develop. In addition, the government's role in technology development will influence the media.

POINTS TO REMEMBER

- The media is driven largely by its need to make a profit. It accomplishes this by advertising to large audiences.

- The media contributes to the success or failure of campaigns for elected office.

- The media helps to determine what agendas will be set in Washington.

- The media helps to shape people's impressions of government, individual officials, and policy problems and successes.

- The media plays a role in "educating" the public, but that role is unclear, uneven, and sometimes quite negative.

- While there is some government control over the media, it does not affect content. Government regulation does not include ownership of any segment of the media.

KEY TERMS AND CONCEPTS

1st Amendment

This opening passage of the Bill of Rights prohibits Congress from establishing a religion and ensures freedom of expression, religion, press, assembly, and petition.

attack ad

Political advertising that denounces a candidate's opponent by name.

Communications Decency Act (1996)

An act that makes the spread of "indecent" materials on the Internet to anyone under the age of 18 a crime.

electronic media

Radio and television broadcasting media. The term derives from their method of transmission, in contrast to print media.

Federal Communications Commission (FCC)

An independent regulatory commission that controls interstate and foreign electronic communications.

feeding frenzy

A process through which members of the media attack politicians or candidates whose performance or character has been called into question.

Through such activity, journalists have become news makers as much as news reporters, propelling some politicians to power, while helping to eliminate others. The term refers to the behavior of hungry animals that encounter a food source.

fractionation

The division of audiences into small, specialized and narrow groups, based on specialized interests. See *narrowcasting*.

freedom of the press

The right to publish and disseminate information without prior restraint, subject to penalties for abuse of the right through such actions as obscenity, libel, incitement to crime, contempt of court, and sedition. Guaranteed by the 1st and 14th Amendments.

front runner

The presidential candidate considered to have the lead at any given time in an election.

gatekeeper function

The power of national media to control the public agenda by deciding what the public will learn about. It gains this power by choosing which topics to report on.

horse race coverage

Media coverage of presidential primaries with an emphasis on who is leading, who is behind, and who has dropped out.

investigative journalism

Journalism in which writers actively seek to uncover detailed descriptions of wrongdoings. See *muckraker*.

issue ad

Political advertisement focusing on a specific issue rather than on a particular candidate.

Kennedy-Nixon debates

The 1960 presidential election debates between John F. Kennedy and Richard Nixon. The debates were televised and broadcast on radio. Kennedy wore a dark suit that contrasted with the background, while Nixon's lighter suit blended into the background and gave him a washed-out appearance. Most of those who watched the debates on television felt Kennedy won, while most who listened on the radio felt Nixon won. These debates were a turning point in the identification of the power of television as a political medium.

libel

Written defamation of a person's character, which may expose the person to hatred or ridicule, damage his reputation through criminal accusations, or harm him within his profession. Libel is usually dealt with in civil court, though sometimes in criminal court. The truth of a statement is generally considered a suitable defense against charges of libel. The 1st Amendment gives the press a limited amount of freedom from libel actions.

managed news

News the government produces that's designed more to make the government and its interests, policies, and action look good (or less bad, as the case may be) than to deliver complete, truthful, and accurate information to the public.

marketplace of ideas

The concept that government has no role in managing or controlling the flow of ideas, arguments, or opinions that occur naturally in a society, and that this flow, if left unhindered, will eventually result in the best ideas rising to the top. This is one of the main justifications of the freedom of the press. The concept was most thoroughly developed by John Stuart Mill.

media consultant

A professional paid by a party, candidate, or government official to help present news stories in ways that reflect positively on a candidate or government official. See *spin doctor*.

media event

A time when government officials or politicians arrange for television and newspaper reporters to see some dramatic evidence of government achievements or decision making.

muckraker

A journalist or writer who investigates and exposes wrongdoings and excesses of corporations and the government.

narrowcasting

Broadcasting whose content and presentation is directed to a small sector of the population.

national newspaper chain

A collection of newspapers owned by one individual or company that are distributed to many cities nationally. In theory, a chain allows wider distribution of political news and ideas. They have also given increased power to those publishers aiming to influence politics.

political advertising

Advertising a political candidate via mass media. Political advertising is a very influential, controversial, sophisticated, and lucrative industry.

press secretary

The person who represents the White House to the media. The press secretary writes news releases, sets up press conferences, and acts as an intermediary between the White House and the nation (through the press) in the dissemination of information from the White House.

prior restraint

Preventing an action before it even happens. Prior restraint relies on censorship instead of subsequent punishment.

public agenda

Issues members of a political community consider worthy of public attention and governmental action. The media has a great deal of influence on the public agenda.

sound bite

A short, catchy, memorable statement that news broadcasters can easily fit into their coverage of political events.

spin

Public-relations campaign interpretation of events or election results that are intended to help a public figure.

spin doctor

An adviser to a political campaign who tries to persuade journalists of a particular interpretation of events. The intent here is to put a candidate or party in a favorable light, and the opposing candidate or party in a negative light.

spot ad

A type of political advertising that generally promotes a candidate, in a positive fashion, by name.

watchdog function

The duty to oversee the administration of the law.

White House press corps

Reporters from various news organizations with the full-time assignment of covering and reporting on the presidency.

yellow journalism

Sensationalistic and irresponsible journalism, often associated with William Randolph Hearst, but seen widely throughout the press. The term is thought to have originated from the phrase "Yellow Kid journalism," which was itself an allusion to the old *New York World* cartoon "The Yellow Kid." The *New York World*, owned by Joseph Pulitzer, was a particularly sensationalistic newspaper.

Multiple-Choice Questions

1. At the turn of the 19th century, the press was:

   A. more partisan than it is today.

   B. pretty much the same as it is now.

   C. less partisan than it is today.

   D. shackled by restrictions that prevented it from reporting negative news about the government.

   E. less prone to muckraking that it is today.

2. Which of the following are true about mass media coverage of presidential elections?

   I. Mass media focuses almost exclusively on substantive issues.

   II. Mass media focuses primarily on the horse-race aspect of the campaign.

   III. Campaigns employ spin doctors in an attempt to obtain favorable media coverage.

   IV. Electronic media largely covers candidates, while print media covers substantive issues.

      A. I and II

      B. II only

      C. II and III

      D. III and IV

      E. II and IV

3. The growth of the Internet has affected American politics in all of the following ways except

   A. it has allowed citizens to learn more about political candidates.

   B. it has allowed citizens to engage in more debate about political issues.

   C. it has contributed to increased reporting of information on the private lives of political figures.

   D. it has enabled more citizens to contact their elected officials.

   E. it has eclipsed the role of television as a source of political information.

4. The majority of mass media campaign coverage tends to focus on

   A. the presidential debates.

   B. third party candidates.

   C. who is currently winning and losing.

   D. the mood of the electorate.

   E. the major issues facing the country.

5. The electronic media versus the print media tend to be

    A. interested in in-depth analysis of news events and candidates for office.

    B. generally more concerned about instantaneous news and events than analysis.

    C. focused on controversial and personal information about candidates.

    D. more heavily regulated by the legal system in this country.

    E. more invasive of personal privacy and intimate details of candidates' lives.

6. The CNN effect is

    A. the caution that television cameras generate for a public official when being interviewed.

    B. the reliability and credibility that viewers have for information and analysis conveyed by the television networks.

    C. the willingness of television to create and even fabricate stories to attract viewers.

    D. the purported ability of television to raise a distant foreign affairs situation to national prominence by broadcasting vivid pictures.

    E. the profound ability of television to raise people's interest in politics and public policy issues.

Essay Questions

1. Identify three ways in which the media depends on candidates for office, and three ways in which the candidates use the media during election campaigns. Explain how these bidirectional efforts at influence or control aid both of these actors.

2. What reasons are there for the government to regulate the content of the Internet? The content of over-the-air television broadcasting? The content of cablecasters? What reasons are there to prevent such regulation? Be sure to present an equally balanced treatment of these reasons.

ANSWER KEY

Multiple-Choice Questions
1. A
2. C
3. E
4. C
5. B
6. D

Essay Questions
1.   The media depends on candidates for:
   • "News" about their positions on issues
   • Information on their reactions to events and other campaign events
   • Information about their personal lives and concerns

   Candidates depend on the media for:
   • Broad coverage of their views and agenda issues, as well as policy proposals
   • Free advertising
   • Framing issues or concerns in ways that favor their candidacy and that support their party

   The interdependent nature of this relationship has led to both sides accepting and tolerating what the other side needs.

2.   Government regulation of the Internet could be justified in part because of the speed and diversity of distribution, as well as the anonymity of the Internet sources. Furthermore, with respect to children, the lack of screening devices or parental supervision makes government regulation justified. Some parents may want to monitor their children, but lack the technical ability to do so.

   Over-the-air broadcasting might be regulated in part because of the limited resource involved. There are not enough airwaves for everyone, so the licensees should be subject to certain limitations.

   Cablecasting is more limited to those who subscribe. They can also choose which channels they wish to receive. Presumably there is little justification for controlling cable content: The cable does not use a limited resource, so anyone who wants to and can afford to use it can do so.

Prohibiting various forms of communication that are detrimental to children is one justification that is widely cited for regulation. Regardless of how the information is transmitted, it includes various kinds of objectionable speech or press. There are legitimate concerns about such obscenity or fighting words. Protecting children from this clearly may justify government regulation. However, the standards for this regulation are controversial and not at all clear, and they often fail to sustain when challenged against the 1st Amendment.

Much regulation does not take place because no definable standards have been set. Until that happens, no censor—government or otherwise—has guidelines with which to regulate. Some justifications for censorship and regulation are not very convincing, since the free market of ideas argues that all voices should be heard and those that prevail in the marketplace should be recognized.

UNIT FIVE:

Institutions of American Government

Chapter 10   *Congress*

Congress is the bicameral legislative body of the national government. It is composed of two chambers: the upper chamber, the *Senate*, and the lower chamber, the *House of Representatives*. The organization of each house is complex, with several subunits that assist the legislature in lawmaking. From small subcommittee units to full conference committees, Congress follows processes that are complicated, nuanced, and convoluted. That makes the legislative process slow, complex, and uncertain.

The relationship between Congress and other policymaking institutions—the presidency, the bureaucracy, and the judiciary—is constantly changing. Individual legislators and their constituents generally have a unique and idiosyncratic relationship. Yet, Congress formulates and considers general legislation for the entire country.

> Congress's authority partly depends on the Supreme Court for its interpretation.

Although not often visible in the legislative process, each congressional chamber resolves conflicts among interests both *inside the legislature* and *within the U.S. population*. In order to both serve their constituents and to push through their policies, legislators tend to balance two styles of behavior, Home Style and Washington Style.

The First Branch of Government

Congress performs a variety of functions, both institutionally and individually. Most of these functions are listed in Article I of the U.S. Constitution.

Lawmaking

The most obvious function of Congress is to make laws or adopt policy for the national government. The Constitution provides only slight guidance about the process by which laws are made, but the function of lawmaking is clearly expected of Congress.

> Congress is the most representative body in our political system, yet it does not always reflect voter preferences. Furthermore, the policy preferences of legislators and constituents do not always coincide.

This very general legislative framework has led to a number of complaints about Congress. Many argue that it does not act quickly or respond to immediate needs. It is likely that the framers did not wish that to occur, but rather expected the Congress to be a deliberative body. Regardless, people expect Congress to adopt policies that will address "problems."

Initially, legislators identify problems and fashion proposed bills or "solutions" to those problems. The bills go on to gain, or lose, support and consequently have different chances of success in the legislative process. While most proposed policies are indeed serious attempts to address problems, many legislative efforts will inevitably fail due to lack of interest and support. Yet even those that fail may serve a symbolic effort to pacify advocates.

Representation of Constituent Interests

A second function of Congress is to represent the interests of constituents. There are both collective interests of the district (or state), and individual interests within that population. Senators and Representatives devote major amounts of time to determining constituent interests and needs—many of which compete or conflict with one another—and balancing them into a single policy position or proposed bill. At the same time, legislators must address and heed the needs of large campaign contributors, who may not even be constituents.

> Some legislators will vote according to the preferences of their colleagues, their party leaders, the president, or even their sense of the public interest.

Casework

Another task of legislators is casework; that is, legislators troubleshoot problems or complaints that individual constituents may have with government institutions. In exchange for their "personal intervention," representatives often win electoral support from those who have had their problems solved. The casework function is different from the function of representing constituent interests, in that it involves interceding with the government on behalf of one person or small group. The latter function, on the other hand, relates to the proposal and adoption of policies or laws.

Legislative Oversight

Another major function of Congress is to oversee the administration of policies. This is called *legislative oversight*. Though not a highly visible or constituent-oriented function, this is something that congressional committees have focused on in recent decades. While Congress may not wish to do this kind of work—it is complicated and does not grab headlines—growing constituent complaints and exposed policy failures by the media have forced this role.

The way in which Congress oversees this process is to investigate and evaluate the work of the responsible administration agency—the bureaucracy. Oversight allows Congress to determine the success or failure of legislative policies. For failures, it enables legislators to place blame on the bureaucracy —a favorite, amorphous target—and perhaps correct policy mistakes. And frequently, once blame has been placed, these same legislators go on to win favor by informing the public about possible solutions. And for policy successes, oversight allows legislators to take credit.

A legislator's mandate is to represent the interests of his constituents. But at the same time, he must also respond to interest groups with specific economic, social, and political demands. As a result, legislators are often forced to compromise on issues and policy proposals, to support policies that others advocate, to allow opponents to succeed, and to see their own preferences lose out to delay or defeat.

Originally, the two houses represented very different constituencies. The House of Representatives represented the people, while the Senate represented the state legislatures. But that changed in 1913, after the adoption of the 17th Amendment provided for the direct election of senators. Now, the Senate and the House both represent the people, but with different perspectives:

- Senators have longer terms in office (6 years) than do Representatives (2 years).

- Senators generally have larger and more diverse constituencies—entire states— than do Representatives. On average, House members represent 550,000 people.

- The legislative process in the Senate is less formal than the House, in part because it is smaller.

- The House (but not the Senate) is affected by the "one person, one vote" concept. Legislative districts are drawn and redrawn every time the total U.S. population is counted; that is done every ten years by the Census Bureau. Based on the current population numbers, reapportionment occurs; that is, the reallocation of the 435 House seats among the states.

Legislator Styles

Being able to respond to competing and conflicting demands is one of a legislator's greatest challenges, and each one handles it differently. It depends on his expertise. It depends on the current district and policy issues. In that the interests and demands are always changing, the challenge to balance them successfully is constant. Legislators know that if they are successful in this delicate balancing act, it will be helpful in their bid for re-election.

There are various "styles" with which representatives take on their functions, and this depends on the individual elected to office:

> Congress performs two kinds of functions: First, individual legislators assist their individual constituents. Second, the full chamber performs some functions, such as law making or legislative oversight. These functions should be kept separate when evaluating the work of Congress and legislators. In part, this accounts for the divided view that many people have in which they love their congressman but dislike Congress.

Once the conflict among policy advocates is resolved and a bill has been adopted by both houses, the final shape of a bill is determined by negotiations in a Conference Committee. In order make the House and the Senate versions of the bill coincide, the final bill is sometimes drastically revised from its original version.

- The *delegate*, or instructed delegate, believes that he should reflect (i.e., mirror) the preferences of constituents without passing judgment or trying to sway their beliefs.

- The *trustee* tends to see his role as one that should filter constituent preferences through his own good judgment and beliefs.

- The *politico* tends to focus on deal-making without close attention to constituent preferences or his own principles and beliefs.

Most legislators concentrate on one of these roles, but can and do blend them. At times, legislators may also consider a "public interest," that is, what is good for the country. For example, in foreign policy, legislators may not be able to help their constitutents, but they will vote for what they believe is in the best interest of the country. Similarly, when a crisis does not directly affect constituents, it may still require a legislator's attention.

Every ten years, when the U.S. census is taken, House members face reapportionment and perhaps redistricting. This involves political and racial gerrymandering. The result is that for many House members, their district boundaries will change and thus their constituent base will change. This means legislators will have to assess and represent their new interests.

Agenda Setting

Agenda setting by the legislature is essential to the policy-making process. Many factors can affect the agenda setting process.

- Congress must be able to work with the president, who clearly has the media's "ear" and has his own "bully-pulpit" as well as his own priorities.

- Congress must be able to work with the congressional caucuses or the parties in each house, who may hold more closely to partisan agendas than would individual legislators.

- Unexpected crises and events, such as energy crises, military interventions, natural disasters, or economic problems, which divert attention and policy efforts from the longer-term needs of the country.

- Constituents become mobilized when they perceive a threat or an opportunity to win or lose something of value—subsidies, favorable policies, symbolic issues.

- Campaign contributors expect legislators to respond when their interests are at stake, and since legislators hope for continued financial and electoral support, they pay close attention to those demands when they arise.

The Organization of Congress

The organization of Congress is complex and cumbersome. Leadership in both houses is based on the majority party—the majority party caucus. Leadership styles vary a good deal depending on partisanship, prior experience, individual leaders, and interpersonal skills. The party caucus, both minority and majority party, determines committee memberships, chairmanships, and other leadership positions. The caucus also sets policy positions on issues as well as selects party leaders in each chamber.

The debates that take place on the floor of each chamber do not often persuade legislators to vote differently, though they do establish public records of Congress's intention. In fact, the public can watch these debates on C-SPAN, which may include symbolic acts of support or criticism of bills.

The legislative process is the most visible and controversial part of the functioning of Congress. In that Congress is designed to be deliberative, the process contains many steps that increase the chances of failure or defeat. Legislation—adopting a bill—is the exception, not the rule, for this process.

The process by which a bill becomes law is complicated. It is slightly different in the Senate than in the House of Representatives, but the common features follow. It is important to note that most bills die at stage 2.

> Although party discipline is fairly weak in the houses of Congress, party caucuses do substantially influence most legislators. When the caucus decides a party's position on a proposal, most members will follow that line, even if it is against the interest of constituents. That is because the caucus can deny valuable campaign funds, or (sub)committee assignments to recalcitrant caucus members.

1. Introduction of a bill by one or more members of the chamber.

2. The bill is referred to subcommittee or committee (in the first house) that has jurisdiction over its subject matter.

3. The committee or subcommittee conducts hearings on the bill at which private and public supporters and opponents testify.

4. The bill is marked up, if it advances that far. Mark-up is where the bill is revised so that it reflects supporters' preferences.

5. The committee approves the bill and refers it to the body for deliberation.

6. In the House, the bill goes to the Rules Committee for a Rule governing the time and kinds of debate. In the Senate, the bill is referred to the majority leader who schedules debate in consultation with the minority leader.

7. In the House, a vote is taken after the debate. In the Senate, the bill can be filibustered or tabled once it is on the floor.

8. If the bill is passed by both houses, it goes to Conference Committee for resolution of the differences between the two versions.

9. If the Conference Committee report is approved by both houses, then the bill is sent to the President for signature or veto.

The legislative process is slow and inefficient, with many pitfalls and hurdles. Gridlock often occurs between the House and the Senate, or between Congress and the president.

- There may be strong partisan differences between the branches and the chambers. This leads to some bitter disappointments.

- Legislator's policy actions reflect various constituent needs and preferences. This leads to pork barrel efforts.

- The stages of the legislative process are filled with disagreement. There may be differences of opinion within a chamber over policy. There may be disputes within each party caucus. There may be disagreement between leadership and rank-and-file members. At the very least, there is always some disagreement between public opinion polls and media attention on the one hand, and other legislative actors, on the other.

- Divided government, in which different political parties control the White House and at least one house of Congress, contributes to gridlock.

- The House Rules Committee manages the flow of legislation to the floor of the House.

- There are various things that can be done to delay Senate consideration of bills. First, a senator can informally stop a bill from being considered. This stop, called a "hold," is usually temporary, though it can be permanent if Senate leadership allows. Second, opponents of legislation can hold a filibuster. Third, the minority and majority leadership can informally collaborate to schedule floor consideration of bills.

When it comes time to vote on bills, there are many things that can influence how a legislator will vote.

- Pork barrel legislation often is the most overriding influence in bills, so that legislators will gain constituent support and reelection.

- Legislators might feel pressure from the party caucus and "whip," depending on party strength, and party discipline. This may also depend on sanctions (or threatened party sanctions) against a wayward "back-bencher." (Sanctions such as favored committee assignments in the next Congress).

- Some legislators take cues from colleagues with expertise on the subject involved or from their party leaders.

- Some legislators might vote-trade or log-roll, doing favors for each other. These votes do not reflect their own interests but rather those of another representative with whom they have a prearranged deal.

Committees

Congressional committees and subcommittees do the bulk of work on proposed bills. Committee hearings investigate problems, provide public displays of concern about issues, and inform legislators about policy proposals and "solutions."

As mini legislatures, these committees are the real workplace of legislation. There are standing, select, conference, and joint committees. Standing committees are made up of the following members:

1. Chairperson, selected by the majority party, often using seniority as the criteria

2. A ranking minority member, who is the senior committee member from the minority party

3. Rank-and-file committee members are determined by party caucuses, on the basis of individual member preference, the size of the party's majority (or minority), and the caucuses leadership's preferences

4. Committee staff, selected by majority and minority committee leaders, who analyze and investigate proposals and issues

Traditions

There are some elements of professionalism in Congress and leadership. The longer a legislator holds office, the more knowledgeable she becomes about the legislative process. That experience generates expertise in policy specialization.

There are also certain unspoken traditions that govern the House and Senate, where compromise is essential for legislative success. These traditions are more visible and effective in the Senate, though they do exist in both houses.

- Seniority is the criteria for leadership selection in most cases.

- Logrolling—when two or more legislators agree in advance to vote for each other's bills—takes place frequently.

- Legislators who are less familiar with specific policy areas commonly defer to those who are more specialized experts in those areas.

- "Holds," "Senatorial Courtesy," and the "Filibuster," which are unique to the Senate.

Women are slowly gaining more seats in Congress. This is likely due to their winning more and more lower-level offices in state and local government. As women gain experience and visibility, they will gain more seats in the national legislature.

The reality of *term limits* is contrary to the work of a professional (career) legislator. Getting "new blood" in a chamber increases the amateurism of that chamber, and reduces the institutional memory and respect that professional legislators have. Limiting the number of terms in office that an official can hold accentuates that turnover and amateurism. It emphasizes new, inexperienced legislators.

Redefining Congressional Relationships

Congress is greatly handicapped when it deals with crises or emergencies. It can react to emergencies only after the president or the bureaucracy has acted. Even then, Congress is usually able to only support or criticize the actions of the executive branch.

The advantages that incumbents have during election campaigns suggest that they are bound to win re-election. However, the most important advantage cannot be controlled or limited: By adopting new laws and responding to constituent needs, legislators can earn high levels of voter satisfaction. The press for term-limits runs directly counter to this effective legislative effort.

In recent years, efforts have been made to reassert legislative control and hegemon over the executive branch. Many call for a structural change in the legislative process, and for a redefining of the relationship between Congress and the Executive.

- The *Budget and Impoundment Control Act* created a more central role for Congress in the formulation of the annual budget by 1) changing the budget process inside the legislature by imposing deadlines; and 2) creating expert support (the Senate and House Budget Committees, and the Congressional Budget Office) for the budgeting process in the legislature.

- The *War Powers Act* (1973), which sought to ensure a legislative role in the deployment of U.S. troops abroad, when there is no declaration of war. More specifically, the Act 1) requires the president to notify Congress of any deployment of troops; and 2) requires Congress to approve continued deployment beyond 60 or 90 days. And while presidents have for the most part complied with the notification requirement, they have also argued that the Act unconstitutionally restricts the power of the Commander-in-Chief.

- The *legislative veto*, which assigned Congress the right to reject an act or regulation, was an attempt to ensure that the executive administers laws in a manner approved by the legislature (though it was declared unconstitutional in 1983).

In spite of the continuing debate surrounding the role of the legislature, and the attempts to strike a new balance among the branches, it is unlikely to result in any concrete or long-term success.

POINTS TO REMEMBER

- Congress relies on the president and the bureaucracy for implementation of policies.

- Congress has multiple constituent interests and perpsectives. The perspectives of these different interests and of the two chambers provide for a very diverse and uncertain legislative output. The perspectives of Congress and the president also differ.

- Congress has links to both governmental actors and private interests. As a result, the legislature must respond to competing interests and conflicting demands for policy action. The legislative process resolves and responds to many of these conflicts.

- Congress reaches its policy goals and serves its varied interests in different ways. That means the processes used by Congress produce uncertain, even unexpected, outcomes. Many proposals never even get acted on, but this can acceptable to some interests since they have been "heard" by the legislature.

- As representatives and senators make decisions, they are affected by various pressures from their constituents (both organized interests and individual voters). Furthermore, organized interest groups can contribute to campaign coffers, or threaten to withhold election support.

KEY TERMS AND CONCEPTS

17th Amendment (1913)

The amendment that provides for the direct election of U.S. senators by the voters of each state.

agenda setting

Determining the public policy questions to be considered by Congress.

apportionment

Granting political representation to a group of people. The apportionment of Representatives between states is done through a complicated statistical method. The apportionment of Representatives to districts within a state is done by the majority party of the state legislature and sometimes leads to gerrymandering.

Appropriations Committee

A standing committee in the House of Representative that recommends how much money to provide to federal agencies.

bicameral legislature

A legislature made up of two parts. The U.S. Congress, composed of the House of Representatives and the Senate, is a bicameral legislature.

bill

The draft of a proposed law presented to a legislative body for approval; the law enacted from such a draft.

bully pulpit

The "soap box" that the president has and uses to his advantage because he has the attention of the press and the public.

calendar

An agenda, or list, that contains the names of bills or resolutions to be considered before committees or in either chamber of a legislature.

capital punishment (death penalty)

A sentence of punishment by execution, now limited to the crime of murder.

casework

Personal work done for constituents by members of Congress.

census

The counting, every ten years, of the population in the United States, conducted by the Bureau of Census.

challenger

A candidate for public office who does not currently hold that office, but rather is challenging the incumbent office holder. In Congress, challengers face very great uphill difficulties in defeating an incumbent.

checks and balances

A major principle of the U.S. governmental system whereby each branch of government exercises a limiting power on the actions of the other branches. Power is distributed among the three branches in order to prevent tyranny.

cloture

A parliamentary technique to end debate and to bring the matter under consideration to a vote in the Senate.

committee chair

The congressional member who heads a particular committee.

conference committee

When bills pass both chambers of Congress in different forms, a special joint committee is appointed to reconcile differences. It is composed of House and Senate members.

constituency

The residents in an electoral district. A group of individuals represented by a legislator.

continuing resolution

A temporary law that Congress passes when an appropriations bill has not been decided by the beginning of the new fiscal year (October 1).

delegate

A person authorized to act as a representative for another.

direct primary

An election within a single party in which voters select the candidates who will run on the party's ticket in the next election.

discharge petition

When a committee has refused to report a bill for consideration by the House, this procedure is used by the House of Representatives to force that bill's discharge (release). The discharge petition must be signed by an absolute majority of representatives (218) and is used only on rare occasions.

enumerated powers

Powers specifically granted to the national government by the Constitution. The first seventeen clauses of Article 1, Section 8, specify most of Congress' enumerated powers.

executive budget

The budget prepared and submitted by the president to Congress.

filibuster

Unlimited speech-making in the Senate, designed to stall the legislative process and halt action on a particular bill.

finance committee

A standing committee in the Senate, in charge in taxes.

first budget resolution

A resolution passed by Congress in May that sets overall revenue and spending goals and, therefore, the size of the deficit for the following fiscal year.

fiscal policy

Government's use of its powers to tax and spend in order to influence the nation's economy.

fiscal year (FY)

A twelve-month period the government uses for accounting purposes. The fiscal year is usually not the same as the calendar year. Until 1974, the FY of the U.S. government was July 1–June 30. In 1974 Congress changed it to October 1–September 30.

franking

A policy that allows congressional members to substitute their fax signature (frank) for postage when sending materials through the mail.

gerrymandering

The practice of drawing legislative district boundaries with an eye toward creating a political advantage for a particular party. In order to increase its electoral strength, the state legislature's dominant party tries to manipulate the shape of a district.

Great Compromise (or Connecticut Compromise)

During the Constitutional Convention of 1787, this was the compromise reached to the opposing New Jersey and Virginia Plans. It created a bicameral legislature: states would be represented equally in the Senate, and by population in the House of Representatives. The Great Compromise gave disproportionate influence to states with small populations by granting them equal representation in the Senate.

gridlock

The circumstances where little or nothing is accomplished at the policy-making level. This occurs either because there is no clear and consistent majority, or because the government is divided with a Democratic president and a Republican House and/or Senate (or vice versa). In other words, the two policymaking branches of government—Congress and the president—are too divided to act.

holds

A Senate tradition that allows a Senator to stop or delay consideration of a bill on the floor because he wishes to be present for the debate and vote, or because he is fundamentally opposed to the legislation. This is connected to Senatorial Courtesy.

Home Style

A style of behavior used by legislators that emphasizes a folksy, "one-of-the folks" attitude. A legislator would adopt this behavior in order to make constituents believe that he is a Washington "outsider," and as such, can accurately represent the district and fight against all those "Washington types." This style can be compared with Washington Style.

House of Representatives

The lower house of the bicameral Congress, in which representation is based on population.

implied powers

Authority possessed by the national government by inference from those powers delegated to it in the Constitution

impoundment

The refusal of the president to spend money that Congress has appropriated.

incumbent re-election

The great likelihood that a current office holder will be re-elected to office because of the advantages he has an incumbent—name recognition, the franking privilege, legislative visibility and success.

instructed delegate

Legislator who votes directly according to the views of the voters who elected him or her, no matter what the legislator's personal views are.

joint committee

A legislative committee including members of both the House and Senate. Committee members are usually split evenly between the House and Senate, and each member has one vote. Joint committees are usually established for specific purposes, mainly for investigations. There are some permanent committees, such as the Joint Committee on the Economic Report.

lawmaking

Process of developing the rules that govern a society. Created by governments, laws may deal with a wide spectrum of activities, from minor affairs to sweeping policies of national concern.

legislative oversight

Congressional responsibility to determine if the laws it has passed are being enacted and enforced in the way Congress intended.

legislative veto

A process placed in a number of bills that presidents signed into law allowing one or both houses of Congress to reject (veto) a decision made by an administrative agency if it disapproves. This process was declared unconstitutional by the Supreme Court in the case of *Immigration and Naturalization Service v. Chadha* (1983).

logrolling

When two or more members of a legislature agree in advance to vote for each other's bills. There are no established penalties for logrolling; there is only the threat of voter disapproval if it is discovered.

majority floor leader

The chief spokesperson of the majority party in the House of Representatives or Senate, the floor leader is very influential. In the House he or she is considered second in influence to the Speaker. In the Senate the floor leader is the most powerful senator in the party. Floor leaders direct the legislative program and the party's political strategy. Party caucuses select floor leaders, who are aided by party whips. Their counterparts in the minority party are known as minority floor leaders.

majority leader of the house

The chief spokesperson of the majority party in the House of Representatives, considered second in influence to the Speaker. This individual directs the legislative program and the party's political strategy. Party caucuses select the leader of the house, who is aided by party whips. The counterpart in the minority party is known as the minority leader.

majority whip

An assistant to the floor leader for the majority party.

mark up (session)

Joint action by a committee of House and Senate members in which a bill is approved or revised on a section-by section basis.

megabill (omnibus bill)

A bill with many provisions attached, with the aim of appealing to many legislators.

minority floor leader

The leader of the minority party in the Senate or House of Representatives. The minority leader directs his or her party's policies and political strategies.

minority leader of the House

The leader of the minority party in the House of Representatives. The minority leader directs his or her party's policies and political strategies.

minority whip

An assistant to the floor leader for the minority party.

necessary and proper clause

The final paragraph of Article I, section 8 of the Constitution, which delegates legislative powers to the Congress. Also known as the elastic clause.

party caucus

A meeting of party members in one of the houses of a legislature to make decisions on selection of party leaders and on legislative business.

politico

The legislative role combining concepts of instructed delegate and trustee concepts. The legislator switches roles according to the issue being considered; sometimes also used as a derogatory term for a politician.

pork barrel (or pork)

Public money appropriated by a legislative body for local projects not critically needed.

position taking, credit claiming, and advertising

Three activities that political scientist David Mayhew claims legislators engage in to satisfy their main goal: reelection. The legislator introduces legislation (position claiming), takes credit for the legislation (credit claiming), and advertises his or her success and hard work in the reelection campaign.

president pro tem (or pro tempore)

The presiding officer of the Senate when the vice president is absent. The president pro tempore is nominated by the leading party of the Senate and is elected by the Senate. The president pro tempore is fourth in line for the presidency in the event that the president, vice president, and Speaker of the House have all died or are unable to fill the office. The position usually goes to the majority party's senior member.

quorum

The minimum number of legislative members who must be present in order to transact business.

reapportionment

The reallocation of seats in the House of Representatives. Reapportionment can take place only after a census has been conducted. For reallocation to occur, population changes within states must be significant enough to justify the change. This is determined through a mathematical formula that considers the national population and the 435 seats allowed to the House. Those states that are earmarked for change then redraw their district boundaries to match their new allotment of representatives. This is done by the majority party of the state legislature and often leads to gerrymandering.

redistricting

The redrawing of district boundaries within each state. Redistricting is performed in states allotted a new number of representatives after the census. The majority party in the state legislature redraws the districts. This often leads to gerrymandering, in which districts are redrawn with an eye toward increasing the political power of that party.

representation

The responsibility that legislators have as elected officials to represent the views of their constituents. Just exactly how they must do that is debated: Some feel that legislators should vote exactly as their constituents wish, while others feel that legislators are elected representatives, and should exercise their own best judgment. It is difficult, though, to determine exactly what citizens want and how much they know about issues. Ultimately, elected officials are accountable to citizens in the next election, and this influences the amount of attention they give to citizen concerns.

resolutions

A measure that one chamber of Congress adopts. Resolutions do not have to be adopted by the president or the other chamber of Congress.

Rules Committee

A standing committee within the House of Representatives that specifies special rules, or conditions, under which the House can debate, amend, or consider a bill. This committee is intended to function as a traffic-cop for bills moving through the House, since there are so many. However, this role allows the Committee a great deal of power to influence the outcome of the bill. The Rules Committee is made up of ten members of the majority party and five members of the minority party.

safe districts

Districts that almost automatically re-elect House of Representative incumbents.

safe seat

A voting district that returns an incumbent legislator with at least 55 percent of the vote.

second budget resolution

A resolution passed by Congress in September of every year, setting binding limits on taxes and spending for the next fiscal year, beginning October 1.

select committee

A temporary legislative committee established by either branch of Congress for a limited period and a particular purpose. Select committees are generally established to handle issues that don't fall within a standing committee's jurisdiction, or to handle issues that standing committees would prefer not to handle. Most select committees deal with investigations, though others deal with supervision, housekeeping, and coordination.

Senate

The upper house of the U.S. bicameral Congress, in which representation is based on the principle of state equality.

senatorial courtesy

A tradition in the Senate that allows an individual senator to object to a presidential judicial nomination for a district court in that senator's state. Its function usually depends on the senator running it being in the majority in the Senate, and of the president's party.

seniority system

A custom that both Congressional chambers follow that gives preference to members with the longest terms of continuous service when selecting committee chairpersons and holders of other significant posts.

Speaker of the House

The presiding officer in the House of Representatives. The Speaker always belongs to the majority party, is nominated by the majority party caucus, and is elected by members of the House. The election is a formality; the majority party caucus makes the real decision. The Speaker has more power and influence than anyone else in the House, and is third in line for the presidency after the vice president. The Speaker recognizes speakers, interprets the rules of the House, and handles matters regarding order. As such, he can exerts a great deal of influence over legislation in the House. Many state legislatures have a Speaker of the House, also.

standing (permanent) committee

A committee within the House or Senate charged with considering bills within certain, specific subject areas. While the committees itself is permanent, its membership changes over time.

subcommittee

Congressional committees formed as a means of easing the legislative workload and dispersing some of the power amassed by long-serving committee chairs.Subcommittees hold hearings on bills, take testimony from interest group representatives and other concerned individuals, and "mark up" or make changes to the text of proposed legislation.

term limits

The movement at the state and federal levels to limit the number of terms in office that elected officials can hold.

three branches of government

Executive, legislative, and judicial branches. The U.S. government is separated into three branches to keep any one group from gaining too much power.

trustee

A legislator who acts according to his or her conscience and the broad interests of the entire society, as opposed to the specific agenda of his or her constituents or another narrow interest.

Tuesday-Thursday Club

The term refers to the House members who go home to their districts for long week-ends. These members have typically been criticized for spending time in their districts, as the work done there was seen as less important than the "real" work taking place in Washington, D.C.

veto

A legislative power of the chief executive to return a bill unsigned to the legislative body.

Washington Style

A style of behavior that relies on a legislator's expertise and specialized knowledge in order to achieve results in Washington. A legislator who adopts this style will emphasize his being an experienced insider who can "get things done" in Washington. He may even disregard constituent preferences.

Ways and Means Committee

The House committee that deals with all tax measures.

whip

A legislator who acts as an assistant and helps the House majority or minority leader, or the Senate majority or minority leader.

Multiple-Choice Questions

1. A descriptively accurate House of Representatives would have what number of women?

   A. 222

   B. 41

   C. 144

   D. 270

   E. 200

2. The majority of the legislative workload in Congress is handled by

   A. rule committees.

   B. standing committees.

   C. select committees.

   D. joint committees.

   E. conference committees.

3. According to the trustee view of representation,

   A. members of Congress should use their best judgment and pursue the broader interests of society as a whole.

   B. members of Congress should act to benefit the poorest and least educated citizens.

   C. members of Congress should act in accordance with the expressed wishes of a majority of their constituents.

   D. members of Congress should vote however they please in the absence of a strong preference by their constituents.

   E. members of Congress should consult with their staff before voting on important issues.

4. Intervening with a bureaucratic agency on behalf of an individual constituent is a congressional practice known as

   A. logrolling.

   B. casework.

   C. oversight.

   D. franking.

   E. agenda setting.

5. Traditionally, the most frequent beneficiaries of the seniority system in Congress have been

    A. southern Republicans and midwestern Democrats.

    B. northeastern Democrats and Republicans.

    C. west coast Republicans and Democrats.

    D. northeastern Republicans and southwestern Democrats.

    E. southern Democrats and midwestern Republicans.

Essay Questions

1. Describe two functions that are performed by Congress in the U.S. political system. Identify one conflict that arises in connection with each function you select. Explain how a legislator might balance or resolve it.

2. Is a descriptively accurate legislature essential for the representation of interests in this country? Explain. How would an electoral system operate that would generate an accurate demographic representative body? Explain why that kind of representational system will not likely be adopted in this country.

ANSWER KEY

Multiple-Choice Questions

1. A
2. B
3. A
4. B
5. E

Essay Questions

1.   The functions of Congress include:

*Representation of interest*s: The conflict here would be in determining what interests to represent from among an entire constituency. A legislator might try to use poll results to determine his constituent's true preferences.

Casework or constituent service: Conflict here usually involves disagreements between a constituent and a government agency over the application of a policy or program. Since casework often involves only the distribution of information to constituents or about the voters to an agency, there is little conflict. In a conflict arising from a constituent who wants an agency to contravene its policies in order to receive help, the legislator may well have to tell the constituent that that would be illegal, unfair to everyone, or is not possible.

Policy (Law) Making: Here, a legislator considers alternative policies that address a problem. Quite often, the problem and its solution are characterized differently by those who are involved. Legislators tend to resolve these differences in terms of the perceived best interest of constituents, the best interest of the nation, the preferences of the party leadership, or the proposal that would generate enough agreement and support.

Legislative Oversight: This is the control and shaping of the administration of policies by bureaucracies. Through legislative hearings, budget reviews, and formal audits by GAO, Congress will assess and possibly revise a policy or process. Conflicts inevitably arise between agency and regulated clientele interests, on the one hand, and legislators' goals on the other hand. Resolution of these conflicts usually involves legislators blaming bureaucracy for policy failures, or claiming credit for successes that policies have achieved.

2. The answer to this question depends on whether such a descriptive legislature is desirable or necessary to achieve representation. The easier and stronger answer is No. A descriptive legislature in which the demographic characteristics of the population are represented is not essential for accurate interest representation. It is not necessary that all representatives possess the relevant demographic characteristics, such as age, sex, race, income, occupation, and religion.

   Given single-member districts, it is virtually impossible to design an electoral system that would produce descriptive results. A proportional representation system would probably provide more descriptive representation, though not necessarily. That is because in any given district, voters (and their votes) are not arrayed according to demographic positions and characteristics; they are arrayed according to policy and ideological preferences.

   If such an electoral system were available in this country, it would run counter to party organization and strengths. Partisan opposition would prevent it from being adopted. Parties aggregate widespread interests and diverse groups of people, regardless of demographic characteristics. As such, it is nearly impossible that such descriptive representation would ever occur.

Chapter 11   *The Presidency*

The presidency is the most visible institution of government in modern America. That is partly because the president is one individual, easy for the media to focus on and to cover. Part of a president's power derives from the expectations of the public; people expect him to lead the nation, and to resolve crises as they arise. It also derives from his personality and interpersonal skills—he may or may not have the ability to engage people. Some U.S. presidents have in fact suffered because of a weakness in this area.

As for his constitutional role, a president's power stems from the expectation that the laws, enacted by Congress, need execution. The chief executive "shall take care that the laws be faithfully executed." In modern times, the power of the president and the executive branch has grown tremendously. That is due to the development of "modern" government, from the time of the Depression in the late 1920s and the New Deal of President Franklin Roosevelt. Since then, the number and complexity of federal laws has grown, and the number of regulations and restrictions on those affected by these laws has virtually exploded. So when bills are enacted into law, Congress delegates tremendous power to the president. The presidency is both an individual president and a large institution that is constitutionally responsible for executing the laws passed by Congress.

While the president has significant authorities, he does not have unlimited powers. The framers devised a system of separation of powers, and checks and balances, so that no single institution or actor could control the national government. And while this system has been successful in separating powers, it has also created gridlock.

The issue of *divided government* and *gridlock* has become a major point of concern in the United States. These concerns are due in part to rancorous partisan conflict between the White House (controlled by one party), and Congress (at least one house of which is controlled by a majority of members from the other party.)

Selection of the President

How a president is selected is a complex process: A candidate gains the nomination of a major political party, and then campaigns for office throughout the country. The final step in this process requires the candidate to win a majority of Electoral College votes. That is, at least 270 of the 538 votes available.

The Electoral College vote is based on the population of each state, and is determined by the number of senators and Representatives apportioned to each state. The total votes in the Electoral College is 538 (535 senators and Representatives plus three for the District of Columbia). The Electoral College was designed to filter the popular vote for president through a mechanism that would ensure careful consideration and weighing of various factors.

The presidential selection process involves a great deal of time, money, and effort. Candidates require the support of party faithfuls both at the national convention (to get the nomination) and at the voting booth (to get enough popular votes). To do this, a candidate must appeal to the extremely partisan views of the party at the convention, and perhaps take fairly extreme positions on policy issues. By doing so, he will attract the ideological support of the party. Once a presidential candidate obtains the nomination of the party, he must attract the large portion of the voting population that is moderate or in the middle of the political spectrum, so he might well moderate his policy positions.

Both during the campaign and after the election, the president must appeal to a variety of constituencies. The president is the only official elected by a national electorate. All other officials represent smaller state-wide or narrower constituencies. As the leader of his political party, the president makes some effort to maintain the support of his fellow partisans while in office. He also focuses on working with some interests that are represented in Congress. These include members of his own party, or those who support his positions on policy proposals.

The Institution of the Presidency

The institution of the presidency is a major element of the executive branch: It focuses largely on administering or executing policies, and on advocating policy proposals. How the presidency is organized largely depends on the individual preferences of a president and his advisers. This set of advisers has grown tremendously in the last half century.

In addition to his own skills and experience, the president's powers depend on a number of other actors, e.g., the media, Congress, and the public.

Executive Office of the President (EOP)

This is the institutionalized presidency. It contains a number of advisers and advisory bodies, installed by each president to serve in an advisory and policy analysis role.

- Council of Economic Advisers
- Office of Management and Budget
- National Security Council
- U.S. Trade Representative
- Council of Environmental Quality
- Office of Science and Technology
- Office of Policy Development

None of these offices performs enforcement or administrative duties. They have no legal authority to execute the laws. Their functions are to provide the president with information and policy advice.

The White House Office

The White House Office is made up of the president's personal staff. These people are absolutely loyal to the president and they are his functionaries—without caution, restraint, or limit. The Office includes some visible people and many who are virtually invisible. The *Chief of Staff* is the individual who literally controls access to the president. The *Press Secretary* maintains close, constant relations with the White House Press Corp and is a direct conduit from the president to the press. *Speech writers* are people whose task is to formulate presidential addresses. *Counsel to the President* serves as a legal adviser to the president. *Congressional liaisons* continually do the president's bidding and bargaining with the leadership (and the rank-and-file) in Congress. This office is essential to the president's legislative agenda.

The White House will sometimes claim that a high percentage of Americans approve of the president's actions, though it rarely conducts scientific polls to back this up. Most often, it simply tallies the number of phone calls, letters, and e-mails received.

The Vice President and the Cabinet

While the vice president's formal powers are minimal, he presides over the Senate, and casts any tie-breaking votes on bills, which can be a significant power. The relationship between the vice president and the president depends on the two individuals in these positions. Former president Bill Clinton used his vice president Al Gore as an adviser and an assistant on particular policy issues.

The Cabinet comprises the departments that have been given cabinet status, by Congress or by the president. The Inner Cabinet is often viewed as the Departments of *Defense*, *Justice*, *State*, and *Treasury*. The Outer Cabinet is the remainder of the Departments.

Cabinets as whole entities can be policy advising bodies, but policy advice more often comes from individual cabinet secretaries with specialized knowledge or from members of the Executive Office. Cabinet secretaries have competing constituencies and loyalties even though they are all appointed by the president. These competing constituencies might be department bureaucracies or policy subgovernments, whose policy support will help to determine how successful the secretaries will be in their positions.

Informal Advisers and the "kitchen Cabinet"

Informal advisers and members of the kitchen Cabinet are generally connected to the president by means of the White House Office. In prior times presidents would surround themselves with trusted advisers who were often cronies. Now the White House Office contains those same advisers, in more formal positions of trust.

The First Lady

The role of the first lady depends on the individual and on her relationship with the president. Many recent first ladies have become spokespersons for particular causes. Some have fought for literacy or advocated the war on drugs. Hillary Clinton took a leading role in developing and then lobbying for the Clinton Administration's health-care proposal, though congressmen often found her policy advocacy threatening.

The Powers of the President

The president has a number of formal powers and plays various roles. His explicit constitutional powers include:

- *Commander-in-Chief of the Armed Forces.* This set of powers relates to the need for civilian control of the military and the need for a single leader—the president—in confronting foreign crises or opportunities. In modern times, this power has involved sending troops to resolve wars or to keep the peace, often without a formal declaration of war by Congress. The Gulf War in 1991, for instance, was not a declared war.

- *Chief Diplomat.* The president is the formal representative of this country in its relations with other countries. This power involves more than just receiving and appointing ambassadors. Treaty-making and the formation of executive agreements are done largely by the president.

- *Veto Power.* The power to veto legislation gives the president some formal control over the legislative process. Note that the Line Item Veto that gave the president statutory authority to veto portions of legislation was declared unconstitutional in the case of *Clinton v. City of New York* (1998).

- *Powers of Appointment.* The president is responsible for appointing the following officials:

  Executive Officers who administer the laws enacted by Congress

  These include cabinet secretaries such as the Secretary of State. The highest levels of these officers are appointed with the "advice and consent of the Senate." Lower-level officers, such as assistant or deputy secretaries, may be appointed by the president alone, if Congress so designates.

Federal Judges

These appointments are made with the advice and consent of the Senate. This is particularly important because judges serve during "good behavior," often much longer than a sitting president serves.

Presidential appointment of federal judges has become highly political in the past 30 years: The president has to be concerned not only with the experience and perspective of the possible nominee, but also with what Senate members prefer, particularly if the opposite party controls the Senate. The Senate can hold up nominations (sometimes using senatorial courtesy) if some members do not like the nominee. The Senate Judiciary Committee Chair is closely consulted or "sounded out" about possible nominees. The White House also consults with senators from the state involved (and in the president's party), particularly for lower federal judgeships. Other times, particularly with Supreme Court nominations, the public, the media, and affected interest groups can make the appointment more partisan and controversial.

Ambassadors

Presidents commonly appoint friends and campaign supporters to these positions, but some ambassadors have been career diplomats with extensive professional experience.

Most of the president's formal power derives from statutes enacted by Congress. In these cases, Congress gives the president authority to execute each law, which often requires that he make discretionary choices. Cabinet secretaries or other agency heads may be the ones to exercise this discretion, but it is done on behalf of the president.

The president also has implicit and inherent powers, although these are largely attached to the status of being the chief executive. These powers have been limited since the Supreme Court, in *Youngstown Sheet and Tube v. Sawyer* (1952), held that the president could not seize U.S. steel mills during the Korean War in order to ensure that the production of war material would not be interrupted. The Court reasoned that the president did not have any inherent, statutory, or constitutional power to seize.

The president also has a variety of informal powers.

- The *power to persuade* is often cited as the president's most important power, if he has that personal ability.

- The *power to inform the nation* about crises or good news. This may be viewed as the power of the "bully pulpit."

- The *power to recommend matters to the legislature*, such as proposing the budget. In this way, he sets much of the legislature's agenda.

- The *head of his political party*. This is an obvious fact, even though the titular head (the National Chair) is in place throughout the president's term. The president campaigns heavily and raises a great deal of money for other candidates in his party.

- *Executive privilege*. This is not a power but rather the understanding and expectation that White House staff and executive officers can give candid advice to the president without it being made public. The case of *U.S. v. Nixon* (1974) held that this privilege was not absolute and did not protect presidential advice from scrutiny and use, if appropriate, as evidence in criminal prosecutions of advisers.

Presidents also bring various role perceptions and personality traits to the office. Some presidents are aggressive and active, while others are more passive and restrained in their exercise of power. Some are positive while others are more negative.

The president's powers are both shared and unilateral. Most of his power is shared with other actors and institutions. In other words, his powers are limited by the preferences and powers of others: legislators, bureaucrats, advisers, states and state leaders. Some power, however, such as commander-in-chief, is quite unilateral and restrained only by legislative appropriations and minimal public scrutiny.

Divided and unified government greatly shape the power of the president. Divided government is a common feature of national politics in the post-war era. Some presidents are very good at using the opportunities and limitations of divided government to achieve their legislative agendas. Others are less able or willing to bargain and negotiate with the other political party to gain legislative success.

There are formal and informal limitations on the power of the president.

- Congress (the House) may impeach the president and if it does, then the Senate will try those charges. This is an extraordinary measure that may cripple the president during and after the impeachment proceedings. It is seldom used.

- The president faces formal term limitations: The 22nd Amendment limits the president to two terms in office. Serious limitations are imposed on the president as a "lame-duck" status during the end of his second term.

- A president's approval ratings and popularity may limit him—legislatively or even abroad. Approval ratings vary over the course of a president's term in office, and a low approval rating means less flexibility in what he can advocate or achieve. Various factors influence and shape a president's popularity: his style and character, his reputation for honesty, for candor, and for energy, people's perceptions of him, and the circumstances of events, both at home and abroad.

Leadership and Execution of the Laws

The execution of laws depends largely on bureaucrats and long-term government employees with expertise and experience. Yet, presidents can hold different philosophical positions about administration and exercising their powers. The two most visible views are Dormant and Overt—the functionary Executive versus the Aggressive Leader. Theodore Roosevelt clearly believed that the president should take an aggressive and positive view toward the office. A number of modern presidents have probably shared this view, often called the "stewardship" theory of presidential conduct.

Roosevelt's successor, President William Howard Taft, held a more passive perspective of the office—that of a constructionist or caretaker. In his view, a president should react when required but should not engage in an excessive or positive form of leadership. A president should respond in a limited or minimal fashion when called on. Few modern presidents have decisively taken this tact, even if their personalities have been more passive in nature.

For many reasons, the president's leadership on domestic issues is more restricted than it is on foreign policy issues:

- There is more direct inter-branch conflict with Congress over domestic policy issues than over foreign affairs issues.

- Congress tends to defer more, though never completely, to the president over foreign policy issues because of the need for a single voice abroad. In addition, the president has more explicit power than does Congress in these matters.

- Domestic issues must take into account various national interests and constituents. Foreign affairs has fewer constituencies. As a result, there will inevitably be more conflicts between the executive and legislative branches when dealing with domestic policy.

- Although not an explicit protagonist in this inter-branch conflict, the Supreme Court may be called on to make determinations about the power of the branches in relation to domestic policy. There are fewer constitutional questions about the president's conduct in foreign affairs than about his exercise of domestic, administrative powers.

The Workings of the President

When a newly elected president begins his term, he must appoint around 5,000 officials to occupy various executive posts. These extend several layers below cabinet-level secretaries to Deputy or Assistant Secretaries. Modern presidents do not know this many people with expertise or experience in the various fields, such as transportation, environment, labor, or defense, so they rely on advisers to provide competent candidates. These administrative and policy making positions may be awarded as political plums to campaign contributors. They may go to policy experts (academics or practitioners), to defeated candidates from the party, or even to industry officials who belong to the party. Since the president does not know most of these people, he must be highly confident of the advisers who recommend them.

In a mutually dependent relationship, the president and the media use each other, and may also try to effect a certain "climate." The president has a "bully pulpit," which gives him a decided advantage in communicating his agendas and goals to the public. And the media uses the president as a major source of news.

It is considered inappropriate for one branch of government to intrude, uninvited, on the turf of another. The president does not go up to Capitol Hill to lobby or persuade legislators to support his policy proposals. Rather, he puts great effort into developing congressional liaisons. In fact, some White House staff have only one task: to monitor Congress and the positions of legislators on particular bills. These White House liaisons contact and try to persuade congressmen (perhaps visiting them on the Hill) of the president's preferences. In addition, the president may meet regularly with the leaders of one or both houses of Congress, especially when they are of his own party. Furthermore, if individual legislators are "on the fence" about an issue, the president may call them to try to sway their position. Congress rarely can speak with one voice to the president in this regard, so this type of conversation helps the president and his advisers.

Though seemingly one-sided, this type of relationship is not unidirectional: Individual legislators certainly convey their own preferences to the president. Some congressmen will make public statements to the media or their constituents about their preferences on important, pending legislation.

It is commonplace for a president to jawbone private interests such as the railroad industry or the telecommunications industry into acting as he wishes. Whether or not a president achieves his goals this way will depend on his connections in the industry, the strength of his arguments, and how closely his objectives coincide with those of the industry in question.

As Chief of State, the president is the country's representative to the rest of the world. In many other democracies, this function is performed by someone other than the chief executive. In this country, few would suggest that the functions of chief of state and chief executive be separated. The president not only conducts business with other heads of state—bargaining and negotiating agreements—he also serves as the ceremonial representative of our government abroad. This may create various strains or conflicts within the executive branch, and it may elicit criticism from the president's political opponents.

Foreign Perceptions of the President

The president is a significant and visible world leader. He leads the most powerful military and largest economy in the world, and represents the most successful democracy ever. That gives him tremendous visibility and credibility. No individual legislator or group can claim this kind of pre-eminence.

In the post–Cold War Era, the president may still think in terms of superpower confrontations. More often, though, these matters relate to small crises in developing countries, or deal with terrorist and non-state threats. And while the solutions to these crises are not at all clear, and are sometimes impossible to solve, the president of the United States is expected to take charge.

POINTS TO REMEMBER

- The president serves a number of roles in our political system, some of which conflict each other.

- The president's role of Chief Legislator has become more important in recent decades.

- The day-to-day operation of the president depends on a developed and elaborate set of assistants in the White House Office and the Executive Office of the president.

- The vice presidency has evolved a good deal in the past three decades. The vice president's role depends largely on his relationship with the president and the functions that he might be asked to do.

KEY TERMS AND CONCEPTS

12th Amendment

The amendment (1804) that calls for separate ballots to be used by the electoral college when voting for president and vice president. Before that, the president was the candidate who received the most votes, and the vice president the candidate who received the second most. Also, in cases when no candidate receives a majority of electoral college votes, this amendment specifies that the House of Representatives is to choose from the candidates with the three highest vote totals. This had been the five highest before.

25th Amendment

The amendment (1967) that establishes guidelines for filling the offices of president and vice president if they become vacant and makes provisions for situations when the president is disabled. This amendment was created on the heels of events including the death of Franklin D. Roosevelt, the serious illnesses of Dwight D. Eisenhower, and the assassination of John F. Kennedy.

advice and consent

Power the Constitution (Article II, Section 2) grants the U.S. Senate to give its advice and consent to treaties and presidential appointment of federal judges, ambassadors, and cabinet members.

appointment power

The president's authority to fill a government office or position. Positions filled by presidential appointment include those in the executive branch, the federal judiciary, commissioned officers in the armed forces, and members of independent regulatory commissions.

"beyond the beltway"

The part of the U.S. outside of Washington DC. The "beltway" is a highway circling Washington DC.

Cabinet

The president's core advisory group. The Cabinet presently numbers 14 department secretaries (State, Treasury, Defense, Justice, Interior, Agriculture, Commerce, Labor, Health and Human Services, Housing and Urban Development, Education, Energy, Transportation, and Veterans Affairs) and the attorney general. Depending on the president, the Cabinet may be highly influential or relatively insignificant in its advisory role.

chief diplomat

The president's role in recognizing foreign governments, making treaties, and making executive agreements.

chief executive

The president's role as head of the executive branch of the government.

chief legislator

The president's role in influencing the making of laws.

chief of public opinion

presidential role as chief communicator for the nation and nation's symbolic leader.

Chief of Staff

The assistant to the president who directs the White House Office and advises the president.

chief of state

The president's role as ceremonial head of the government.

civil service

A collective term for the employees working for the government. Generally, civil service understood to apply to all those who gain government employment through a merit system.

commander in chief

The president's role as supreme commander of the military forces of the United States and of the state National Guard units when they are called into federal service. This power is granted by Article II, section 2 of the Constitution.

Council of Economic Advisers (CEA)

A staff agency, established in 1946, that advises the president on measures to maintain stability in the nation's economy.

economic chief

The presidential role involving management of the national economy. In this role, the president is responsible for smoothing out the rough edges of the capitalist business cycle by taking action to curb inflation, lower unemployment, and adjust the international trade balance.

emergency power

An inherent presidential power exercised during a period of national crisis, particularly in foreign affairs.

executive agreement

A binding international agreement between chiefs of state. Unlike treaties, these do require the consent of the Senate.

Executive Office of the President (EOP)

Established by President Franklin D. Roosevelt by executive order under the Reorganization Act of 1939, the EOP now consists of nine staff agencies that assist the president in carrying out major duties.

executive order

A rule or regulation issued by the president that has the effect of law. Executive orders can implement and give effect to provisions in the Constitution, to treaties, and to statutes.

executive privilege

The right of officials in the executive branch to refuse to appear before, or to withhold information from, a legislative committee or judicial proceeding. Executive privilege is enjoyed by the president and by those executive officials accorded that right by the president.

expressed powers

Presidential powers expressly written into the Constitution or congressional statute.

federal budget

The estimate of the income and expenditures need by the federal government to carry out its program in some future period, usually a fiscal year.

Federal Register

A publication of the executive orders, rules, and regulations of the executive branch of the U.S. government, as well as bureaucratic rules.

formal presidential roles

Chief diplomat, chief executive, chief legislator, chief of party, chief of state, commander in chief.

gridlock

The circumstances where little or nothing is accomplished at the policy-making level. This occurs either because there is no clear and consistent majority, or because the government is divided with a Democratic president and a Republican House and/or Senate (or vice versa.) In other words, the two policymaking branches of government—Congress and the president—are too divided to act.

impeachment

A formal accusation by the House of Representatives, accusing the president, vice president, or any civil officer of the United States of "treason, bribery, or other high crimes and misdemeanors." The Senate must then try the impeachment. Impeachment is authorized by Article I of the Constitution. Military officers and members of Congress cannot be impeached.

informal presidential roles

Roles not assigned by the Constitution that the president fills along with the formal roles that come with the position, including party chief, economic chief, and chief of public opinion.

inherent power

Authority and power held by the national government but not specifically granted to it by the Constitution. These powers most commonly relate to foreign affairs and international relations. The powers of the federal government are delegated powers, meaning they must be directly or implicitly granted. In foreign affairs, however, it's presumed that the federal government has the same powers as other nations.

kitchen Cabinet

Informal advisers to the president. The phrase originated during the presidency of Andrew Jackson, who frequently met with friends and trusted advisers in the White House kitchen to discuss policy. The kitchen Cabinet may include members of the official Cabinet. This does not mean that the kitchen Cabinet will give the president the same advice as the official Cabinet. In fact, presidents often follow the advice of their kitchen Cabinets instead of the advice of their official Cabinets.

"leader of the free world"

The belief that the United States, and in particular the president, is responsible for safeguarding the freedom and liberty of all nations. This belief grew from hostilities between the U.S. and USSR during the Cold War.

line-item veto

Executive power to veto specific items included in a piece of legislation without vetoing the entire piece of legislation.

National Security Council (NSC)

A staff agency in the Executive Office of the President that advises the president on matters relating to national security, both domestic and foreign. The NSC is made up of the president, vice president, secretary of state, and secretary of defense. The director of the CIA and the joint chiefs of staff are statutory advisers; others may serve at the president's request.

Office of Management and Budget (OMB)

A division of the Executive Office of the President charged with running the government efficiently and economically, helping to prepare the annual budget as well as clear and coordinate the budgets of all departmental agencies, and helping to create fiscal policy. The OMB was created by executive order in 1970, replacing the Bureau of the Budget. The OMB includes the Office of Information and Regulatory Affairs and the Council on Competitiveness, a secret body established by President George Bush in 1989 and headed by Vice President Dan Quayle.

pardon

Power to release a person from the punishment or legal consequences resulting from a crime. The president and governors of 30 states have the right to grant pardons within their respective areas of authority. In the other states, governors share the power with special pardon boards. An "absolute pardon" fully restores the person to his or her position before conviction. A "conditional pardon" sets conditions that the person must meet before the pardon is granted.

party platform

A document prepared by a political party, outlining its policies and objectives and used to win voter support during a political campaign. Candidates do not feel obligated to fulfill the items laid out in a platform if elected to office.

patronage

Appointing government jobs and contracts to faithful party workers as a reward for their contributions. Unrestricted patronage came about with Andrew Jackson's spoils system and began to lose influence with the Civil Service Act of 1883.

plebiscitary presidency

A model of presidentially centered government in which a president seeks to govern through direct support of the people. Under this theory, presidential power and legitimacy emanate from citizen support, as measured in public opinion polls; presidents directly link to citizens through television; and presidents find themselves unable to deliver on promises made to citizens due to structural barriers inherent in our governmental system.

pocket veto

The chief executive's special veto power exercised after the legislative body adjourns. By not signing a passed bill within a specific time, the chief executive in effect "vetoes" the bill. If the legislature wishes to have the bill passed, it must reconsider the bill again in its next session.

political party chief (chief of party)

The role of the president as the nation's partisan political leader.

power to persuade

A president's ability to bargain with political actors and get them to fall into line with his agenda. It was claimed by political scientist Richard Neustadt to be the most important of the president's powers, in his 1960 book *Presidential Power*.

split-ticket voting

Voting for a candidate from one party for one office and a candidate (or candidates) from another party for another office(s).

State of the Union message

The message to Congress in which the president lays out a legislative program. The Constitution requires the message be given "from time to time," but it has become customary for the president to deliver it every January, at the beginning of the legislative term. The State of the Union was not originally a very dramatic event; early presidents sent it in the form of a letter. Radio and television greatly increased its importance by making it a media event and providing the president an audience with the American people and the rest of the world.

statutory power

Power created by laws that Congress establishes. These powers may be given to the president or to other political actors such as bureaucratic agencies.

veto message

A presidential explanation to Congress detailing reasons for vetoing a piece of legislation.

veto power

A legislative power of the chief executive to return a bill unsigned to the legislative body.

vice president

The second highest executive officer of the U.S., who is also the presiding officer of the Senate.

War Powers Act (1973)

A law specifying certain conditions the president must meet to commit U.S. troops without the approval of Congress. The War Powers Act attempted to close a loophole by which presidents were able to get around the constitutional requirement that only Congress can declare war.

Washington community

People who play a regular role in Washington, D.C.'s political scene.

White House Office

The group of advisers set up by the president without Congressional ratification who tend to his political needs, advise him, and act as his intermediaries with the press and Congress. Included in this group is the Chief of Staff.

Multiple-Choice Questions

1. Which of the following receives a lifetime appointment?
   A. the ambassador to the United Nations
   B. a judge of the U.S. Court of Appeals
   C. the clerk of the U.S. Senate
   D. the attorney general of the United States
   E. the chairman of the Federal Reserve Board

2. What presidential role is largely ceremonial in nature?
   A. Chief Executive
   B. Commander-in-Chief
   C. Chief Diplomat
   D. Chief of State
   E. Chief Legislator

3. Which of the following is a constitutional duty of the vice president?
   A. accompanying the president to meetings with foreign heads of state
   B. signing legislation when the president is out of the country
   C. breaking a tie vote in the U.S. Senate
   D. assisting the president in nominating members of the U.S. Supreme Court
   E. presiding over meetings of the Cabinet

4. "Going public" refers to the ability of presidents to
   A. use the mass media to take their case for a particular policy directly to the electorate.
   B. hold press conferences whenever they want.
   C. travel around the country and attend various civic functions.
   D. sign important legislation with a number of "average" citizens present.
   E. cite opinion polls in an effort to pressure Congress to adopt their legislative proposals.

Essay Questions

1. What presidential function below is most removed from his explicit constitutional powers? Explain why.

   - Chief Legislator
   - Commander-in-Chief
   - Chief Diplomat

2. Richard Neustadt once indicated that the "power to persuade" was the greatest power the president possessed. What is this presidential power? List three factors on which this power depends.

   Using two presidents from the past 30 years, illustrate one successful and one unsuccessful case of presidential exercise of this power.

ANSWER KEY

Multiple-Choice Questions

1. B
2. D
3. C
4. A

Essay Questions

1.   Chief Legislator is the most removed from the formal constitutional powers of the president. Although the president does have the constitutional power to render the State of the Union message to Congress, there is no clear indication that it should include a formal proposal of a legislative agenda, which is what this role permits the president to do.

   The reason this role is the most removed from the Constitution is that it most closely moves the president to the legislative function of initiating legislation. This moves closest to violating the spirit, if not the letter, of the principle of the separation of powers and boundaries of the chief executive, whose job it is to merely execute the laws given him by the legislature.

   Commander-in-Chief is the most difficult function to argue is removed from explicit constitutional powers. That is because it is an explicit role specified in Art. II of the Constitution for the Chief Executive.

   Chief Diplomat is not an explicit constitutional grant of power, so this role could be argued as "removed from the explicit constitutional powers" of the president. If you selected this function for your answer, you should have communicated that the president's role as diplomat and representative of the country places him far beyond the Constitution's powers. In this capacity, the president bargains and cajoles foreign governments on matters of economic policy and social programs, as well as military and formal treaties.

2.   The "power to persuade" is the ability a president has to persuade or cajole other influential people—legislators, actors in the private sector, even diplomats representing foreign governments—into doing what he wants. This ability is used primarily in executive–legislative relations.

   How strong a president is in this area depends on his persuasive powers and interpersonal skills. It may also depend on how clear he is on his own goals and on his formal powers.

Ronald Reagan was exceptionally good at this kind of warm joking and cajoling. A Republican, Reagan was very successful at getting legislators, particularly Democrats, to understand his perspective and accept his preferences, even when they were opposed. Reagan would give and take, compromise, smile, and accept half-a-loaf in order to get legislative support for his policy preferences.

At the other extreme is Jimmy Carter, a prominent example of a leader unable to persuade others. Carter would be considered a "weak" president in Neustadt's terms: Though he did not lack a willingness to compromise, he little understood the art of bargaining and the kinds of skills needed to win over recalcitrant legislators. He seemed psychologically unwilling to cajole and assert his objectives on others, perhaps out of a lack of purpose or direction. The end result was an unwillingness for even legislators of his own party to agree to his views.

Chapter 12   *The Bureaucracy*

"The bureaucracy" is defined as the administrative and implementation functions of the U.S. political system. Though the president is the chief executive of the nation, one individual cannot possibly administer all the laws enacted by the legislature. As a result, a large and elaborate administrative structure helps to manage government policies.

The bureaucracy is generally considered part of the executive branch, but given its size and unique organization, it has been termed the "fourth branch" as though it were a separate branch of government. And while it does operate quite independently from the chief executive, the president has the ultimate responsibility to "take care that the laws be faithfully executed."

Historically, there has been much controversy surrounding the bureaucratic institution. Many people consider it to be evil because it involves anonymous individuals who make broad policy decisions. Others see it as largely unsuccessful and wasteful, calling for the elimination of government programs altogether. At a minimum, opponents of bureaucracy want a devolution of government programs; that is, the transfer of powers to state and local governments. Some have even argued for privatization of certain government agencies, e.g., prisons and garbage collection, which would shift the responsibility of these services to private contractors (often the lowest bidder).

Most government tasks are very difficult, even impossible, to accomplish, yet policy-makers (presidents as well as legislators) will set goals, appropriate money, and authorize bureaucracies to pursue those goals. But because of their size, bureaucracies cannot move quickly or implement changes as soon as they would like; the process by which they act involves too many steps and too many actors.

Yet without bureaucracies to administer policies and distribute government benefits, the complex tasks of modern society could not be performed. Who would take on the difficult challenge of safely disposing toxic waste, created by our nation's industries? Who would register voters at the Motor Vehicle Bureau, as per the Motor Voter Law? Who would issue driver's licenses?

Bureaucratic Organization

The administrative bureaucracy has several distinguishing characteristics.

- First, the bureaucracy is composed of specialized experts. These experts must make sense of the statutes enacted by Congress, and so by default, have great personal discretion to "make policy." Since congressional statutes are usually quite vague, bureaucrats must fill in the gaps and set the standards. But even when Congress has been quite specific in a statute, it is the bureaucrat's role to clarify the details and translate it into policy.

- Second, bureaucrats are not typically subject to political pressure, so they have the freedom to fashion policies as they wish. In that they are selected for their expertise, bureaucrats are given tenure; that is, if their political preferences do not coincide with those of a new, incoming administration, they cannot be fired for that reason alone.

- Third, the president appoints—and is served by—the higher echelons of administrative agencies (though with some advice and consent of the Senate).

The "headless" fourth branch of government performs tasks essential to implementing public policy. The specific tasks vary according to the laws passed by Congress and the regulations of the agency involved. An agency that provides social services has a different undertaking than does an agency that regulates a market. Some agencies provide services themselves, such as the Postal Service (formally the Post Office Department). Other agencies produce public goods, such as national defense.

While government agencies have a great deal of expertise about the problems they deal with, they may lack clear solutions. Regardless of this, people and legislators expect agencies to solve those problems.

Since 1932 and the beginning of the New Deal, government policy has expanded greatly. The initial policies were aimed at regulating various markets—securities, labor, agriculture, product, communications, transportation. The intent was to correct market imperfections, or to provide the public with services at more acceptable prices, whether providers' costs were covered or not. In order to administer these types of policies, administrative agencies were developed. Today, it is common for federal policy to be administered and monitored by state and local bureaucrats, because government programs often involve channeling federal money to those levels.

Government Agencies

There are four kinds of government agency. Though all agencies administer policy, they do so in very different ways. Regardless of an agency's specific statutory authority, it has one of two agendas: (a) to focus on the expenditure of funds (tax revenues) to address a problem identified by Congress, as with the Federal Emergency Management Authority, or (b) to implement a specific legislative objective by regulating private actions, as with the Safe Drinking Water Act administered by the EPA.

- *Cabinet–Level Executive Departments*

  These are the traditional kinds of bureaucracy—Justice, Treasury, Commerce, Labor, among others.

- *Independent Executive Agencies*

  These are separate from cabinet departments, but are still lodged in the executive branch. These include the Environmental Protection Agency (EPA), the Central Intelligence Agency, and the Nuclear Regulatory Commission.

- *Independent Regulation Agencies*

  Designed to function (largely) independent of the president and the executive branch, these include the Securities and Exchange Commission (SEC), the National Labor Relations Board, and the Federal Communications Commission (FCC).

- *Government Corporations*

  These provide consumers with a service or product that depends on at least some government capital investment. The Postal Service, the Tennessee Valley Authority, and the Pension Benefit Guaranty Corporation are all government corporations.

There are two kinds of procedures by which bureaucracies reach decisions and administer policies: rule making and adjudication. *Rule making* is a quasilegislative process that permits agencies to formulate rules that govern the conduct of a category of actors. First, the agency notifies the public of the proposed rule. Then, everyone, including citizens, is given a chance to provide written comments or relevant suggestions. And last, the revised rule is publicly recorded in the *Federal Register* and becomes binding.

Adjudication is a quasijudicial procedure that allows an agency to enforce a rule by applying it to an individual situation that is in violation of the rule. This requires adjudication before an administrative law judge, which includes standard (due process) protections for taking oral and written evidence. Agencies are often given the authority to impose fines or revoke a license by means of such adjudication.

Agency procedures are intended and designed to treat everyone alike. They use Standard Operating Procedures (SOPs) to respond to every request or task that is being addressed.

Adjudication is also used to examine proposed rate changes by regulated companies whose rates are governed by the agency. Some agencies frequently conduct inspections in order to ensure compliance or to examine alleged problems. For example, the Environmental Protection Agency examines point source pollution sites, and the Occupational Safety and Health Administration inspects workplaces for hazardous working conditions. Though they rarely involve criminal liability, such inspections may be governed by Search and Seizure protections covered in the 4th Amendment.

Characteristics of Bureaucracies

Bureaucracies are organized hierarchically. This means that individuals are supervised by those with wider responsibilities. This Weberian model of bureaucracy, developed by Max Weber in the 19th century, does not exist in perfect form in government, though each bureau has some of these characteristics.

The head of a bureau is often a political appointee of the president's choosing. Though many agency decisions actually are made by lower level bureaucrats based on facts rather than partisan ideology, appointment of a bureau head by the president means that the general tenor of the agency will reflect the preferences of the executive branch.

The first bureaucracies in this country were staffed using the spoils system of political appointment. In other words, friends and supporters were selected to agency posts, regardless of their competence or knowledge in a particular program. Today, administrators are chosen by the Office of Personnel Management through a process of merit selection, based on educational qualifications, work experience, and performance on examinations.

The function of a bureaucrat is to perform specialized functions based on his knowledge and experience. Depending on how narrowly his job is defined, the administrator will usually be a technical policy expert in a specialized field.

Management of the Bureaucracy

Bureaucracies are controlled and influenced by various political actors.

The *president* has essential control over the operations of the bureaucracy, in that he appoints executive officers and cabinet heads. The president sets policy priorities. His mandate includes some budget control as well, by means of the Office of Management and Budget. In order to further his own agenda, a president may also propose significant changes in an agency's authority (whether to expand it or contract it).

The *federal courts* also manage the bureaucracy, in the sense that they can restrain or direct agencies through interpretation of statutes. The courts can reverse an agency decision if the agency did not follow proper procedures or if it did not interpret its legislative authority correctly. Should this happen, this judicial review would most likely be done by the U.S. Court of Appeals, though the Supreme Court has been known to get involved in such interpretations.

Recipients of government benefits can also influence bureaucracies. They can bring political pressure on an agency. Since they too will be affected by an agency's policy decisions, beneficiary groups will typically generate media exposure to oppose a program, or to demand changes in the way the agency is exercising its authority. Government watchdog groups, such as the Environmental Defense Fund, or Common Cause, may similarly use the media to publicize agency practices.

Congress has the most expansive controls over the bureaucracy. These legislative control functions are often referred to as *legislative oversight*.

- Congress enacts the statutes; that is, adopts new policies. But since Congress lacks technical policy and expertise in certain areas, policies are often written in vague terms. As a result, agencies are given great discretion with which to "define" what policies mean.

- Congress, particularly the Senate, plays a key role in confirming many presidential appointments to head various agencies.

- Congress plays an extensive role in budget allocations for programs and for operating budgets of various administrative agencies. This influence, which extends through the period of a given program (often multiple years) will greatly affect how much an agency chooses to accomplish. In other words, the amount of money an agency is allocated will determine its goals as outlined by Congress.

- Congress can scrutinize what an agency has done with a policy during a reauthorization hearing. It is at this time that policies are reapproved and refunded, or cancelled. In hopes of getting programs reauthorized, agencies devote much time and effort to complying with Congress.

- Congress can formally request a governmental audit of how an agency has spent its funds. This allows the GAO and the Congress (usually the relevant committee) to determine if the funds were properly spent, and what the affect of those expenditures has been.

In its most extreme form, bureaucratic control comes in the form of *iron triangles*. That is, three-way connections between an agency, its clientele/beneficiary groups, and the relevant Congressional committees. It is generally believed that iron triangles hinder the political process by putting their own interests ahead of national interests.

In addition to all of these players, there are also broader sets of players that affect some policy areas. These can be referred to as *issue networks*—loose, competitive relationship among policy experts, interest groups, congressional actors, and agencies. These networks of interested and affected parties participate in agency rule-making and try to influence agency decisions. However, a network is not as powerful as an iron triangle if one exists in a policy area.

Policy Administration

Administrative agencies exercise a great deal of power in the course of administering policies. Congress often delegates a great deal of administrative discretion to agencies; that is, the power to interpret legislative mandates. This is often because Congress cannot decide on a precise way to remedy a problem, so it hands over that power (e.g., establishing safe air travel or cleaning up the environment) to the agency.

In efforts to gain compliance with agency or congressional policy, many regulatory agencies take on informal advising roles, in which they cajole parties into doing something. This brings agencies additional influence (above and beyond their formal authority) over segments of the public.

POINTS TO REMEMBER

- Bureaucracies try to be responsive—albeit slowly—to political demands and pressures, but since they are not elected bodies, their constituencies differ from those of an elected or a representative body.

- Federal agencies are rarely affected directly by elections, though the heads of agencies are likely to change with a new presidential administration. Moreover, if an agency feels attacked by a presidential candidate who claims that "government should get off the backs of the people," it may respond slowly, or even not at all.

- There are bureaucracies connected to the judicial and the legislative branches of government. However, these generally provide support to the Congress and to the federal courts, rather than administer policies directly to citizens. They're also much smaller-sized administrative instruments than those in the executive branch.

KEY TERMS AND CONCEPTS

acquisitive model

A model of bureaucracy in which top-level bureaucrats seek to expand their budgets and staff to gain greater power and influence in the public sector.

administrative agency

An agency that is part of the executive branch, an independent agency, or an independent regulatory agency. Examples are the Federal Trade Commission and the Securities and Exchange Commission. State and local governments also have administrative agencies.

agency imperialism

A common problem with governmental bureaucracies (and other bureaucracies as well), in which the agencies grow with no limit and without an eye to the benefits they're intended to provide. See *bureaucratic pathologies*.

appropriation

Congressional passage of a spending bill, specifying the amount of funds previously authorized that will actually be allocated for an agency's use.

authorization

A legislative action establishing or continuing a certain amount of funding for an agency. Some authorizations terminate in a year; others are automatically renewed without further action.

bureaucracy

An administrative system that executes policies and carries out specific functions by using standardized procedures in a hierarchical structure.

bureaucracy problem

A collection of incentives and constraints facing those working to make government more efficient. They include accountability, equity, responsiveness, efficiency, and fiscal integrity.

bureaucratic pathologies

Problems shared by all or most federal bureaus or agencies. They include bureaucratic red tape, mission conflict, mission duplication, agency imperialism, and bureaucratic waste.

bureaucratic red tape

Probably the most common complaint about bureaucracies, red tape refers collectively to the complex rules and procedures that cause delays and sometimes make it difficult to get something done.

bureaucratic reform

The effort to make bureaucracies operate more efficiently.

bureaucratic waste

Unnecessary bureaucratic spending of money without providing real benefits.

Cabinet

The president's core advisory group. The Cabinet presently numbers 14 department secretaries: State, Treasury, Defense, Justice, Interior, Agriculture, Commerce, Labor, Health and Human Services, Housing and Urban Development, Education, Energy, Transportation, and Veterans Affairs, plus the attorney general. Depending on the president, the Cabinet may be highly influential or relatively insignificant in its advisory capacity.

capture

The act of gaining direct or indirect control over a regulatory agency's personnel and decision-makers by the industry that is being regulated.

Civil Service Commission

The central personnel agency of the national government, created in 1883. The Civil Service Reform Act of 1978 abolished the CSS. The Office of Personnel Management assumed most of its functions at that time, except for its quasijudicial functions, which the Merit System Protection Board assumed.

Civil Service Reform Act (1978)

An act that reformed the federal bureaucracy. It established the Office of Personnel Management and the Merit Systems Protection Board.

contracting out

Replacing services provided by the government with services provided by private firms, through contractual agreements with the government.

deregulation

The elimination of government controls, especially over private companies.

division of labor

Method of splitting the responsibilities associated with a job amongst different workers. Division of labor is used in bureaucracies.

entrepreneurial government

New model of government advocated as a replacement for our current bureaucratic government system. Promotes competition among service providers, empowerment of citizens, focusing on outcomes, reaching goals and missions, redefining clients as customers, preventing problems before they surface, earning money, decentralizing authority, use of market mechanisms, and serving as a catalyst to promote action in the public, private, and volunteer sectors of communities.

Executive Order 12291

Order made by President Ronald Reagan requiring that the Office of Management and Budget review all proposals for new executive branch regulations.

fourth branch of government

A term referring to the federal bureaucracy.

garbage can model

Bureaucratic model that views bureaucracies as directionless, with little formal organization. According to this model, bureaucracies make decisions without the benefit of forethought and rational policy planning, relying instead on trial and error.

General Service (GS) system

Basic pay system for the federal government's white collar employees.

government corporation

A government agency that runs a business enterprise. Its activities are mainly commercial and produce revenue for continued existence. Government corporations have more freedom of action than do regular departments of government. Examples include the Federal Deposit Insurance Corporation, and the U.S. Postal Service.

Government Accounting Office (GAO)

A governmental agency created by Congress in 1921 to review government agency performance, and the receipt and distribution of public funds.

Government in the Sunshine Act

Law passed in 1977 requiring all multiheaded federal agencies to perform their duties in open sessions. Closed meetings are permitted for only specific subjects, such as national defense, but participants must keep minutes of those meetings. The act was a reaction to governmental secrecy and expanded the public's "right to know."

Hatch Act (Political Activities Act)

A law passed in 1939 that limited contributions to political parties and spending by political parties. Most importantly, the Hatch Act made it illegal for individuals and companies under contract with the federal government to contribute to political candidates or to political parties. This was due to concerns over federal employees being pressured to donate to political campaigns through threats to their job security or chances for promotion.

hierarchy

A principle of organization in which each person or office is under control of and responsible to the next highest level.

incrementalism

A doctrine that holds that change in a political system occurs only by small steps, each of which should be carefully considered before proceeding to the next one.

independent executive agency

A federal agency that reports to the president but isn't part of a Cabinet-level department, including the Small Business Administration and the Office of Personnel Management. These agencies' officials often have terms that overlap those of presidents to avoid undue control by the president.

independent regulatory agency

A multiheaded agency outside the major executive departments and responsible for making and implementing rules and regulations to protect the public interest. They include the Federal Trade Commission, the Securities and Exchange Commission, and the Federal Reserve Board. These agencies can establish rules for the industries they regulate and prosecute those who break the rules. Members are appointed by the president, subject to the Senate's consent.

inner Cabinet

Refers to the oldest and most important Cabinet departments, which play roles in day-to-day government decision making. They include the Departments of State, Treasury, Justice, and Defense.

iron triangle

A three-way alliance between political organizations or agents. It is generally thought that iron triangles hinder the political process by putting their own interests ahead of national interests. A well-known iron triangle involves the Pentagon, defense contractors, and the Congressional committees in charge of defense spending.

issue network

A loose collection of parties interested in a policy area and affected by government policy. These interests include policy experts, industry players, interest groups, congressional committees and government agencies.

line organization

A government or corporate unit responsible for providing services or products to the public, in contrast to a staff agency, which serves other agencies.

merit principle

The principle that in employment individuals should be selected, retained, and promoted based solely on their ability, knowledge, and skills.

merit system

A system for selecting employees through competitive testing, and retaining and promoting them based on their abilities, knowledge, and skills.

mission conflict

A bureaucratic pathology in which the roles of different agencies within the bureaucracy.

mission duplication

A bureaucratic pathology in which the roles of different agencies within the bureaucracy are the same, or overlap.

monopolistic model

A bureaucratic model that compares bureaucracies to monopolistic businesses. Without competition, the bureaucracy results in inefficiency and higher costs. And since there's no penalty for its inefficiency, the bureaucracy has no incentive to reduce its costs or use its resources more efficiently.

National Partnership for Reinventing Government

A plan for bureaucratic reform launched under former President Clinton and headed by Vice President Al Gore. It's commonly known as "the plan to reinvent government."

Office of Personnel Management

The federal agency that administers civil service employment.

outer Cabinet

The outer Cabinet refers to Cabinet departments that are less important to the day-to-day functioning of the government and were created to look after the needs of various constituencies. It includes the Departments of Agriculture, Labor, and Veteran's Affairs.

patronage system

A system in which elected officials make appointments to office or to confer contracts or other special favors based on party affiliation.

Pendleton Act (Civil Service Reform Act) (1883)

A law that made national government employment dependent on open, competitive exams. The Pendleton Act brought the patronage, or spoils, system developed by Andrew Jackson to an end. The Act was passed as a direct result of the assassination of President James Garfield at the hands of someone who had wanted, but had not received, a government job. The Act created the Civil Service Commission to handle the national government's personnel. Though it originally applied to only ten percent of national government employees, it has been expanded so that now more than 90 percent of government positions are included.

political appointments

Presidential granting of federal jobs to reward friends and supporters. See *patronage spoils system.*

reinventing government

A bureaucratic reform effort instituted by President Clinton and headed by Vice President Gore. It is driven by four guiding principles: 1) increase customer satisfaction, 2) institute less centralized management, 3) empower front-line employees, and 4) cut government services back to basics.

Senior Executive Service

An elite group of governmental mangers outside the regular merit system, established by the Civil Service Reform Act of 1978.

specialization

Area of responsibility and expertise associated with a job.

spoils system

A system of awarding government jobs to political supporters and friends. Also known as *patronage*, the spoils system is generally associated with President Andrew Jackson, who felt that government work was so simple anyone could do it and that bringing new people into government employ kept the government vital. This system began to lose influence with the Civil Service Act of 1883. The term is based on the saying "to the winner go the spoils."

standard operating procedures

Established methods routinely followed for the performance of specific operations or in specific situations.

sunset legislation

A law with provisions that call for the law's expiration after a certain period of time. After that time, the law can be renewed after consideration by a legislative body. If the law isn't renewed, the law is no longer valid, or provisions set forth under the law for what to do if it's not renewed go into effect.

symbolic politics

A cause of incrementalism, whereby politicians give the appearance of taking decisive action, in order to please the voting public, while they're actually avoiding making substantive policy changes in order to please specific interest groups.

Weberian model

German sociologist Max Weber developed the Weberian model of bureaucracy, which holds that bureaucracies are hierarchical organizations that direct power from top to bottom and make decisions by analyzing data and reasoning logically.

whistleblower

An employee who publicizes illegal, inefficient, or unethical actions in a government department or contractor working for the government.

Multiple-Choice Questions

1. The existence of iron triangles or "subgovernments" calls into question which theoretical model of American politics?

   A. elitism

   B. constitutionalism

   C. hyperpluralism

   D. federalism

   E. pluralism

2. All the following statements are true except

   A. most presidents meet infrequently with their entire cabinet.

   B. there are presently 14 cabinet departments.

   C. presidents often rely on advice from an informal group of advisers and friends known as a "kitchen Cabinet."

   D. heads of cabinet departments are always chosen because of their extreme loyalty and devotion to the president.

   E. All nominees to head cabinet departments must be approved by a majority of the Senate.

3. The Federal Election Commission is an example of a(n)

   A. independent regulatory agency.

   B. part of an iron triangle.

   C. cabinet department.

   D. government corporation.

   E. line organization.

4. A bureaucracy has all of the following characteristics except

   A. tenure in office.

   B. specialized skills and tasks.

   C. clear lines of bureaucratic authority.

   D. a set of complex hierarchical departments.

   E. performs staff functions.

5. Executive orders are

   A. carried out by the Joint Chiefs of Staff in the Department of Defense.

   B. executive directives from cabinet secretaries to department bureaucrats.

   C. presidential directives providing guidance to agencies for executing the laws.

   D. explanations that accompany the president's legislative proposals to the Congress.

   E. informal agreements with foreign governments that are binding to the U.S..

6. Before the Department of Veterans Affairs was created in 1987, its functions were performed by what department?

A. Labor, and Health, Education and Welfare

B. Health and Human Services, and Education

C. Labor, Education, and Defense

D. Health and Human Services

E. Labor, and Education

Essay Questions

1. Select three of the following items and explain how each one contributes to the power of the bureaucracy.

- Agency policy expertise

- Close connections between the regulated interests and the agency

- Congress' infrequent attention to agency work

- The federal courts' deference to agency expertise

- Congress' general or vague grants of authority to agencies

2. List three reasons that bureaucratic growth in size in the post–World War II era has largely been at the local level, with state bureaucracies a distant second. Explain why there has been such growth in the size of these bureaucracies and why it has not occurred at the federal level where many programs are adopted.

ANSWER KEY

Multiple-Choice Questions

1. E
2. D
3. A
4. E
5. C
6. B

Essay Questions Questions

1. *Agency policy expertise* is the bureaucracy's specialized and unique knowledge about a policy area and problem. Other actors may also have some policy knowledge, but the combination of knowledge with real legislative authority makes an agency's policy expertise a powerful institution. Its strength lies in its knowledge about policies, problem solutions, and pitfalls to be avoided.

    Connections with the regulated industry means an agency can develop strong political support and protection against legislative challenges. By making policy that is favored by regulated interests, an agency earns their political support. It also makes the agency virtually invulnerable to legislative threats or efforts to control its policies.

    Congressional inattention means that an agency can develop long-term goals and policies that are not open to legislative attack or correction. While Congress can always remove bureau authority through legislative retraction, inattention often leads to a strong momentum for agency policy directions when faced with legislative scrutiny.

    Federal court deference to agency expertise: The judiciary can and does exert some control over agency statutory authority through judicial interpretation of statutes. However, since many modern-day statutes are complex and open-ended, agency expertise is often used to deflect judicial inquiries and scrutiny. Called Chevron Deference after the name of the case in which the Supreme Court first indicated that an agency would be given deference to interpret its own statutory authority, courts are reluctant to intrude on agency exercise of statutory power unless in clear violation of the statutory wording. It is not essential to use the phrase Chevron Deference in your answer, but the principle of judicial deference is an important feature of agency power and independence.

Vague legislation is due to several features of modern legislation. It results in a great deal of agency independence. First, Congress may not be able to agree on precise narrow statutory wording. Second, there may not be a known solution to a problem, but raised awareness and concern pushes Congress to assign an agency authority to treat the problem. Third, Congress may wish to give the agency a good deal of latitude so that if the bureaucracy is successful, Congress can take credit. Similarly, if the bureaucracy is unsuccessful, Congress can blame the agency.

2. The growth in bureaucracies since World War II is largely due to the development of federal funding (grant-in-aid) to solve various problems. Congress gives local governments money and directs them how to administer or spend the money. This results in increased local bureaucracies that must administer the federal programs.

    State bureaucracies have grown somewhat as well for the same reason. Federal programs and funds may require states to administer policies and monitor their expenditures, but are given virtually no increase in federal bureaucracy to administer those programs.

Chapter 13   *The Courts*

The United States federal system has two layers of law: state and federal. As a result, there are 51 court systems in this country. The courts are hierarchically organized, with trial courts, e.g., federal district courts, at the bottom, hearing cases initially. Appellate courts, such as the U.S. Courts of Appeals and the Supreme Court, ensure that trials proceed correctly and that the law is applied correctly.

Although at the time of the Federalists the judiciary was considered the least dangerous (powerful) branch of government, the courts have become increasingly involved in making policy. From the Supreme Court's decision justifying the exercise of judicial review by courts in *Marbury v. Madison* (1803), to the more recent Supreme Court decision to stop a recount of the Florida popular vote in a presidential election (*Bush v. Gore* (2000)), courts make public policy.

Most policy making done by courts is through interpretation of statutes enacted by legislatures. Though less dramatic than the exercise of judicial review, this comprises the bulk of courts' workload. Implementation of court decisions is left to the other branches of government since courts lack "the power of the purse" and "the power of the sword." Furthermore, unpopular court decisions often produce recalcitrant behavior and challenges to the legitimacy of courts.

The federal system has three-tiers: The Supreme Court is at the top, intermediate appellate courts (Courts of Appeals) in the middle, and trial courts (District Courts) at the bottom.

Court Organization

The only court mentioned in the Constitution is the Supreme Court. The lower federal courts are creatures of statutory enactments by Congress. Each state has its own court system. Each judicial system administers different constitutional, statutory, and common laws.

Courts are organized according to constitutional or statutory arrangements. The Constitution specifies there is to be a Supreme Court, and such "inferior courts as the Congress may from time to time ordain and establish" (Article III). In addition, Congress is given power to "constitute tribunals inferior to the Supreme Court" (Article I).

Article I courts may have judges who serve for fixed terms of service, with limited or specialized jurisdiction. These judges may be removed for various reasons, as specified in a statute. Appointment of Article I judges may be done by the president alone, or by the legislature. Article I judges face standard threats by Congress to implement pay reprisals for unpopular decisions.

Article III courts exercise most of the judicial authority in this country. Article III judges are federal judges, and district court judges, and are appointed by the president and confirmed by the Senate. Once appointed and approved, federal judges never have to run for election. They are protected from removal, except by means of impeachment and conviction, and they serve during good behavior. Similarly, they enjoy protection from salary reductions while they serve.

Federal Court Structure

The federal courts have a three-tiered structure: The Supreme Court is at the top, the Courts of Appeals below, and District Courts at the bottom.

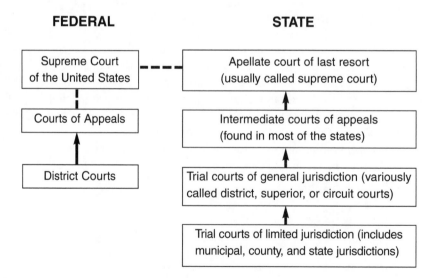

Apex Learning

Jurisdiction

District Courts have original jurisdiction over cases involving federal law, even though federal questions can be raised in state courts. When an appeal is sought from a trial conducted in District Court, it usually goes to the Court of Appeals, which has appellate jurisdiction to consider alleged errors of law (procedural or substantive law) made in the District Courts. In addition, the Court of Appeals considers appeals from administrative agency adjudications.

The Supreme Court has a mixture of jurisdiction. Its original jurisdiction is limited to a few kinds of cases outlined in Article III of the Constitution, but the bulk of its work comes from its appellate jurisdiction, which is regulated and controlled by Congress. Most of this work comes on appeal from the lower federal courts. The Supreme Court will also hear an appellate case from state courts if it contains federal questions.

The Court's appellate jurisdiction is discretionary. That means the Court need not grant a Writ of Certiorari when it is sought by a petitioner unless the Court (actually four members of the Court) think the questions in the petition warrant the Court's attention. The Court decides a very small proportion of the cases brought to it—something less than two percent.

All courts must wait for cases to be initiated by litigants who claim they have suffered a legal wrong. The particular jurisdiction of federal courts involves federal law—U.S. statutory or constitutional law. State courts resolve disputes that arise under state law, and if a state case raises a federal legal question as well, then that portion of the case may be appealed from the state courts to the U.S. Supreme Court for resolution.

Types of Law

Courts apply different kinds of law to decide the cases that are brought to them. The foundation is the common law tradition of England which was inherited at the time of the Revolution.

- *Common law* is law made by judges as they decide cases brought to them. After a certain point, a set of governing rules is developed—contracts, torts, property. Common law establishes a large body of precedent so that as like cases arise, prior decisions can be applied. Unfortunately, common law is a collection of cases, scattered through different court reporters, over perhaps a hundred or more years, and to find its meaning requires a lot more work than reading a statute.

- *Statutory law* is enacted by legislatures, and comprises the vast bulk of law in this country today. Unlike common law, it is explicit and codified into one book of laws, written so that it can be found and interpreted easily by those in the legal system. Statutory law is more visible and "compelling" than common law, since it is written by elected representatives of the people.

Courts devote much of their energy to interpreting and applying statutory law, and to developing the meaning of statutory words and phrases. Since legislation is often vague and general, court decisions often become the significant and governing law in the country.

- *Administrative law* is developed by administrative agencies (bureaucracies) in the course of performing their functions and of exercising their rule-making powers. Administrative laws are complex and pervasive features of our legal system today because of the tremendous amount of legislation that must be administered by agencies.

- *Constitutional law* involves the provisions of the Constitution. This is law made generally by appellate courts, including the Supreme Court, and is considered supreme or ultimate, prevailing over any contrary statutory or common law. The principle for this was established in *Marbury v. Madison*, which struck down an act of Congress as unconstitutional.

There are also criminal and civil laws in this country:

- *Civil law* outlines the obligations, duties, and rights between private citizens, which govern how social, commercial, and even political relationships should be conducted in society.

- *Criminal law* governs our actions in connection with wrongful acts against society, e.g., murder, robbery, embezzlement. Violations of these laws carries sanctions: fines, imprisonment, and even capital punishment.

How Courts Function

Courts are largely passive institutions, and must wait for a litigant to initiate a lawsuit before they can exercise their power. Judicial process is based on an adversary model that presumes that the two parties to a case will present all the necessary evidence and arguments. The judge or the jury goes on to determine the true facts of the case, and the governing law is applied to resolve the case. Courts cannot initiate cases, but must wait until a dispute arises. Once a legal case does arise, then the court may be able to develop and apply (i.e., interpret) the relevant law. In the course of that interpretation, it makes policy.

In the process of hearing a case, a court, particularly the Supreme Court, can signal an interest in a particular legal question, though it is uncommon. Such a signal does not means that the initiator will win the case but rather that the court has doubt about the existing state of the law, has a desire to "correct" an earlier decision, or has an interest in changing substantive law.

Some interests have become expert litigants because their claims are amenable to judicial attention and because they have a flair for litigating. Their skill and experience in litigating help them to get the outcomes they desire. Some litigants use courts to achieve their policy goals, even if there is some doubt about whether the court's decision will actually benefit their goals. Furthermore, these litigants may articulate minority positions, e.g., Jehovah's Witnesses, the American Civil Liberties Union, or the NAACP, whether as prosecuting parties or as *amicus curiae* (friends of the court).

Selecting Federal Judges

Supreme Court Justices

Nine justices serve on the Supreme Court. Their seats are lifetime; vacancies occur only when a justice dies, resigns, or retires.

The process for selecting a Supreme Court justice is an elaborate one. It involves the president, the Senate, and various advocacy groups.

1. Advisors, friends, and interest advocates recommend certain individuals to the president.

2. The Department of Justice examines their backgrounds, and comes up with a "short list" that reflects the president's preferences or criteria.

3. The president selects, and then nominates, an individual. That nominee is forwarded to the Senate for consideration.

4. The Senate Judiciary Committee conducts public hearings on the nomination, at which time advocates and opponents can place their views on the public record. This is an open media show that has become more controversial since the nomination of Abe Fortas to Chief Justice by President Johnson in 1968. At that time, the Senate Republicans were so angry at the Warren Court's liberal decisions that they decided to politicize the nomination process. Strom Thurmon led these efforts and the result was the defeat of Fortas as Chief Justice. Since then, senators and interest groups who oppose nominees and have taken on the task of defeating presidential nominations to the Court on any grounds they choose.

5. Confirmation by the Judiciary Committee either takes place or not. Confirmation is not a foregone conclusion; some nominees are rejected by the Committee, others are sent to the Senate floor with unfavorable recommendations. Most of the recent nomination defeats have not been on the floor of the Senate, but rather in Committee. Since the 1968 rejection of Justice Fortas as Chief Justice, three more nominees have failed to obtain Senate confirmation, and a fourth had his name withdrawn due to damaging public disclosures.

Some justices who achieve Senate approval do so by narrow margins, amid much controversy and opposition. Most Supreme Court Justices have been white middle-class males: They have attended Ivy Leagues schools and have engaged in some type of public service, including serving on lower federal courts. In earlier years geography or religion were important criteria for appointment, including a supposed "Catholic" and "Jewish" seat. Now race and gender are the visible criteria, in part because of underrepresentation and significant pressure from interest groups and advocates.

Though expected to be impartial, judges do bring their judicial philosophies, their ideologies, and even their partisanship to the bench. Those preferences may be reflected in court decisions.

One significant but uncertain criteria that the president uses when considering a nominee is his political ideology and judicial philosophy. Assessing these views beforehand is difficult: Some people think that a nominee's prior decisions in lower court is sufficient to reflect his ideology. Others believe that asking a nominee his views on a subject such as affirmative action or abortion is a litmus test. Some advocate the appointment of "strict constructionists," or those who believe in the views of the founding fathers. Others believe that justices should be active, open-minded, and more flexible interpreters of the Constitution.

A president frequently has two things in mind when he appoints a justice with shared ideology and political philosophy, though neither one can be assured. First, it strengthens the president's legacy to carry those views into the future, far longer than his term in office. Second, it produces court decisions that enhance the president's policy preferences, at least in the short term.

Lower Federal Judges

Lower federal court judges are also appointed by the president, when there are vacancies on the bench, and he does so with the advice and consent of the Senate. Senate confirmation of the nominee will depend most importantly on the politics of the president, the Senate, and the nominee.

Although these nominees are appointed by the president, the Senate or the relevant senator (from the state in which the federal judicial vacancy exists), play a more direct and explicit role in selecting an appointee. The senator might suggest someone. Given the acceptance of senatorial courtesy, a senator can veto a presidential nominee if she strongly opposes the individual. Given the rules of procedure in the Senate, a senator can virtually block the nominee by communicating her opposition to her fellow senators.

The Supreme Court

The Workings of the Supreme Court

The Supreme Court has had a number of different ideological complexions over the years. The major controversy surrounding Supreme Court justices has been whether they are judicial activists or judicial restraintists. *Judicial activists* are judges who interpret the Constitution to reflect current conditions and values, or to achieve modern, practical results. Judicial *restraintists* are those who believe the Constitution should be interpreted as the framers originally intended, and according to what the words of the Constitution mean literally.

In addition to this debate over judicial philosophy, there remains the traditional controversy over the political philosophy of justices: liberal or conservative. The Warren Court (1953–1969) was viewed as a politically liberal and judicially active court. The Burger Court (1969–1986) was considered politically conservative but judicially active, as is the current Rehnquist Court (since 1986). The Burger and Rehnquist Courts have declared a high number of statutes to be unconstitutional, which is the mark of a liberal, activist court. Though they include more politically conservative judges than did the Warren Court, neither the Burger nor the Rehnquist court has overruled its decisions on racial integration and the rights of individuals. Furthermore, the Burger Court decided the controversial case of *Roe v. Wade* (1973) establishing that a pregnant woman can choose to have an abortion during the first trimester of her pregnancy.

In their dealings with each other, justices sometimes persuade each other, but more often bargain in order to reach a decision. In doing so, they might have to compromise their strong ideological positions. Justices do not always hold one firm philosophy throughout their tenure on the bench. That is, their views tend to change with time and experience.

The Process Used by the Supreme Court

Supreme Court decision making is a labor intensive and slow process. The Court reaches two decisions. The first is the "decision to decide." The second is the "decision on the merits," i.e., a substantive decision on the case, if the Court grants certiorari at the first stage. Since the Court has discretionary appellate jurisdiction, it need not decide cases brought to it on appeals. Rather, it can deny certiorari to any case it feels does not warrant review. That means on the vast majority of appeals, the Court does not reach the second decision.

Most appeals—well over 99 percent of the approximately 7,000 appeals per year—are denied review by the Court. It takes four justices to support a grant of certiorari before a case will be heard on the Merits. Petitions for certiorari are filed continually throughout the year, but the Court reviews them as promptly as it can, with a three month gap for vacation from July–September, and another month around January.

Poor litigants who cannot afford counsel will have legal counsel appointed. The Court has procedures that allow them to proceed *in forma pauperis* (in the form of a pauper).

Filing and printing costs may also be waived. Each year, about one half of the petitions for writs of certiorari are filed in forma pauperis. Very few of these petitions are granted review by the Court.

Once a petition is received, it is read and summarized by the certiorari pool, a small group of law clerks, who in turn distribute their memorandum and recommendation to the justices. (There is one exception: Justice John Paul Stevens has chosen not to join the cert pool and to do the work himself. He prefers to rely on his own clerks to assess the value of a case.) The pool memorandum recommends granting or denying certiorari, but each justice can make his own assessment about the worthiness of a petition. If he thinks it warrants discussion by the Court, in Conference, he may place the petition for certiorari on the Discuss List. If a petition is not placed on the Discuss List, then certiorari is automatically denied by the clerk, at the direction of the Chief Justice.

The Decision on the Merits is the formal decision that is rendered by the Court once it has decided to grant certiorari. This decision is based on two sets of information presented for Court consideration.

1. Written legal briefs are filed by both parties to the case, once certiorari has been granted. These are carefully prepared by the attorneys for both parties and they focus on the questions of law in the case and the constitutional, statutory, and/or prior decisions that are both intended to persuade the Court to decide in favor of each side in the case.

2. Oral argument, a closely timed presentation before the justices, is the only display of Court activity open to the public. The attorneys for each side can take 30 minutes to argue their position. The justices often use this period to get clarification on matters presented in the briefs, or to argue publicly with one another, with counsel "in between them" fielding their questions.

The Court reaches a decision within days of the oral argument, in Conference. The Conference is secret and closed to the public. *Amicus curiae* participants may also submit briefs if they have been permitted to appear in a case. These parties are outsiders who will be affected by the decision in the case and wish to present the Court with views and arguments that neither of the two parties can be expected to present. *Amicus curiae* participants rarely if ever are allowed to argue before the Court, even if they have filed legal briefs.

The decision of the Court is usually announced by a single opinion. This majority opinion is assigned by the chief justice to one member of the majority. That justice and his clerks write drafts of the opinion until they are satisfied. The final draft opinion is circulated among all the justices for their acceptance or their disagreement. During this period, any justice may change his mind and his vote about the decision, and a good deal of bargaining can occur. In fact, it is assumed that the vote will change somewhat in the bargaining process, as justices vie with each other over points of law. Justices may even use the bargaining process in a strategic way, using threats of dissenting or disclosure, to win over colleagues.

Once a Supreme Court decision is announced, i.e., published, the opinion is printed and made available to the public. Any concurring or dissenting opinions are also presented.

The Supreme Court lacks the power to enforce its decisions. Rather it must rely on lower courts, from where the case arose, to comply and follow the decision. Whether or not a party complies with the decision depends not only on whether he "accepts" it, but also on the visibility of the case, and on the public's acceptance of the decision.

The Court's Authority

In the U.S. political system, the role of the judiciary in general, and of the Supreme Court in particular, are not always clear. The Supreme Court relies on a degree of legitimacy and respect from the nation's citizens, even when they do not agree with a decision. Within this context, many of the controversial decisions that the Court has made in recent decades have presented some challenges to its legitimacy.

The Court's legitimacy has not always been great or durable. After the *Dred Scott* decision in 1857, which held that African Americans were not entitled to the rights and privileges of citizenship, many people lost faith in the Supreme Court for decades.

Further damaging was the Court's *Brown v. Board of Education* decision, which declared in 1954 that racial segregation in public schools was unconstitutional. This decision produced a highly violent response even though many Americans believed in the need to achieve racial desegregation. Many of the opponents were southerners who believed in racial segregation. Others believed that states, not the federal government, should control education and school policy. Still others did not believe that the Supreme Court should be making liberal decisions relating to race, or overturning the established separate-but-equal doctrine of *Plessy v. Ferguson* (1896).

The Supreme Court will continue to be a focal point for some policy advocates who are technically skillful at litigating but not successful in other policymaking arenas. These groups will see the Court as a policy-making body in which their views prevail. Courts make public policy when they interpret statutes and provisions of the Constitution. They also distribute and redistribute wealth—resources such as money and symbolic legitimacy—when they reach decisions in civil cases. Litigants will seek such decisions from courts when they believe they can win in the political arena.

The Role of the Courts

Though it is less directly involved in policy making than are the executive and the legislature, the judiciary in this country is a powerful, policy making branch of government. This is particularly the case because of the power of judicial review; this controversial power is in effect antidemocratic since the federal judges who exercise it are not elected, are not representative, and are not answerable to any constituency.

As Congress enacts laws under its constitutional powers, the courts will continue to scrutinize them for constitutional validity, and thus will interpret the meaning of those statutes. This places courts in a policy making position, even though judges are supposedly "above" politics and partisanship. The respect given the courts in the future will depend on the acceptance and understanding of court decisions by litigants, opponents in other political institutions, and the general public.

POINTS TO REMEMBER

- The judicial process is based on an adversary view of presenting evidence and arguments. It presumes that the truth will emerge from the competitive presentation of evidence.

- In this country, the law is composed of constitutional provisions, legislative statutes, administrative regulations set by agencies, and judge-made common law. These are the policies that determine the outcome in a case that is litigated.

- For a case to be litigated, it must meet several rigid and specific requirements. While many cases appear to have circumvented these obscure and technical requirements, they have in fact usually been met. Courts can use these requirements as a way to decline to decide some issues if they so wish.

KEY TERMS AND CONCEPTS

ACLU

American Civil Liberties Union, a nonprofit interest group with approximately 275,000 members dedicated to preserving the liberties guaranteed in the Bill of Rights.

advice and consent

Power the Constitution (Article II, Section 2) grants the U.S. Senate to give its advice and consent to treaties and presidential appointment of federal judges, ambassadors, and cabinet members.

affirm

In an appellate court, to reach a decision that agrees with the decision reached in a lower court.

***amicus curiae* brief**

A brief is a document filed with a court containing a legal argument supporting a desired outcome in a particular case. An amicus curiae brief is filed by a party not directly involved in the litigation but with an interest in the outcome of the case. Amicus curiae is Latin for "friend of the court."

appellate court

A court that hears appeals on points of law decided by trial courts.

appellate jurisdiction

Authority of a court to review legal decisions by a lower court.

Brown v. Board of Education of Topeka, Kansas

The U.S. Supreme Court decision establishing that segregation of the races in public schools violates the equal protection clause of the 14th Amendment.

certiorari (cert)

A writ (request) from a higher court to a lower court to send up a case's record so that the higher court can review it. Most cases come to the Supreme Court in this manner instead of through an appeal. A party must petition a court to issue a writ of certiorari, and fewer than five percent of the petitions are granted.

civil law

The law regulating conduct and allowing for the settlement of disputes between private persons over noncriminal matters such as contracts, domestic relations, and business relations.

class-action suit

A lawsuit filed by an individual seeking damages for himself and for "all persons similarly situated."

common law

A system of law originating in England in which judges make decisions according to prevailing customs. Decisions are applied to similar situations and thus gradually become common to the nation. Common law forms the basis of legal procedures in the United States.

concurring opinion

A separate statement, prepared by a judge who supports the decision of the majority of the court, but who wants to clarify a point or to voice disapproval of the grounds on which the decision was made.

constitutional law

Law that involves the interpretation and application of the Constitution.

courts of appeals

Courts of appeals are the intermediate federal appellate courts. These decide appeals from federal district courts and from administrative agencies.

criminal law

The collection of laws defining crimes and establishing punishment for violations. The government prosecutes criminal cases because crimes are against the public order.

defendant

The party against which a criminal legal action is being brought.

discretionary jurisdiction

Discretionary jurisdiction is court jurisdiction that may or may not be exercised by the court. The Supreme Court's appellate jurisdiction, in particular, is discretionary. This means the Court can decline to decide a case that comes to it on appeal from a lower federal or state court.

dissenting opinion

A separate opinion in which a judge explains his or her own views about a case, in dissent from (disagreeing with) the majority opinion or conclusion reached by the majority of the court.

district courts

District courts are the trial courts of original jurisdiction in the federal system. The vast majority of federal cases begin and end in these courts.

Dred Scott v. Sandford (1857)

A case that held that African Americans could not be considered persons under the Constitution nor were they entitled to the rights and privileges of citizenship.

federal circuit court of appeal

A special court established by Congress in 1982 to be on the same footing as the existing 12 Courts of Appeals but with nationwide jurisdiction based on subject matter rather than geographic area. It covers, in particular, business, trade, and civil service.

federal court system

The court system of the federal government. It is divided into three levels: The bottom level is made up of 94 federal district courts. At the next level are 13 federal circuit courts of appeal. The top level is the Supreme Court.

grand jury

A jury of 12 to 23 people called to weigh evidence and determine if there is enough evidence to warrant a trial against someone suspected of committing a serious crime. Grand juries meet in private. If a majority (not a unanimous vote) believes there is enough evidence, the grand jury presents a "true bill" and the suspect is indicted and held for trial. If it believes there is not enough evidence, the suspect is freed. The 5th Amendment requires that grand juries be held for crimes that call for a punishment of death or imprisonment.

judicial activism

A doctrine holding that judges should take an active role in making decisions that lead to socially desirable ends, primarily by exercising the power of judicial review. Others feel judges should show restraint and allow the legislative and executive branches to do this, since judges are not elected officials accountable to the voters.

judicial implementation

How court decisions are turned into actions.

judicial restraint

A doctrine holding that judges should not take an active role in making decisions that lead to socially desirable ends. Instead, judges should restrain their own opinions and defer policy decisions to legislators and the executive branch-elected officials who are accountable to voters.

judicial review

The power of courts to judge legislative or executive acts unconstitutional. All national and state courts hold this power, though the highest state or federal court usually makes the final decision. Judicial review is not mentioned in the Constitution. The Supreme Court claimed this power in *Marbury v. Madison* (1803). Judicial review is based on the following assumptions: the Constitution is the law of the land, acts that violate the Constitution are void, and the judicial branch is best suited to protect and interpret the Constitution.

jurisdiction

A court's authority to decide certain cases. Not all courts have the authority to decide all cases. Two factors that decide what court has jurisdiction for a case are 1) its subject matter; and 2) where the case originated.

justiciable dispute

A question or dispute that's appropriate for settling in the judicial branch of government. Some disputes may be ruled "political," and therefore more appropriate for consideration by the legislative or executive branches.

lifetime appointment

A length of term in office granted to most federal judges as required by Constitution. Once appointed, these judges can stay in office as long as they wish. Judges are granted lifetime appointments in order to free them from partisan battles and the possibility that the fear of losing their jobs will influence their legal decisions.

litigant

A party engaged in a lawsuit.

litigate

To take part in a legal action or attempt to settle dispute in a court of law.

majority opinion

A written statement, prepared by an appellate court, that states the opinion of the majority of the judges who heard the case. A majority opinion explains the rules of law that relate to the case, advises lower courts on how to proceed, and justifies the ruling to the public. The majority opinion may be accompanied by a dissenting opinion, which disagrees with the ruling. This is especially true for the U.S. Supreme Court. A concurring opinion may also come with a majority opinion, in which a justice agrees with the court's decision but offers another reason for the validity of the decision.

mandatory jurisdiction

Mandatory jurisdiction is court jurisdiction that must be exercised by the court that possesses it. This usually involves trial courts which must decide those cases brought to them over which they have jurisdiction, and appellate courts which have been given mandatory jurisdiction over appeals.

***Marbury v. Madison* (1803)**

This case that struck down for the first time in U.S. history an act of Congress as unconstitutional. It declared the Constitution to be the supreme law of the land, and that it is "the duty of the justice department to say what the law is."

oral argument

The verbal arguments presented in person by attorneys to an appellate court. Each attorney presents reasons why the court should rule in his client's favor.

original jurisdiction

The authority of a court to hear a case in the first instance. Usually courts of original jurisdiction are minor courts or trial courts.

plaintiff

The party that initiates a suit in court.

political question

A question that a court feels is more appropriately dealt with by the executive or legislative branch of government, and is inappropriate for judicial consideration. This is generally invoked when a decision would place the courts in conflict with other governmental branches or in a political controversy, or when a decision would lead to enforcement problems. Examples include the power of the president to recognize foreign governments and the power of Congress to determine if a Constitutional amendment was passed in timely fashion. If a question is appropriate for judicial consideration, it's a *justiciable question*.

precedent

A previous court ruling that bears on a later court decision in a similar or related case. Lawyers try to persuade judges that certain precedents should be considered in deciding a case. It is the judge's role to determine which precedent applies most directly. Courts are free, however, to overrule a precedent and establish a new one.

Rehnquist Court

The period (1986 to present) during which William H. Rehnquist has served as Chief Justice of the Supreme Court.

remand

Sending a legal case back to the court that heard it previously.

reverse

To nullify or invalidate a legal judgment.

rule of four

A procedure that requires four votes in favoring of hearing a case before the entire U.S. Supreme Court.

senatorial courtesy

A senate tradition under which the Senate will almost always reject a presidential nominee for a federal office within a state if the senator from that state and of the president's party objects. This means that the president must consult a state's senator or senators from his party before appointing someone to fill a federal office within that state. In fact, most appointments are actually recommended by the senators, and the president usually follows their recommendation. If neither senators from the state are of the president's party, the president usually consults the party leaders of that state.

stare decisis

Court policy to follow precedents established in past cases; to stand on decided cases.

state court

Each of the 50 states has its own courts with jurisdiction over all cases that arise under its own laws. The state court system is organized in a similar fashion to the federal court system.

statute

A law enacted by Congress or by a state legislature.

statutory law

Law passed by a legislative body.

trial

The examination of a civil or criminal action in accordance with the law of the land before a judge who has jurisdiction.

trial court

The court in which most cases usually begin and in which questions of fact are examined.

U.S. Supreme Court

The court of last resort in the federal system. Most states also have courts of last resort.

unanimous opinion

A legal opinion or determination that all the judges agree with.

Warren Court

The Supreme Court when Earl Warren was Chief Justice. The Warren Court was known for its judicial activism.

Multiple-Choice Questions

1. Which of the following are not Article III courts?

   I. Federal District courts

   II. Court of Federal Claims

   III. Tax Court

   IV. the Supreme Court

   V. Court of Appeals for the Armed Forces

   A. II, III, and V

   B. I, II, and IV

   C. I, II, and V

   D. III and V

   E. III, IV, and V

2. Judge-made law is also known as

   A. civil law.

   B. criminal law.

   C. common law.

   D. constitutional law.

   E. statutory law.

3. When the Supreme Court decides to hear a case, it issues a(n)

   A. writ of mandamus.

   B. majority opinion.

   C. amicus curiae brief.

   D. order of stare decisis.

   E. writ of certiorari.

4. All of the following serve as potential checks on the Supreme Court except

   A. public opinion.

   B. lower court decisions.

   C. presidential reluctance to enforce Supreme Court decisions.

   D. Congressional ability to rewrite legislation overturning Supreme Court rulings.

   E. Congressional control of the Court's appellate jurisdiction.

5. Advocates of judicial restraint believe that

   A. the Supreme Court should play an assertive role in setting social policy.

   B. the Supreme Court should never overturn an act of Congress.

   C. the Supreme Court should generally defer to the wishes of the two elected branches of government.

   D. the Constitution should be interpreted in accordance with the intentions of the framers.

   E. the Constitution should never be interpreted in a way that contradicts public opinion.

6. Which of the following is true about presidential nominations of Supreme Court justices?

   A. Fewer than four presidential nominations to the Supreme Court have been rejected by the Senate since 1950.

   B. Senatorial courtesy has been used a number of times with regard to Supreme Court nominees.

   C. Presidents have consulted interest groups in selecting a nominee for the Supreme Court since the 1950s.

   D. Presidents must nominate members of their own political party.

   E. Presidents have generally selected judges from the Court of Appeals to fill Supreme Court vacancies over the past several decades.

Essay Questions

1. Under the leadership of Chief Justice Earl Warren in the late 1950s and 1960s, some people characterized the Supreme Court as activist for its rulings on civil liberties and civil rights. Is this characterization true? Explain your answer in terms of judicial activism and judicial review, using two of the following cases to illustrate.

   - *Brown v. Board of Education* (1954)
   - *Mapp v. Ohio* (1963)
   - *Miranda v. Arizona* (1966)
   - *Reynolds v. Sims* (1964)

2. The judiciary has been characterized by some as the least dangerous branch of government. Others believe that the courts, and the Supreme Court in particular, have so much power that they now play the central role in making policy at the federal level. Discuss your position on this issue. Explain how the following features of the Supreme Court's decision-making process support your conclusion.

   - Discretionary appellate jurisdiction
   - Life tenure
   - Legitimacy of the Supreme Court

ANSWER KEY

Multiple-Choice Questions

1. A
2. C
3. E
4. A
5. C
6. E

Essay Questions

1.   This thesis regarding the activism of the Warren Court is probably true. Certainly the listed cases are examples of such activism. Make sure to define judicial activism, which means the use of judicial review to invalidate statutes (federal or state) that violate a Constitutional provision, here particularly the Bill of Rights.

   Brown declared racial segregation in public schools to be inherently unequal and therefore a denial of the Equal Protection Clause of the 14th Amendment. This overturned the Separate but Equal Doctrine first announced in *Plessy v. Ferguson* at the end of the 19th century. Therefore, it illustrated judicial activism by over-turning a state and local government policy followed in many southern states.

   Mapp v. Ohio illustrated judicial activism by applying the federal exclusionary rule to state law enforcement practices. These law enforcement practices violated the 4th Amendment's prohibition against unreasonable searches and seizures. While different than just invalidating a state statute, it still illustrates judicial activism in the sense that it imposed a federal standard on a 4th Amendment violation.

   Miranda v. Arizona required that persons suspected of criminal activity be informed of their constitutional right to counsel, to remain silent, and to be provided with an attorney if unable to afford one. This too, does not overturn a state statute, but it aggressively outlined a right that was not explicit in the Constitution.

   Reynolds v. Sims first articulated the "one person, one vote" rule for both houses of state legislatures. This decision invalidated several apportionment schemes used by states, including state constitutional provisions, as well as state statutes. These clearly reflect an aggressive, activist effort to ensure that the popular vote of people have approximately equal weight in the selection of state legislators.

2.   This question asks you to take a position on the issue of court power and policy making. It is much easier to support the power thesis than the nonpower thesis using of the items in the list, so it is probably wise to select the thesis that the judiciary is powerful.

Discretionary appellate jurisdiction gives the Supreme Court the ability to pick and choose the cases it will decide on appeal. This does not apply to the lower courts because they have little or no discretion in their jurisdictional authority. The Supreme Court can select particularly important, controversial cases if it wants to, and decide those in an effort to settle controversial issues. Examples of this would be the selection of racial segregation cases (*Brown v. Bd. of Education*) or abortion cases, such as *Roe v. Wade*. More recently, the Supreme Court selected and decided the Florida election case of *Bush v. Gore*. The question does not ask you to list or use a case, but such examples would indicate that you know the importance of case selection in the exercise of judicial power.

Life tenure is a traditional point of judicial insulation. This means that justices on the Supreme Court, and lower federal judges, need not worry that their decisions, even in controversial cases, will produce threats or reprisals from opponents. Though not part of this list, the constitutional protection against lowering judicial salaries illustrates the same aspect of insulation from political pressure. These elements contribute to the independence of the judiciary and its freedom to decide cases, no matter how controversial.

Supreme Court legitimacy has to do with the Court's reputation, and the respect that people show it regardless of their agreement with its decisions. This "store of good will" encourages tolerance among people and even acceptance of controversial decisions. Legitimacy may be the most tenuous and fragile of the three items listed in this case, since the Court can "use up" its legitimacy with controversial cases. If the Court continues to make controversial decisions, there may be dwindling tolerance for it into the future.

The counter position to this argument—that the Court is not powerful—is very difficult to support, given the items listed in the question. Even if you truly believed that this position is favored, you must be able to make an effective argument. Keep in mind that the "right" answer in this situation is one that you can argue effectively, as the analysis of politics and government should be done without regard to beliefs.

UNIT SIX:

Civil Rights and Civil Liberties

Chapter 14   *Civil Rights and Civil Liberties*

Civil rights and civil liberties have become an important, even central, feature of American politics in the past half century. They set out the relationship between the government and individual citizens. And while rights and liberties could be treated separately, they are more often treated as one core issue.

Civil rights are the rights citizens have to equal treatment. Derived largely from the Equal Protection Clause of the 14th Amendment, these are rights that all Americans enjoy, such as the right to equal protection of the law, the right to vote, and the right to privacy. One common civil rights issue is racial discrimination—both *de jure* and *de facto* discrimination—where certain groups of people are denied equal access or opportunity. Because of it, this country has seen a great deal of racial violence over the last half century.

Civil liberties are fundamental rights that protect citizens from governmental intrusion, and focus more on the freedoms that people enjoy and exercise. Many of these liberties were defined in the original Constitution, but they have been developed and expanded since then. In fact, their expansion has been a defining element of late-20th century American politics.

There have been two significant developments in civil rights and liberties over the past 100 years. The first is the selective incorporation (that is, the nationalization) of the Bill of Rights and its application to the states by means of the Due Process Clause of the 14th Amendment. This nationalization has forced states to conform to most of the civil liberties contained in the Bill of Rights.

The second major development has been the expansion and definition of civil liberties by the Supreme Court—equal protection of the law. The expansion of the equal protection of the law has given various groups of people the protection of equality or equal treatment.

History of Civil Rights and Civil Liberties

The original U.S. Constitution did not contain significant rights and liberties. The framers thought it unnecessary to define limits on the new government with respect to individual rights. In opposition to that, the Anti-Federalists argued for explicitly defined individual rights and liberties. They felt that the proposed central government was too powerful and that without formal and written protections against it excesses, the people would be severely disadvantaged.

After much debate, the two sides agreed to a compromise: the Bill of Rights (the first ten amendments to the Constitution). Along with the Reconstruction Amendments, the Bill of Rights provides the template for the rights and liberties Americans enjoy today. Some rights and liberties have been expanded through litigation. For example, in order to expand the liberties protected in the 1st Amendment, the American Civil Liberties Union litigated cases that had tried to restrict or expand free expression. In addition, litigation has added rights and liberties through constitutionalizing some claims, such as the right to privacy which now has constitutional statute. Other rights, like the Americans with Disabilities Act and the Civil Rights Act of 1964, have gained status through legislation.

> Civil rights and liberties are an essential part of liberal democratic principles.

The expansion of the Bill of Rights is a 20th century phenomenon. Over most of the 19th century, few issues were based on the Bill of Rights, and as a result, there were no Supreme Court decisions during that time. In fact, in *Barron v. Baltimore* (1833) the Supreme Court held that the Bill of Rights did not limit states or apply to the states. With incorporation, this all changed.

The adoption of the reconstruction amendments changed the relationship between states and the Bill of Rights. Each of these amendments granted Congress "the power to enforce, by appropriate legislation, the provisions of this article." This added to the powers that Congress exercised and extended those beyond the powers itemized in Article I of the Constitution. In other words, Congress became able to enact laws requiring states to treat people equally or with due process.

The Reconstruction Amendments are:

- The 13th Amendment (1865) prohibited involuntary servitude (slavery) in the United States.

- The 14th Amendment (1868) granted such things as "national and state citizenship." It also prohibited states from various things: States could not deny their citizens the privileges and immunities that U.S. citizens enjoy; they could not deny anyone life, liberty or property without due process of law; and they could not deny anyone the equal protection of laws.

- The 15th Amendment (1870) granted citizens the right to vote, regardless of race, color or previous condition of servitude.

Litigation, usually initiated by those who claimed they were denied rights and liberties, has significantly helped to expand and develop rights and liberties in the past century. The NAACP litigated the issue of segregated educational facilities on the grounds that racial segregation—no matter how close to equal—denied racial minorities equal protection of the law. Eventually, in *Brown v. Board of Education*, this claim prevailed in the Supreme Court.

Another significant aspect to the expansion of rights and liberties in the 20th century has been the selective incorporation of provisions of the Bill of Rights to the states through the Due Process Clause of the 14th Amendment. Though it was accomplished incrementally, one provision at a time, the nationalization of the Bill of Rights now makes the following provisions uniform across the country. It applies federal standards to judge infringements of these rights. The application of these parts of the Bill of Rights now protects against state, as well as federal, infringements and intrusions.

- **Just Compensation** (5th Amendment)

  Chicago, Burlington & Quincy Ry Co. v. Chicago (1897)

- **Free Speech** (1st Amendment)

  Gitlow v. New York (1925)

- **Free Press** (1st Amendment)

  Near v. Minnesota (1931)

- **Right to Counsel in Capital Cases** (6th Amendment)

  Powell v. Alabama (1932)

- **Freedom of Religion** (1st Amendment)

  Hamilton v. Regents of the University of California (1934)

- **Free Assembly and Right to Petition Government** (1st Amendment)

  De Jonge v. Oregon (1937)

- **Free Exercise of Religion** (1stAmendment)

  Cantwell v. Connecticut (1940)

- **Separation of Church and State** (1st Amendment)

  Everson v. Bd. Of Education of Ewing Township (1947)

- **Guarantee of a Public Trial** (6th Amendment)

  In re Oliver (1948)

- **Freedom from Unreasonable Searches and Seizures** (4th Amendment)

  Wolf v. Colorado (1949)

- **Freedom of Association** (1st Amendment)
  NAACP v. Alabama (1958)

- **Exclusionary Rule Relating to Searches and Seizures** (4th Amendment)
  Mapp v. Ohio (1961)

- **Protection against Cruel and Unusual Punishment** (8th Amendment)
  Robinson v. California (1962)

- **Right to Counsel in Felony-Level** ("Serious") **Crimes** (6th Amendment)
  Gideon v. Wainwright (1963)

- **Prohibition against Self-Incrimination** (5th Amendment)
  Malloy v. Hogan (1964)

- **Right to Confront Witnesses against the Accused** (6th Amendment)
  Pointer v. Texas (1965)

- **Right to Privacy** (1st, 3^{rd,} 4th, 5th, and 9th Amendments)
  Griswold v. Connecticut (1965)

- **Right to an Impartial Jury** (6th Amendment)
  Parker v. Gladden (1966)

- **Right to a Speedy Trial** (6th Amendment)
  Klopfer v. North Carolina (1967)

- **Right to Compulsory Process for Obtaining Witnesses** (6th Amendment)
  Washington v. Texas (1967)

- **Right to Jury Trial for Crimes Above the Petty Level** (6th Amendment)
  Duncan v. Louisiana (1968)

- **Guarantee against Double Jeopardy** (5th Amendment)
  Benton v. Maryland (1969)

Civil Rights

Civil rights involve constitutional rights that are afforded to people as individuals, largely by the Equal Protection Clause of the 14th Amendment. While these liberties are claimed by individuals, the issues that arise under equal protection generally involve the treatment of categories of people, such as racial categories, age categories, or gender classifications. This set of rights does *not* require that all people is all settings be treated equally.

In order for state or federal governments to enact policies, they must usually classify people into categories. A welfare program or a student loan program sorts people into two groups: qualified and nonqualified (excluded) individuals. Such differentiation is not always a violation of equal protection, because the Supreme Court has recognized that many classification schemes are considered appropriate and justifiable.

There are, however, some instances when excluded individuals may have just cause to litigate for inclusion in these programs. In these cases, the government must establish that the classification scheme used, whether it be race, wealth, or age, for example, is legally justified. As a rule, a classification of race is far more difficult to justify than a classification of age.

Courts have developed several tests to determine if a government classification violates the Constitution. The easiest test for the government to meet is the *rational basis* test, which requires only that the state prove that the classification scheme is rational. The *strict scrutiny* test is another, and it is the most difficult to pass. To allow this kind of classification to stand, the state must show a compelling state interest and the classification, such as race, must be narrowly tailored to meet that interest. A law based on a suspect classification scheme, such as race, will always be subject to strict scrutiny.

> Individual rights are not absolute, and governments can and do infringe on them. One classic example is that free speech does not permit shouting "Fire!" in a crowded theatre.

The Supreme Court has developed a third kind of scrutiny test, called *intermediate scrutiny*. This test seems to apply mostly to gender, which might be an acceptable classification if it is substantially related to achieving an important governmental objective.

The issues involved in equal protection cases are whether the classification sentence, such as race, is "suspect," because that determines what test the courts will apply to the case. Certain categories of classification, like race, have attracted most of the courts' attention, and have also produced most of the civil rights litigation in this country. Not just matters of equal protection for individuals, these classifications involve the application of rights to identifiable groups of people.

Gender

One of the most fundamental and long-standing criteria used to classify people in this country is gender. The law has long differentiated and discriminated against women. In fact, women were not allowed to vote until 1920, when the 19th Amendment was passed. There are other challenges that women face today, particularly in the workplace.

- Women are limited from advancing in their jobs because of a "glass ceiling."
- Women are often paid less than men for comparable work.
- Women are sometimes the subjects of sexual harassment in the workplace.

Some people have tried to address these situations, through constitutional change, as was the case with 19th Amendment, and the proposed Equal Rights Amendment. Some remedies are statutory, enacted by legislatures, to give women legal rights and protections or to remove traditional differential treatment. Title VII of the Civil Rights Act (1964) prohibited sexual harassment in the workplace. Note that the right to be free from sexual harassment extends beyond the state to private employers if they are involved in interstate commerce. Statutory remedies for gender discrimination are based on Congress' power to regulate interstate commerce. The Supreme Court has never held gender as a suspect classification, so it allows more gender classification than racial classification. And while gender gap may not be totally overcome by law, the more overt segments of such discrimination can be removed.

Race

Race as a discriminatory practice clearly goes back to slavery and the founding of the Union. African Americans, Latinos, Asian Americans, and Native Americans have all been targets of unequal treatment, and many are still today.

African Americans were subjugated by slavery until the Civil War and the Emancipation Proclamation. Even after that, discrimination against races by states, society, and others has continued. However, the development of equal protection with regard to race has been gradual. After the 1868 adoption of the Equal Protection Clause, the doctrine of "separate but equal" treatment of races was considered constitutional. Only gradually before *Brown v. Board of Education* (1954) did the courts decide that the treatment given African Americans denied equal protection. With the *Brown* decision, the Supreme Court declared separate but equal to be inherently unconstitutional, at least with regard to de jure racial segregation in schools. After 1954, the Court expanded the meaning and the reach of the Equal Protection Clause. In addition, Congress enacted a far-reaching statute prohibiting racial segregation in places of public accommodation that was related to interstate commerce. This is the Civil Rights Act (1964), and it is focused on various forms of private discrimination.

The Voting Rights Act of 1965 focused on racial discrimination in voter registration practices. This was an effort to overcome strong southern resistance to the 15th Amendment.

The efforts to achieve equal treatment for African Americans have led to the widespread and aggressive civil rights movement in the last part of the 20th century. That has spilled over and reached the problems of other discriminated minorities, whether they be homosexuals, the elderly, or persons with disabilities.

Political equality is only one aspect of the civil rights movement. Economic opportunity, employment opportunity, educational opportunity, housing opportunity are all areas of concern for minorities. In order to address these areas, statutory enactments have been passed by legislatures prohibiting discrimination in the workplace and requiring affirmative action in the workplace to compensate for past racial discrimination.

Some discrimination continues because of voter efforts using initiatives and referenda in some states. However, the advocacy of equality for various groups will continue but has not achieved the same stature or had the same impact as that relating to African Americans or to women.

Civil Liberties

Civil liberties are essential for successful self-governance and representative democracy. They are also basic for the exercise of personal freedoms in society. They protect individuals from the "tyranny of the majority." That is, they protect minorities with unpopular views from intimidating majorities. These liberties are guaranteed by the Bill of Rights and the Due Process Clause of the 14th Amendment. Note that these Liberties are afforded people against states as well as the federal government by means of the selective incorporation of the Bill of Rights through the 14th Amendment.

Free Speech

Free speech is a fundamental liberty firmly established in this country. It has a high value in our society because it presumes that ideas, competing in a "free exchange," are basic tenets of a free and open society. In order for open exchange to take place, people must be able to convey their ideas, no matter how extreme or unpopular.

One aspect of free speech is that speech may not be censored in advance of its utterance. That is, censorship is anathema to the basic propositions of a free and open society. Words can lead to action, and violent action can be restrained, but it is extremely difficult to establish beforehand when words will cause some future illegal action.

All speech, however, is not absolute. Rather, some utterances are protected by the 1st Amendment from government censure or limits. Determining what speech is protected has always been difficult. The Court has gradually expanded the definition of what constitutes "speech," and thus, what is protected by the 1st Amendment.

Symbolic speech is actions or nonverbal expressions that convey opinions and ideas. For example, burning the American flag was treated as a protected right in *Texas v. Johnson* (1989). Wearing a black arm band to convey a particular message—opposition to the war in Vietnam—was also protected speech, see *Tinker v. Des Moines Independent County School District* (1969).

Hate speech is intended to impose emotional distress or defamation on an identifiable ethnic minority, and that expression has been protected in some Court decisions, namely *R.A.V. v. St. Paul* (1990).

Libel and slander is printed and spoken material that causes personal injury to an individual, his reputation, and credibility. That means free speech and press protect these kinds of utterances. However, if they cause the subject damage, a libel or slander suit can result in large damage awards against the speaker or the writer. These damaging materials can form the basis for lawsuits after the injury for damages. Libeling public figures, such as movie stars, is more difficult to prove than libeling private citizens. Public figures voluntarily seek or benefit from "being famous" and so seek such attention. Their reputations can be damaged by scandal, but proving the damage is more difficult than for a private citizen. Public officials also face a more difficult task in establishing injury from news coverage of their actions and statements. That is because they willingly subject themselves to such scrutiny.

The Supreme Court has sought to specify whether certain statements are protected by the free speech provision. It has devised several tests to determine when speech can be limited in order to prevent action. The *Clear and Present Danger* doctrine, first outlined in *Schenk v. United States* (1919), provides that speech is protected unless the language gives rise to a clear and present danger that could be prevented. Establishing a direct correlation between words and bad actions, though, has never been easy.

The Court has also used a balancing test that requires the value of the speech to be balanced with the public's interest in peace and tranquility. For example, in *Dennis v. United States* (1951), the Court upheld convictions for speaking and teaching communist doctrine as though they were criminal activity. The Court thought this speech was advocacy, and that was considered *action* when balanced against speech.

The government can regulate speech but only if it can "prove" to a court that it has a compelling interest in such regulation, and as always regulating or penalizing speech after it is uttered is possible. That heavy burden on the government has not easily supported restrictions on speech.

Obscene materials are not protected by the 1st Amendment. However, there has been no clearcut way to define "obscene." Though the Supreme Court has applied several tests in recent decades, none is workable, and the court now seems inclined to stay away from these cases. The only exception is child pornography, which the Court has been willing to restrict or sanction.

Fighting words that can or do cause violence are not protected by free speech. Such speech incites people to riot or to engage in fighting or criminal activity.

Religion

All Americans have a right to the free exercise of religion. As a rule, government cannot intrude on one's religious practices. Yet this freedom is not absolute; while one's beliefs are his own, his actions based on beliefs may not be. That is, the way one practices his religion may be restricted.

Freedom of religion cannot be used to justify violating the law. So polygamy, hallucinatory substances used in worship, snake handling, or refusing to vaccinate children may be prohibited by government against the justification that one's religious beliefs dictates such regulation.

On the other hand, there have been cases in which the actions of religious organizations have been protected. Requiring people to salute the flag or say the Pledge of Allegiance violates the free exercise clause if those actions are contrary to beliefs. Similarly, requiring people to work on their Sabbath is in violation of the free exercise clause. Even animal sacrifice for purposes of worship has been recognized, with some restrictions for public health safety, as protected by the free exercise provision of the 1st Amendment.

Anti-establishment of religion is a right that ensures that the government will not favor or fund one religion over another. The would-be wall of separation between church and state posits that the state should not encourage or discourage any religion. This means that the government must take a neutral position with regard to religions.

The *principle of separation* means that church and state are formally separate. There cannot be complete separation between the two entities in this country, because some overlap does occur. (Government purchase of textbooks for parochial schools would be an overlap of church and state.) The principle of separation prohibits direct governmental assistance to any religion. Rather, it allows only for indirect and uniform governmental assistance to religions, such as through tax exemptions. However, the penetration of the wall of separation causes worry for some people, often small minority religions who perceive discrimination or disadvantage from such overlap.

Posting the Ten Commandments or the Lord's Prayer in a public school classroom in a public school would violate the separation between church and state. Conducting prayers in public schools and at school events can raise strong objections and has usually been considered a violation of the wall of separation. Moments of silence in the class room have been invalidated on the basis of this separation. On the other hand, placing a nativity scene on a courthouse lawn is permitted as long as any religion is able to display its symbol as well.

Regardless of what the Supreme Court decides in cases involving religious issues, people will continue to follow their preferences and local practices. Public opinion polls often indicate that a majority of people favor prayer in schools, as well as other forms of religious observance, despite its clear violation of church and state separation. It is quite likely that in spite of any objections that small minorities may make, these observances will continue.

The Press

Freedom of the press is a long-standing protection that has come to mean the entire press, not just the print media. It is based on the proposition that information about government and society must be available the citizenry. That includes criticism of government actions, not just information about such actions.

Prior restraint on publication is not allowed under the 1st Amendment. That would be government censorship, and with the exception of military secrets or national defense issues, this cannot occur. While the press may be constrained by libel law and government confidentiality, those limitations can be imposed only after publication of the information.

The Freedom of Information Act provides a statutory basis that allows both the press and individuals access to some governmental information. This has become very important in recent decades as the size of government has grown and the amount of personal information maintained by government agencies has increased.

There is a difficult balance struck in this connection between the freedom of the press and the need for a fair trial, including pretrial publicity or the disclosure of evidence and the conflict.

Criminal Prosecution

An individual who faces criminal prosecution has many rights available to him. In recent decades, these liberties and protections have been defined more clearly than simply the "general right to due process of law." In addition, these rights have been expanded to apply in cases outside of traditional criminal law. Most state constitutions contain these protections, but they have been expanded nationwide by Supreme Court decisions through the incorporation of the rights of the 4th, 5th, 6th, and 8th Amendments.

- The *right to a jury trial* in a criminal case is available in state prosecutions *Duncan v. Louisiana* (1968). On their own, states may not afford the right to jury trial for some criminal charges, until the Supreme Court required it.

- The *right to legal counsel*, expanded beyond *Gideon v. Wainwright* (1963) to other, less-serious (misdemeanor) criminal prosecutions.

- *Unreasonable searches and seizures* are protected against state as well as national intrusions *Wolf v. Colorado* (1949).

- The *right to a speedy jury trial* is also available to anyone in state proceedings.

Privacy

The right to privacy is a right not specified in the Constitution. Rather, it was constructed by the Supreme Court through a series of cases in the late 20th century. Many people support this right and believe in it, though its precise meaning and extent of its reach varies. This allows widespread claims of privacy for all kinds of people and circumstances. To date, the courts have not extensively elaborated on this right, but the matter of privacy has generated widespread claims. The issue of privacy has become the cornerstone for several modern-day issues:

- The right to have an abortion
- The right of couples, married or unmarried, to obtain contraceptives
- The right of consenting adults to have a homosexual relationship in their homes

Changing the Status Quo

As fundamental features of liberal democracy, rights and liberties form a significant part of political culture in this country today. As civil rights litigation continues to challenge the status quo, courts will continue redefining these rights, whether to expand or to limit them. And in the face of increased civil rights advocates and organizations who use their funds to push for rights through legislation, the courts will face further pressure to clarify our constitutional rights and liberties.

POINTS TO REMEMBER

- Many claims for rights and liberties have been unsuccessful, both historically and currently. For example, homosexual couples have not been granted the same status and rights as heterosexual couples, despite their efforts. Still, the principles of protecting the basic rights of minorities from a majority rule is fundamental and widely recognized in this country.

- While some people tend to think of rights and liberties as synonymous, they are in fact different; liberties focus on individual rights in relation to government control, while rights concentrate on the equality of government treatment of groups of people—women/men, elderly/young, ethnic minorities/white majority.

- The most important feature of the expansion of rights and liberties in the 20th century has been the nationalization of rights and liberties. In other words, most of the Bill of Rights has now been applied to limit state and local governmental actions so that they coincide with the limits of national government.

  These rights have become homogenized throughout the country, e.g., the exclusionary rule and the limits of unreasonable searches and seizures. They are applied to all circumstances with the same federal standards, without regard to differences among the states.

KEY TERMS AND CONCEPTS

13th Amendment

The amendment (1865) that prohibits slavery.

14th Amendment

The post–Civil War amendment (1868) that forbids a state to deprive any persons of life, liberty or property without due process of law, or deny any person equal protection of the law. It made African Americans citizens with full rights.

15th Amendment

The amendment (1870) that forbids a state to deny a person the right to vote because of race, color, or previous condition of servitude.

19th Amendment

The amendment (1920) that forbids a state to deny a person the right to vote because of their sex.

AARP

American Association of Retired Persons, a nonprofit interest group concerned with the welfare of retired Americans. In 1998 the AARP had more than 30 million members (about 45 percent of Americans aged 50 or over).

affirmative action

A policy in hiring that gives consideration or compensatory treatment to traditionally disadvantaged groups in an effort to overcome the present effects of past discrimination.

age discrimination

Action taken based solely or primarily on a person's age, without regard to actual qualifications or abilities. The Age Discrimination in Employment Act protects persons age 40 and over from employment discrimination based on age.

Americans with Disabilities Act (1990)

An act providing protection against discrimination in employment, pubic service, transportation, and telecommunications for disabled people.

Brown v. Board of Education of Topeka, Kansas

The U.S. Supreme Court decision establishing that segregation of the races in public schools violates the equal protection clause of the 14th Amendment of the Constitution.

busing

Transportation of public school students from areas where they live to schools in other areas, with the goal of eliminating de facto school segregation based on residential patterns.

civil disobedience

Refusal to obey a law, usually on the ground that the law is morally reprehensible. Civil disobedience is often used as a protest tactic to call attention to questionable laws.

civil liberties

Those personal freedoms possessed by all individuals and protected from arbitrary interference by government. They include the protection of persons, opinions, and property.

civil rights

Those powers or privileges guaranteed to individuals or protected groups by government, which are protected from arbitrary removal by government or by private individuals. In the United States, they include the right to vote, equal treatment before the law, and equal access to and benefits from public facilities.

Civil Rights Act of 1964

An act that forbids discrimination on the basis of race, color, religion, national origin, and sex.

Civil Rights Act of 1991

An act that reaffirmed and expanded protection against discrimination in employment.

civil rights movement

A citizen's action movement during the 1950s and 1960s led mainly by African American religious leaders in support of equal rights and the end of racial discrimination and segregation.

comparable worth

The concept that compensation for work performed should be based on the worth of the job to an employer, and that unrelated factors, such as the sex of the employee, should not affect compensation.

criminal law

The collection of laws defining crimes and establishing punishment for violations. The government prosecutes criminal cases because crimes are against the public order.

de facto segregation

Segregation that occurs not because of a deliberate governmental intent to separate groups, but because of past social and economic conditions and residential patterns. *De facto* is Latin for "by fact." De facto segregation most often refers to racial segregation, but can equally apply to other forms, for example segregation by ethnicity.

de jure segregation

Racial or other forms of segregation that occurs because of laws or administrative decisions by public agencies. *De jure* means "by law."

double jeopardy

A second prosecution for the same crime once the first one is completed. This is prohibited by the U.S. Constitution.

Dred Scott v. Sandford (1857)

A case that held that African Americans could not be considered persons under the Constitution nor were they entitled to the rights and privileges of citizenship.

Emancipation Proclamation

The announcement issued by President Lincoln freeing the slaves.

Equal Employment Opportunity Commission (EEOC)

A federal commission established by the 1964 Civil Rights Act that 1) sets regulations, investigates, mediates, and brings suit against private employers, unions, or community organizations to end employment discrimination based on race, color, religion, gender, national origin, and age, and 2) promotes voluntary action to foster equal job opportunities.

Equal Pay Act (1963)

This act requires equal pay for men and women doing similar work.

equal protection clause

A provision of the 14th Amendment, which says that states may not arbitrarily discriminate against persons.

Equal Rights Amendment (ERA)

The amendment proposed in 1972 to establish the equal rights of men and women. The amendment failed to be ratified by the required 38 states.

freedom ride

Civil rights demonstrations in the early 1960s in which interracial activists rode buses together through parts of the southern states to protest racial segregation and discrimination.

gender gap

A phrase frequently used to describe the different voting patterns of men and women. It was widely used to explain the different percentage of votes received by candidates in the 1980 presidential election.

gender discrimination

Discrimination in employment, education, or delivery of social services that denies a person or group of people their right to equal treatment on the basis of their gender. Usually directed toward women.

glass ceiling

The invisible barriers in businesses and government that prevent women and minorities from being promoted into top management positions.

grandfather clause

In the south, states created taxes and literacy laws with the intent of keeping African Americans from voting. The grandfather clause restricted the right to vote to those who could prove their grandfathers had voted before 1867. In 1915, the Supreme Court declared the clause unconstitutional.

just compensation

Compensation for private property taken by the government that gives a property owner fair market value.

literacy test

A reading or "understanding" test that a voter had to pass before voting. Literacy tests were frequently used to prevent African Americans from voting. Literacy tests were banned by the Voting Rights Act of 1965, which was expanded in 1970, 1975, and 1982.

mandatory set-aside

An aspect of affirmative action programs in which a specific number of construction contracts are allocated to minority-owned businesses. Ruled illegal in 1989.

minority

A racial, religious, political, national, or other group regarded as different from the larger group of which it is a part.

NAACP (National Association for the Advancement of Colored People)

An organization formed in 1909 to ensure the political, educational, social and economic equality of African Americans and other minority group citizens of the United States. It is the oldest, largest, and strongest civil rights organization in the United States.

nonviolent protest tactics

Peaceful actions to gain political or social ends.

Plessy v. Ferguson (1896)

The case that upheld a state law requiring segregation of the races in public transportation. The Court ruled that a state could provide separate but equal facilities for African Americans.

poll tax

A tax a person must pay in order to vote. The 24th Amendment to the Constitution outlawed poll taxes in national elections. A 1966 Supreme Court ruling declared poll taxes illegal in all elections.

prior restraint

Preventing an action before it even happens. Prior restraint relies on censorship instead of subsequent punishment.

private discrimination

Discrimination done by individuals in their private capacity. This type of discrimination is not prohibited by the 14th Amendment, and Congress cannot prohibit it unless it affects interstate commerce or there is some state involvement. This is in contrast to discrimination by a state agency or governmental body, which is prohibited.

racial equality

The equal treatment of all persons regardless of their race.

racial segregation

The separation of the races in public and private facilities.

reconstruction amendments

The 13th, 14th, and 15th Amendments to the U.S. Constitution, which remove various barriers to freedom for former slaves. These were adopted during the Reconstruction period, and their ratification was required of the former states in the Confederacy for readmission to the Union. Their meaning and reach, particularly the 14th Amendment, has changed greatly since their adoption.

Reconstruction period (1865–1877)

The period following the Civil War during which the states of the Confederacy were controlled by the federal government.

reverse discrimination

Discrimination against those who do not have minority status within a community. Reverse discrimination may result from affirmative action programs that require preferential treatment for minority members of society.

***Romer v. Evans* (1996)**

A Supreme Court ruling benefiting gay and lesbian rights. In this case, the Court struck down a Colorado constitutional amendment that denied protection from discrimination to homosexuals. The Court held that the equal protection clause of the 14th Amendment didn't make homosexuals "unequal to everyone else."

school desegregation

The elimination of the separation of races in public schools; racial integration.

separate but equal doctrine

In 1896, the U.S. Supreme Court held that racial segregation, or "Jim Crow" laws, were constitutional under the "separate-but-equal doctrine." This doctrine held that it was all right to segregate the races as long as both races had access to equal services and facilities. This led to segregation in schools, transportation, housing, and elsewhere. In practice, few of the services or facilities were actually equal—those for African Americans were generally inferior. The separate-but-equal doctrine began to weaken in the 1940s, when the Supreme Court began to insist on true equality. This eventually led to the Court's 1954 decision striking down the doctrine entirely.

sexual harassment

Unwelcome physical or verbal behavior or abuse of a sexual nature. Sexual harassment interferes with the receiver's job performance, creates a hostile environment, or is accompanied by a direct or indirect threat to the person's continued employment or opportunity for promotion.

sit-in

An organized protest demonstration in which participants seat themselves and refuse to move.

slavery

The practice of owning people as property.

social movement

Activation of a segment of the public for political, economic, or social change.

strict scrutiny

A test used by the Supreme Court for issues such as affirmative action. Legislation in these areas is highly suspect and will be closely watched and allowed to stand only if it's "narrowly tailored" and serves a "compelling government interest."

suffrage

The right to vote, also called the franchise. To allow a person to vote is to enfranchise them. Throughout its history, the United States has enfranchised more and more of its population.

Title IX of the Civil Rights Act (1964)

The provisions of the Civil Rights Act that prohibit recipients of federal education aid from discriminating in services provided people on the basis of gender.

Voting Rights Act (1965)

The act that eliminated restrictions on voting that had been used to discriminate against African Americans and other minority groups.

wage discrimination

Paying different people different wages for the same or similar job based on their sex, race, or other discriminatory factors.

white flight

Movement of large numbers of white people from cities to suburbs. This movement was precipitated by the desegregation of public facilities.

white primary

A state primary with voting rights granted only to whites. The Supreme Court outlawed white primaries in 1944.

"with all deliberate speed"

Reference made in the Supreme Court decision *Brown v. Board of Education* about undertaking racial integration of schools quickly. The term "deliberate" was used as a loophole by some officials who wanted to delay desegregation.

women's suffrage

Women's right to vote.

Multiple-Choice Questions

1. Which of the following are true about the constitutionally guaranteed rights of criminal defendants?

   I. They have a right to legal counsel, and if they cannot afford adequate counsel, the government will provide them with an attorney.

   II. They have a right to a trial free from press coverage.

   III. They have a right to a trial by a jury.

   IV. They have a right to subpoena witnesses to appear in court.

   A. I and II

   B. I and III

   C. I, II, and IV

   D. II and IV

   E. I, III, and IV

2. The 5th Amendment protects citizens against which of the following?

   I. Illegal search and seizure

   II. Testifying against oneself

   III. Double jeopardy under the law

   IV. Deprivation of life, liberty, or property without due process of law

   A. I and II

   B. I, II, and III

   C. II only

   D. II, III, and IV

   E. IV only

3. The 1954 Supreme Court decision in *Brown v. Board of Education of Topeka, Kansas*, and the 1955 follow-up case known as *Brown 2*, had all of the following effects except

   A. It declared de jure segregation unconstitutional.

   B. It declared de facto segregation unconstitutional.

   C. It ordered public schools to desegregate "with all deliberate speed."

   D. It declared separate facilities inherently unequal.

   E. It overturned *Plessy v. Ferguson*.

4. Which of the following civil liberties has not been applied to state governments through the Supreme Court's selective incorporation of the 14th Amendment's Due Process Clause?

A. freedom of speech

B. the right to bear arms

C. the right to privacy

D. the right to counsel when accused of a crime

E. the right to avoid cruel and unusual punishment

5. The Civil Rights Act of 1964

A. prohibited discrimination on the basis of race, color, religion, sex, or national origin in places of public accommodation.

B. was declared unconstitutional by the Supreme Court in *Katzenbach v. McClung* (1964).

C. lowered the minimum voting age in federal elections to 18 years.

D. established the policy of affirmative action for public contracts.

E. made it easier for African Americans in the south to vote in national elections.

6. Which of the following are not true about the Bill of Rights?

I. It was the product of a compromise agreement between the Federalists and the Anti-Federalist.

II. Most of it has been incorporated into the 14th Amendment and applied to the states.

III. Several proposed amendments are still awaiting ratification like the 27th Amendment was until 1992.

IV. It was the result of efforts during the Reconstruction Period to ensure equal rights and treatment for newly freed slaves.

A. I only

B. I and II

C. II and III

D. III and IV

E. I, II, III, and IV

7. Which of the following is true about the civil rights of Native Americans?

   A. Members of organized tribes can choose to be protected by the Bill of Rights when they join the tribe.

   B. The right to establish commercial gambling establishments on tribal property is the only right protected by the Due Process Clause of the 5th Amendment.

   C. While Native Americans are not permitted to consume prohibited substances in the course of worship, they have nearly complete access to traditional sites on government land for worship.

   D. The Bill of Rights has been applied to the members of the Treaty nations as part of the usual provisions contained in treaties with Indian tribes during the late 19th century.

   E. The Bill of Rights does not apply to them because Native Americans were considered members of a foreign nation at the time the Bill of Rights was drafted.

Essay Questions

1. Select one of the following Supreme Court decisions, and use it to explain what it demonstrates about the relationship between the state and the individual in the United States.

   - *Gideon v. Wainwright* (1963)

   - *Texas v. Johnson* (1989)

   - *Brown v. Board of Education of Topeka* (1954)

2. What is the difference between de jure and de facto racial segregation? Select one case from each of the two columns below and explain how the Supreme Court has treated these two forms of discrimination in these cases. What did the Court say about the type of discrimination involved in each of the two cases you select, and how did the Court decide the issue of racial discrimination in each case?

• *Milliken v. Bradley* (1974)	• *Brown v. Board of Education of Topeka* (1954)
• *Keyes v. School District No. 1 Denver* (1974)	• *Plessy v. Ferguson* (1896)

ANSWER KEY

Multiple-Choice Questions

1. E
2. D
3. B
4. B
5. A
6. B
7. E

Essay Questions

1. This question expects you to be able to articulate what the selected case illustrates about the government–individual relationship. All three cases have the same general thesis; that is, protections from government power and control do exist.

    Gideon v. Wainwright is the famous case of Clarence Earl Gideon which established that to try anyone for a serious crime, the state must provide legal counsel. The basic meaning of this holding is that the state (government) must incur the expense of providing counsel when the accused is indigent, though this may mean only that the defendant may retain (hire) counsel himself. For anyone accused of a crime, the state must ensure a person's protection of criminal procedure. In order to accomplish that, the state must provide adequate legal counsel.

    Texas v. Johnson is the case which held that burning a U.S. flag can be a protected means of expression when symbolically done to convey a message. The importance of this holding is that it protects a form of speech that goes beyond utterances and that are critical of government.

    Brown v. Board of Education held that racially segregated schools denied individuals equal protection of the law. As a result, students, particularly those of color, had a constitutional right to be free of such state imposed segregation.Individuals' civil rights could not be classified or separated on the basis of race. Many subsequent Supreme Court cases have enhanced this principle, but the fundamental meaning still stands and continues to protect various categories of people from government segregation or classification.

2. Begin this answer with a brief explanation about the difference between de jure and de facto discrimination. *De jure* segregation is segregation that occurs because of laws or administrative decisions made by public agencies. Formal school segregation adopted by a school board is de jure segregation. *De facto* segregation, on the other hand, occurs in the absence of any formal segregation policy. It occurs more because of past social and economic conditions and residential patterns. Schools can be segregated de facto if they draw their students from highly segregated surrounding neighborhoods.

The two cases in the left column involve court decisions relating to *de facto* segregation. Those on the right involve *de jure* segregation. In two of these cases, *Keyes* and *Brown*, the Court invalidated the racial segregation involved. In the other two cases, *Milliken* and *Plessy*, the Court upheld the racial segregation. Clearly, you must know the case facts and holding in order to answer the questions.

Milliken involved forced busing of children across school district lines in Detroit to achieve racial integration where de facto (housing pattern) segregation existed. This had been ordered by a federal district court because there were so few white students in the Detroit metropolitan schools. The district court felt that the only effective way to integrate a predominately black school district was to bus in students from the largely white suburban neighborhoods. The Supreme Court went on to invalidate the busing plan on the grounds that crossing school district lines was an inappropriate remedy to de facto segregation. The Court held that the schools were not responsible for the racial segregation, and so they could not be required to remedy the housing segregation.

Keyes involved the school system in Denver, where there was de facto segregation. No formal segregation policy had been adopted by the school board; rather, it had been caused by housing and residential patterns. Here the Supreme Court held that such patterns of segregation violated the Constitution's Equal Protection Clause, and that although the school system did not intend to segregate, it could be required to remedy that separation.

Brown is the famous case in which the Supreme Court held that de jure racial segregation of schools inherently denied equal protection, and that this situation must be remedied by desegregating the schools. In other words, it established the principle that such racial separation was unconstitutional, and that schools would no longer be able to segregate students on the basis of race. This watershed case generated much opposition and open violence on the part of many segregated schools.

Plessy v. Ferguson is the original case in which the Supreme Court upheld the de jure segregation of people on railroads. At the time, the state of Louisiana required segregation of passengers in railroad cars. The Supreme Court held that as long as the segregated facilities were equal, such separation did not deny equal protection. This Plessy doctrine—that separate but equal facilities were constitutional—established the principle that de jure racial segregation did not violate the Equal Protection Clause. This doctrine stood in one form or another until the 1954 *Brown* decision.

UNIT SEVEN:

Public Policy in American Government

Chapter 15   *Domestic Policy*

Policy is a governmental plan of action designed to address a problem. Domestic policy focuses on problems that are internal to the United States and as a result, may have enormous consequences for millions of people. Domestic policy making is often viewed as more complicated and uncertain than foreign policy because of the complexity and variables in the process.

Some policies involve simple issues, such as the speed limit on a highway or the legal drinking age in a state. These kinds of issues can generate a great deal of debate, but in the end, result in a clear "line" such as 65 miles per hour, or 18 years of age. Other domestic policies are more complex and amorphous, such as the protection of the environment. The nature of the problem, as well as the appropriate solution for it, is debatable and uncertain. The impact of policies that would address this type of problem are also unclear. Complicating facts even more is the fact that some domestic policies are formulated at the state level. For example, a state can impose its own speeding limit or its own legal drinking age. In many other contexts, domestic policies are set by the federal government and applied uniformly throughout the country.

There are various aspects to the complexity and unpredictability of the domestic policy making process. First, it is difficult to implement and evaluate domestic policies. Second, administrative bureaucracies may not be able to achieve the policy goals set for them by legislatures, and so it is difficult to measure the success of their policies. As a result, it is quite common for actors to attempt only partial policy changes, rather than to address a problem in its entirety. It is even more rare for a policy to "solve" a problem completely.

The domestic policymaking process is inherently filled with obstacles. It must simultaneously incorporate the often conflicting interests of individuals, interest groups, elected officials, and appointed policy-making officials. In addition, since so many institutions are involved, no one of them can be held directly responsible.

How Domestic Policy is Made

The policy making process is not a single process, but rather involves several institutions—legislatures, bureaucracies, courts, and/or executives. The process affects outcomes and determines or favors different winners and losers (people and interests who do or do not get the policy they want). When all is said and done, though, the status quo is the most likely outcome of any public policy process, because of the complexity of interests and processes and because of inertia in the political system. Opponents to policy change decidedly have the political advantage.

Policy making implements and evaluates policy. Of course, evaluation is subjective, and perceptions of how well a policy has worked are bound to differ among observers. Policy making is limited by several parameters:

- The political power of the actors involved in the process shapes policy. Each actor (private interests and government officials) is not equally involved, or even equally successful in the course of the process. Not everyone has the same interpersonal ability or resources with which to influence policy making.

- The economic situation in the country influences the likelihood of some policy adoptions. A budget surplus, for example, will increase the likelihood of new or redistributive policy adoption.

  1. The "mood" of the country or public opinion generates a climate in which policy proposals must "stew." A national emergency or crisis, e.g., a natural disaster, will affect the likelihood of policy adoption in that area.

  2. The support of some (and opposition of others) to paying taxes affects the adoption of policies that involve expenditures of large amounts of government revenue. That is because government revenue (income) is essential to most public policies.

The sequence of stages in domestic policy making is detailed below. Though it omits some of the finer points, this sequence provides a general breakdown of the process.

1. The first step in making domestic policy is *agenda building*, which means recognizing and characterizing the problem. This initiative usually comes from individuals or the media seeking to correct a problem, rather than from government officials. Most often, initiation comes from a policy entrepreneur who is an expert and deeply interested in the problem. Once it has been recognized by policy makers, the problem is debated: Some may think it severe, others may think it minor. These debates will effectively shape the policy making agenda to come in Congress or in another governmental institution. As a result, how the problem is characterized in this early phase is crucial.

2. The second step involves the development of proposals to address the problem. This might be called the *policy formulation* stage. In this stage, bureaucrats or legislators who are advocating a policy begin discussions among themselves, as well as with the public and the media. Possible solutions are discussed, and "aired" as trial balloons. Factors such as cost, likelihood of success, and strength of support will propel some proposals ahead of others. It is at this time, and into the policy adoption stage, that elected officials interact most with the advocates/opponents of the issue. This stage is like a gestation phase when advocates inside and outside of government discuss, try to persuade, and air their preferences to mobilize support among policy makers.

3. The third step is *policy adoption*. At this stage, the policy formulations that have been prepared will take on only marginal changes. For that reason, step 2 is crucial: The policy design will have been set by the most vocal proponents or opponents. By step 3, the basic proposal has been set. Policy entrepreneurs (citizens or even legislators who actively push a policy area) will likely lobby for changes in the final version.

4. *Policy implementation* is the fourth step. This phase continues to involve both private actors—advocates and would-be beneficiaries—and administrative bureaucracies at the federal, or lower levels. Implementation might be difficult, or it might be straightforward, depending on the complexity of the policy. Implementation also might be quick, or it may be delayed, depending on the complexity of the policy and the degree of acceptance among the affected interests. At the very least, implementation is likely to be only partially successful or satisfactory to those involved.

5. The fifth stage of policymaking is *evaluation*. The evaluation process is not a single process: It may involve several agencies working together. *Congressional oversight* is one type of evaluation. A more formal type of evaluation is *GAO auditing for Congress*. The items considered when a policy is being evaluated are:

    • Whether the policy had the intended consequences
    • What the negative or unintended consequences of the policy were
    • Whether changes to the policy would be beneficial

This policy making process does not always move from stage 1 through stage 5. Sometimes, for virtually decades, an issue will make it to stage 2 but will never be adopted by Congress. Furthermore, once a policy is adopted and implemented, it becomes subject to attack and modification all over again. This set of challenges, moving the issue through the stages again, may be raised by opponents who did not want the policy in the first place and by advocates who are not satisfied with the policy that was actually adopted.

In spite of advocates' efforts, it is important to note that this process is unlikely to result in policy adoption. The hurdles are great. And because it is easier to keep the status quo than to change the system, policy advocates often lose out to those who would rather not change anything. Some may even sabotage proposals so that the status quo prevails.

There are a variety of policy agendas that are involved here. The agendas below are listed in *descending size*, but *ascending importance*, suggesting the places where policy proposals may gain or lose ground.

1. *Public Agenda* is a large set of items that a segment of the population wishes to have addressed by the political system. Any issue of concern to any segment of the population might be on this agenda. In order for an item or problem to be placed on the public agenda, it would need to have advocates, publicity, and some public awareness or concern.

2. *Systemic Agenda* is the broad set of general issues that might be considered by the system if the policymaking institutions were willing to consider them. These issues have been recognized by one or more policy makers. The president may address the concerns of a group, recognizing their view of the problem or suggesting some action should be taken. Some decisions by a bureaucracy (an agency) or a court might heighten attention for an policy issue.

3. *Institutional Agenda* is the list of policy items that an institution is likely to consider seriously for adoption. This agenda is the policy proposals that are introduced into Congress, those rules being considered by a regulatory agency, or those cases decided by a court. By mentioning an issue in his State of the Union address, the president would clearly elevate a problem to the institutional agenda.

There is no guarantee that an item placed on an agenda will result in policy. For an agenda item to progress to the next step means that an issue is important to many individuals in the system.

Some domestic policies affect narrow and specific interests by giving them a clear benefit. Other policies broadly affect the "context" in which all Americans live.

There are many possible actors and many possible processes (legislative, executive, or judicial) involved in policy making. Yet when a particular policy is involved, such as agricultural price supports or approving a new prescription drug, there will likely be a narrow set of actors, institutions, and issues involved: iron triangles or issue networks.

Types of Public Policy

There are several types of public policy in the United States: They are not mutually exclusive, but rather overlap in areas. Thus, regulatory policy may have some distributive or even redistributive qualities.

- *Distributive Policy* covers programs that distribute direct government benefits to identifiable groups of beneficiaries. Farm subsidy programs, and medical assistance programs such as Medicare fall into this category. Congress has a tendency to distribute broadly these benefits so that they reach as many people as possible. By doing so, it may net more political support for policymakers.

  A distributive program is often initiated by those people who will most directly be affected by it: first, the beneficiaries, and second, those who believe they will have to pay for it. To the extent that "payers" are not a clearly identifiable group, e.g., all taxpayers, they may not have a concrete way to oppose these policies, but inasmuch as they see beneficiaries just lining their own pockets, payers may voice their opposition.

- *Regulatory Policy* is designed to regulate or change behavior, as well as to educate the public. The "war on crime" and the Safe Drinking Water Act are regulatory policies. If they are directly and overtly regulatory, these policies are bound to be actively opposed by the groups they target. This is particularly true if these groups are organized and have resources to oppose the policy. If they do not have resources with which to oppose the regulatory policy, its adoption will be quicker and more inevitable.

- *Redistributive Policy:* Some policies redistribute wealth from those who are rich to those with little wealth. These might be called "Robin Hood" policies. In the form of welfare programs, education subsidies, and social security (old-age assistance programs), these policies are most notably opposed by those who are wealthy, and who would expect to have to "pay" for this redistribution.

The Scope of Public Policy Making

The controversies that arise over specific policy proposals form the heart of government and politics in this country. Much of the nature of policy depends on who benefits and who pays for that policy. The more narrowly defined the payers are, i.e., the smaller the group of interests that pays for a policy, the more opposition there will likely be to the policy. The more identifiable the beneficiaries, the more likely the policy will be supported. Retired people who would benefit directly from a change in Medicare benefits are likely to be active in advocating that change.

The degree to which policy proposals are supported or opposed depends on several things.

- It depends on the resources of the parties involved: money, organization, knowledge, skill, and strength of belief about the issue.

- It depends on the positions those individuals occupy within government institutions, and outside in society. Vocal advocates of a policy who occupy leadership positions in Congress are more likely to attain their policy preferences than are homeless people, who may lack even an articulate spokesperson.

- It depends on whether or not policy proponents are active. Many policies do not have widespread support or opposition. That is, they may have only a few actively interested people. The more active they are, the more likely their chances for policy adoption, unless there is some vocal opposition.

The form that a policy takes is largely affected by how the problem is characterized. Is it a national crisis or a national disaster? It is also affected by how vocal and how successful advocates are in claiming the attention of the media, the institutions, and the public. In order to effect any change, advocates must fight the power of inertia and the strength of those interests who wish to maintain the status quo.

POINTS TO REMEMBER

- Government has, in the past 70 years, increasingly developed policies that address all kinds of problems. This was not the case before the New Deal and the Depression of the 1930s. Prior to the New Deal, laissez-faire government precluded the federal government from making social policies and economic regulation.

- The policies enacted and administered by governments cost a great deal and rarely solve the problems they were enacted to address.

- The circumstances under which policy proposals emerge greatly affect their outcome. A crisis can mobilize immediate support for a policy that, in the long term, might otherwise prove ineffective. On the other hand, a long-standing problem may go largely ignored because there is no urgency to it.

KEY TERMS AND CONCEPTS

affirmative action

A policy in hiring that gives consideration or compensatory treatment to traditionally disadvantaged groups in an effort to overcome the present effects of past discrimination.

agenda setting

Determining the public policy questions to be debated or considered by Congress.

Capitalism

An economic system based on individual and corporate ownership of the means of production and a supply-demand market economy.

Clayton Anti-Trust Act

A major antitrust act aimed at increasing competition in business.

Clean Air Act

Environmental legislation that set standards limiting the amount of pollutants generated by automotive and industrial emissions.

Consumer Product Safety Act (1972)

This act created the Consumer Product Safety Commission, which is responsible for protecting consumers from injury caused by products sold to them.

deregulation

The elimination of government controls, especially over private companies.

deserving and undeserving poor

Categorization of poor by many Americans into "poor who deserve welfare help" because they can't help themselves, and those who "don't deserve welfare help" because it is assumed they can help themselves but choose not to.

distributive benefits

Programs, such as military contracts, that legislators try to secure for their constituents, who gain much by receiving them.

distributive policy

A policy that distributes political benefits to organized interest groups.

domestic policy

Those public plans or courses of action that concern issues of national importance, such as poverty, crime, and the environment, in contrast to foreign policies.

elite groups

Groups of people who exercise a major influence on or control the making of political, economic, and social decisions. They gain their power positions through wealth, family status, caste systems, or intellectual superiority.

entitlement

A government benefit to which recipients have a legally enforceable right.

Environmental Protection Agency (EPA)

An independent agency, established in 1970, to administer federal programs aimed at controlling pollution and protecting the environment.

Federal Open Market Committee (FOMC)

The FOMC decides how monetary policy should be carried out by the Federal Reserve and is the most important body within the Federal Reserve System.

Federal Reserve Bank (the Fed)

America's central banking system that establishes monetary policies, regulates the amount of currency in circulation, and determines the price of money (through interest rates). Its seven-member board of governors works with 12 regional banks and thousands of member banks to implement its policies.

fiscal policy

Government's use of its powers to tax and spend in order to influence the nation's economy.

Food and Drug Administration (FDA)

The agency charged with safeguarding consumers from impure food and medications.

food stamps

A federal government welfare program that issues coupons to low-income individuals. The recipients can use the coupons to purchase food.

Freedom to Farm Act (1996)

The Act that phased out price supports for American farmers and left agricultural prices to be determined by market forces.

GAO (Government Accounting Office)

An agency created by Congress in 1921 to review government agency performance, and the receipt and distribution of public funds.

government agenda

The list of issues the government chooses to address, as distinct from the public agenda, the list of items the public would like the government to address.

income transfer

The practice of taking income from some (usually the wealthy) and giving it to others (usually the poor). Usually performed by the government, this is a "transfer" because the recipients of the income render no current services.

in-kind subsidy

A good or service the government provides to lower-income groups, such as food stamps, housing, or medical care.

interstate commerce

The buying and selling of commodities, transportation, and other commercial dealings across state lines. It includes radio, television, telephone, and telegraphic transmissions.

Interstate Commerce Act (1887)

The act that established the Interstate Commerce Commission and regulations over business operations, services, and rates of interstate carriers.

Interstate Commerce Commission (ICC)

An independent regulatory commission that regulates business operations, services, and rates of interstate carriers. The ICC was created by the Interstate Commerce Act of 1877.

iron triangle

A three-way alliance between actors who are largely in charge of a policy area. These would include the relevant legislators from appropriate committees, the bureaucrats charged with implementing a policy, and the beneficiaries of a policy. It is generally thought that iron triangles hinder the political process by putting their own interests ahead of national interests. A well-known iron triangle involves the Pentagon, defense contractors, and the Congressional committees in charge of defense spending.

issue network

A loose collection of parties interested in a policy area and affected by government policy. These interests include policy experts, industry players, interest groups, congressional committees and government agencies.

Keynesian economics

Economic theory named after English economist John Maynard Keynes. Keynes claimed the free market would not always produce the best economic conditions and that government should try to influence the economy by increasing or cutting spending, taxes, and interest rates.

laissez-faire government

The political philosophy that states government is best when it governs least. In other words, a political system works best when there is no interference by government.

lobbying

Efforts by individuals or organizations to pass, defeat, change, or influence the crafting of laws and the decisions, policies, and actions of the government.

market economy

An economy in which buyers and sellers interact without government interference, and exchange money for goods and services. The U.S. does not have a pure market economy, but one based on the concept. Market economies were most fully and clearly developed in the writings of Adam Smith.

means-tested programs

Programs such as AFDC and Medicaid in which those who receive benefits must prove a need for them.

Medicaid

A federally supported state health insurance program, established in 1960 to provide medical care to impoverished people.

Medicare

A national health insurance program that provides medical care for the elderly, enacted in 1965 as an amendment to the Social Security Act.

military-industrial complex

An informal alliance of key decision makers within the military, government, and defense industry that tries to implement policy that's beneficial for all three. See *iron triangle*.

monetary policy

Policy in which the government attempts to influence the economy through its control over the amount of money in circulation and the availability of credit. The Federal Reserve (the Fed) directs our nation's monetary policy. In order to restrict inflation, the Fed will try to reduce the amount of money in circulation and raise interest rates. To avoid or get out of recession, the Fed will increase the amount of money in circulation and decrease interest rates.

monopoly

Exclusive control by one group of the means of producing or selling a commodity or service.

national debt

Total debt owed by the federal government, including interest that has accumulated on the debt. If revenues are more than expenditures in a year, the surplus can be used to lower the national debt. If spending is more than revenue, however, that year's deficit is added to the public debt.

National Labor Relations Board (NLRB)

An independent regulatory commission established in 1935 by the National Labor Relations Act (officially, the Wagner Act). It regulates unfair labor practices and labor-management relations, and guarantees labor's right to organize and bargain collectively through representatives of their choosing.

National School Lunch Act (1946)

An act that provided lunch for school children who couldn't afford their own.

National Traffic and Motor Vehicle Safety Act

An act that established safety standards for motor vehicles and tires. This act came into existence mainly through the persistent efforts of consumer advocate Ralph Nader.

non-contributory welfare

Welfare programs that don't require a contribution to receive a benefit. Examples include AFDC and Medicaid.

Occupational Safety and Health Act (OSHA) (1970)

A comprehensive industrial safety program that requires employers engaged in inter-state commerce to furnish a workplace free from hazards to life or health.

policy

A plan or course of action designed to influence and determine decisions, actions, and other matters.

policy adoption

The third stage of the policy cycle, in which public officials select a specific strategy to achieve their policy goals. This is usually in the form of legislation, regulations, or court orders.

policy cycle

Stages through which policy passes, including, in order : agenda setting, policy formu-lation, policy adoption, policy implementation, and policy evaluation.

policy entrepreneur

An individual or group that strongly advocates a policy it believes will solve a problem or address an issue of importance.

policy evaluation

The fifth stage of the policy cycle, in which the results of the implemented policy are studied by public officials and private organizations.

policy formulation

The second stage of the policy cycle, in which government officials consider various policy proposals and attempt to respond to the concerns of interest groups and other segments of the public.

policy implementation

The fourth stage of the policy cycle, in which a law or regulation is put into effect with the goal of obtaining public compliance. Implementation takes place through a variety of government channels, such as the bureaucracy, courts, and police.

pork barrel (or pork)

Appropriations made by a legislative body providing public money for local projects not critically needed.

price fixing

The unlawful agreement between manufacturers or dealers to set and maintain specified prices on typically competing goods.

price support

A process by which government buys surplus goods from producers to keep prices stable. Most price supports occur in the agriculture industry. Used together with production controls since 1933 to manage farm production, price supports may be in the form of an outright purchase or in the form of a loan, with the farmer's stored crops serving as collateral. The farmer can, in effect, turn the loan into a purchase by not paying it off and giving up the crops. However, if prices are high enough to make selling the crops and paying off the loan attractive, the farmer can do that.

Progressive Period

Movement that began after the Civil War and peaked during the early 20th century. Most progressives wanted to remove corruption and partisanship from politics. The progressives can be seen as a reaction against the Jacksonian model.

progressive tax

Any tax in which the tax rates increase as the tax base (the amount subject to taxation) increases. The federal income tax is an example.

public agenda

Issues members of a political community consider worthy of public attention and governmental action. The media has a great deal of influence on the public agenda.

public debt

Total debt owed by the federal government, including interest that has accumulated on the debt. If revenues are more than expenditures in a year, the surplus can be used to lower the national debt. If spending is more than revenue, however, that year's deficit is added to the public debt.

public debt financing

When the national government spends more than it brings in, and pays for the difference by issuing U.S. Treasury bonds, which increase the debt.

redistributive policy

Government policy designed to shift government burdens and benefits from one group to another.

regressive tax

Taxes in which rates go down as income goes up. Regressive taxes are mainly used by state and local government, though the national government uses them to levy payroll taxes. Perhaps the most common example is the sales tax, which takes a higher percentage of total income from poor people than it does from wealthier people. The opposite of a regressive tax is a progressive tax.

regulatory policy

Policy designed to regulate certain activities, such as environmental pollution, financial transactions, and automobile safety.

safety net

A guarantee, as of professional, physical, or financial security.

Sherman Anti-Trust Act (1890)

The basic federal antimonopoly law that prohibits monopolies in trade, or commerce.

social security

A government program that provides economic assistance to persons faced with unemployment, disability, or age, financed by assessment of taxes on employers and employees.

subsidy

Financial aid the government gives to individuals, business firms, groups, or other levels of government. Subsidies can be direct (money is given directly to the other party) or indirect, as is the case when tariffs are levied against a company's foreign competitors.

Taft-Hartley Act (Labor-Management Relations Act)

A major revision of the Wagner Act of 1935 that sought to equalized the power of employers and labor unions. It placed limitations on labor union practices and strengthened the position of the individual worker.

U.S. Treasury Bond

Certificate of debt issued by the U.S. federal government. U.S. Treasury bonds are like corporate bonds (by issuing of corporate bonds a business borrows money and agrees to pay the amount back later with interest), but the government is the one borrowing the money.

underground economy

The sector of the economy that doesn't pay taxes and isn't directly measured by the government. Also known as the subterranean or unreported economy.

Welfare Reform Act (1996)

The act that eliminated the federal AFDC (Aid to Families with Dependent Children) program and replaced it with block grants to the states so they could administer their own welfare programs as they saw fit.

Multiple-Choice Questions

1. The Federal Communications Commission is
    I. a regulatory agency
    II. a distributive agency
    III. a government corporation
    IV. a redistributive agency

    A. I
    B. I and II
    C. I, II, and III
    D. II and III
    E. IV

2. Which of the following have redistributive policy effects?
    I. The Securities and Exchange Act
    II. The Aid to Families with Dependent Children Program
    III. The Federal Election Commission
    IV. The Small Business Administration

    A. I
    B. I and II
    C. II and III
    D. I, II, III, and IV
    E. II, III, and IV

3. Tax policy is an example of
    A. regulatory policy.
    B. retributive policy
    C. redistributive policy.
    D. distributive policy.
    E. destructive policy

4. In the two-year confrontation between President Clinton and the Republican controlled Congress from 1995–1997, targeted programs for poor people were cut and targeted programs for the elderly were not cut. The reason for this was

   A. the Supreme Court held it unconstitutional to cut budgets of programs for the elderly, but upheld cutting welfare programs that benefited the poor.

   B. the mood of the country supported programs for the elderly, but opposed welfare programs.

   C. the president was a strong advocate of programs for the elderly, but did not support the policies in place for the poor.

   D. the elderly are relatively well organized and represented in the legislative process but the poor are not.

   E. there was insufficient time for Congress to devote to targeted policies for the poor.

5. All of the following justify government regulation except

   A. external costs should be internalized by producers and consumers.

   B. information about products needs to be provided in uniform and useable form.

   C. large corporations should be reduced in size so that they can be understood by individuals.

   D. the safety and efficacy of consumer products should be regulated or ensured.

   E. the prices of products and services offered by natural monopolies should be controlled.

Essay Questions

1. Selecting a policy area below, explain the policy formulation stage in terms of likely opponents and proponents. Identify the organized and visible interests that would be present in this stage, and outline their likely positions for a policy proposal.

   • Student Loan Programs

   • Dairy Price Supports

   • Low and Moderate Income Housing Programs

2. Explain the possible effect of policy evaluation on subsequent policy proposals in the "Aid to Families with Dependent Children" policy area. Identify three sets of interests that would be interested in such a policy evaluation. How would each of those interests try to influence evaluation of the program?

ANSWER KEY

Multiple-Choice Questions

1. B
2. D
3. C
4. D
5. C

Essay Questions

1.　This question focuses on one stage of domestic policy making. The stage should be clearly defined at the outset as the legislative stage. You must identify the actors involved in one of the listed policies, including formal policy makers and informal interested parties. As long as you can identify these actors clearly, you should be able to develop a sound analytic essay. Plan on writing two paragraphs.

Student Loan Programs are government loan guarantees that ensure students can obtain low-interest loans. At the formulation stage, relevant actors would be:

(1) Legislators (representatives and senators, majority and minority) on the committees that have jurisdiction over the policy

(2) Beneficiaries of such programs, including students, educators, and banks. Educators could be considered beneficiaries because with low interest loan programs to underwrite the cost of education, they would have more students. Banking interests could be considered beneficiaries because they would benefit from making the guaranteed loans

Undoubtedly, these interests would be interested in supporting an expanded low-interest loan program. Students are likely to be the least well organized, and so probably would be the least vociferous and articulate policy advocates.

Legislators are not at all likely to support a single policy proposal; in fact, some may even advocate a reduction in low-interest loans. But for the most part, all of these interests, with their different perspectives, will support the program.

Dairy Price Support programs have a fairly clear, though small, set of supporters by the time they reach the policy formulation stage. These supporters tend not to be highly visible: dairy farmers and dairy product manufacturers, and legislators from districts with strong dairy interests. These actors would all welcome additional support and change in the status quo. Though this should not be considered pork barrel legislation, it shares two of those characteristics: It has clearly identifiable and concentrated beneficiaries, and its payment comes from general tax funds or the entire taxpaying population.

Low and Moderate Income Housing Programs would benefit low and moderate income families but these groups are not likely to be very visible in policy formulation: Typically, they are not well organized, they are not very politically active, and they tend not to be very knowledgeable about the process or about policy advocacy. However, construction interests, real estate developers, and local government officials would benefit directly or indirectly from these kinds of programs. In the case of local governments, these programs could improve their housing stock. Legislators who represent developers and the like (e.g., in urban areas where houses are in decay) might advocate such programs.

2.   Policy evaluation would be carried out by either a private evaluating agent such as a policy advocate, or by a government agency like the Government Accounting Office, at the request of a legislative committee. Try to establish what actors might be evaluating the program. A policy advocate may well conclude that the program is successful and needs to be expanded. An independent evaluator may present a mixed or negative review of the policy's impact.

Three sets of interests that might be identified are:

a. The beneficiaries: the recipient families, as well as the bureaucrats who administer the policy. Recipient families are not likely to have a visible position, nor are they likely to be actively engaged in an evaluation or its use

b. The legislators who are policy entrepreneurs and advocates for these types of programs

c. Charitable organizations including religious groups and private advocacy groups that believe in helping the needy

Each set of interests has a different perspective on the policy and its evaluation. While all will want this type of program expanded, they each have different reasons. Recipient families would be eager to receive more aid. Administrative bureaucrats would want to maintain a program that provides them with jobs and job security. Legislators would want to see this kind of program expanded so that it benefits their constituents, who might in turn vote for them in reelection. Charitable groups may have a more philosophical perspective about the program.

Chapter 16   *Foreign and Defense Policies*

In the United States, foreign policy formation and domestic policy formation involve fundamentally different sets of considerations. First, the constitutional authority to make and conduct foreign policy is largely lodged with the Chief Executive, rather than with Congress. Congress' role in foreign policy is much less central than it is in domestic policy. Second, very little of the policy that relates to foreign affairs involves traditional "law making." Third, foreign policy affects largely different interests than does domestic policy, though there is some overlap.

For over 50 years, the United States has been a "superpower," and that has led to its political, military, and economic domination in the world. But as countries continue to identify their own economic, military, and cultural needs, conflicts will continue to arise. In all likelihood, the United States will not be able to continue to dictate outcomes or force others to accept its international goals. The dynamics of the international arena are no longer clear-cut or bipolar. This is difficult for some Americans—even some foreign policy experts—to accept. As a result, American foreign and defense policy may sometimes appear antiquated or reactive.

> Though the president has the key role in the foreign policy arena, a number of external things affect foreign policy formation: alliances, international organizations, and multinational corporations.

The Making of Foreign Policy

In contrast to domestic policy making, the president is the central figure in foreign policy making. As Chief Diplomat and Commander-in-Chief, the president plays a singular role, and as such, commands the most attention in areas of foreign and defense policy. And while Congress does serve in some capacity, it is far more limited than in the domestic policy making arena.

The president has a great deal of autonomy in conducting foreign relations, and faces fewer limitations than he would in the domestic arena. There are several elements to the president's foreign policy-making power.

- The president can make treaties with other governments, though the Senate must give its advice and consent to treaties and to the appointment of ambassadors.

- The president can develop executive agreements with foreign governments. These do not require the Senate's consent, yet they are binding for the countries involved. In modern days, executive agreements have largely replaced treaties as the means by which foreign governments agree to certain terms.

- As Commander-in-Chief of the Armed Forces, the president has the power to make war, and that gives Congress little role in actual military decisions. A Declaration of War must be made by Congress, though this legislative power has been modified by modern circumstances and technology. Today, Congress retains its power to appropriate funds for the military, for foreign aid, and to meet treaty obligations. If a treaty requires money, Congress must appropriate and authorize it before implementation can occur.

The Bureaucracy of Foreign Policy

The bureaucracy involved in foreign policy is more limited than for domestic policy. It originally arose after World War II, with the emergence of the Cold War. Unlike many of the other bureaucracies in the U.S. government, this bureaucracy has few policy administration duties. Rather, its mandate is to gather foreign intelligence.

Congress serves a different function in foreign affairs than it does in domestic affairs. That is because of the Constitution, and because fewer constituents are actively interested in and affected by foreign policy.

The "intelligence community" is a unique feature of the foreign policy domain. These agencies, including the CIA and the National Security Agency, provide policy makers with critical and detailed intelligence information about foreign governments and threats to U.S. security. While these agencies have no formal policy implementation duties, they receive significant annual budgets with which to implement surveillance systems throughout the world.

The State Department is the bureaucratic institution focused on diplomacy. It staffs embassies with country specialists and it does country-by-country analyses of our relations with those countries.

The Department of Defense is responsible for maintaining our military and its preparedness for invasions or needs abroad. Organized into the services Army, Air Force, and Navy (including a separate Marine Corp.), the Department devotes a good deal of effort to assessing and preparing for possible military threats to our security.

Another aspect to U.S. foreign defense is what is called the *military-industrial complex*. This is an informal alliance between leaders in the military, government, and defense industries. This relationship seeks to promote all three of their interests. Arms manufacturers rely on large government defense contracts to design and build new weapons systems, and for permission to sell weapons to foreign governments. Similarly, the military is always looking for new weapons sustems.

The Mechanisms of Foreign Policy

Whether in times of peace or war, foreign policy promotes interdependency among countries through diplomacy and negotiations. In that context, the United States is expected to "speak" with a single voice. The president is that voice and is expected to lead and to make foreign policy. In times of crisis, he must do so quickly and decisively.

Many international challenges have no military component, such as poverty or population growth. Foreign aid may be given to support allies or to oppose perceived enemies. Economic and military aid may be used to overthrow opponents or weaken those states.

Public opinion and foreign policy involve a peculiar blend of technology, military technology, and amateurism. That is, the general public is often misinformed or uninformed about foreign policy matters.

There are two primary ways in which the United States can control or influence the international stage.

- *Economic Aid*

  Economic aid is often used to influence foreign affairs, though it is also given as humanitarian assistance for emerging countries.

- *Military Aid*

  Military intervention or funds may involve mutual defense pacts (the promise of one country to provide military aid to the other if it is attacked). Military threats involve changing technologies like biological warfare, and changing delivery systems for mass destruction.

Economic Interests in Foreign Policy

Foreign policy has relatively few economic interests compared to other policy areas. One exception might be multinational corporations. These are emerging as influential players who focus on labor markets, production costs, and international markets in need of their products. Some corporations sell weapons systems abroad. Others export agriculture commodities and consumer products. These actors will often use their power and influence to seek benefits in the foreign arenas in which they want access.

There is also a "national interest" here, though there is a great deal of debate about just what defines the national interest. The content of national interest is always unclear given the diversity of interests in this country. However, the president and his advisers seek to identify what this country's interest is, and act on that, in any international crisis.

Foreign governments can be very active in trying to influence U.S. foreign policymaking, setting their own agendas and goals. They may even challenge the sovereignty and hegemony of the United States.

Some individuals, isolationist legislators in particular, strongly object to U.S. participation in international organizations and arms limitation treaties. They fear that this country's sovereignty will be limited or harmed.

- International organizations such as the United Nations and NATO sometimes limit the options that the U.S. can pursue abroad. Some Americans believe this harms our national sovereignty and independence. Others believe that, rather than try to dictate unilateral outcomes, the U.S. needs to cooperate and collaborate with foreign governments and institutions.

- Non-governmental organizations (NGOs) can play very major roles in U.S. foreign policy and in international policy. An organization such as the Red Cross or Amnesty International can assist in shaping our foreign policy in connection with its interests, or in influencing the public's perception about an international situation.

- Rogue states such as Iran and Iraq do not always "play by the rules" and so these interests are not predictable. They are sometimes viewed as major threats.

- Terrorists can provide a severe threat to the United States at large and to American interests abroad, as well as to individual Americans who travel.

Ideology in Foreign Policy

At least for the attentive public, the American population holds a strong ideology with regard to foreign and military policy. One dimension of this ideology is the traditional *isolationism* that has been present in this country since the Revolutionary War. This policy focuses on remaining uninvolved in foreign affairs or foreign conflicts and free from entangling alliances. While this approach has significantly declined since World War II, it still appears from time to time.

Another dimension of this ideology derives from the Cold War and the post–World War II *competition* between communism and the former Soviet Union, on the one hand, and liberal democracy and Western Europe/NATO on the other hand. However, these ideologies are not uniform throughout the nation, and many people have a practical, humanitarian perspective on foreign policy.

There may be a third dimension as well. A strong *humanitarian* ideology may underlie some actions by this country abroad. Similarly, humanitarian ideology may promote views held by those with an international perspective, such as some church groups.

More and more Americans have come to recognize the interconnectedness of their own, economic well-being and that of the world economy. Increasing globalization of companies, products, and economies makes foreign policy a central feature of even domestic politics in this country. As our corporations seek to do business abroad, whether to sell or to manufacture products, the United States government will be become more deeply involved in international economies and foreign policy.

Public Support for Foreign Policy

The attention of the American public is not constantly focused abroad. At times of international crisis, when the entire country is focused on a particular country or episode, popular opinion largely supports the president's actions. People may take positions and advocate policies based on little knowledge, which often unfolds into unquestioning support for the president, particularly because the president must act quickly and decisively. In the absence of an international crisis, Americans tend to focus on domestic issues, and less consistently back the president.

This may change as more people in this country become more deeply and negatively affected by international affairs. As jobs go abroad where labor costs are lower, or where raw materials are cheaper, more and more Americans may develop and act on sophisticated understandings about foreign policy.

POINTS TO REMEMBER

• The U.S. military is controlled by civilians; first and foremost, the president. The framers had worried about a "strong man on horseback (a military leader) taking over control of the executive branch." As a result, there can be conflict between the objectives of civilian leaders and military experts.

• A few powerful business interests may benefit greatly from foreign and military policies. Agricultural corporations or weapons manufacturers, for example, see foreign markets as desirable for their products, and so work to expand those markets through foreign policy.

• Foreign policy challenges are continually changing: They now include population, hunger, energy resources and fuel, religious extremism, environmental degradation, drug traffic, and chemical and biological weapons. Previously, these challenges focused more on containing the spread of Communism.

KEY TERMS AND CONCEPTS

attentive public

The part of the general public that pays attention to policy issues.

Central Intelligence Agency (CIA)

An agency that functions under the National Security Council to collect and analyze information about political and military activities in other countries.

Cold War

The ideological, political, and economic impasse between the United States and the Soviet Union following World War II.

Cold War era

The period from 1946 to 1989 when the Soviet Union and the United States threatened one another with mutual nuclear destruction.

collective security

A worldwide security system by which nations agree in advance to take collective action against any state or states that break the peace.

commander in chief

The president's role as supreme commander of the military forces of the U.S., and of the state National Guard units when they are called into federal service. This power is granted by Article II, section 2 of the Constitution.

Communism

A political, economic, and social theory based on the collective ownership of land and capital and in which political power lies in the hands of workers.

containment

A diplomatic policy adopted by the Truman administration to "build situations of strength" around the globe to contain Communist power within its existing boundaries.

Defense Department (DOD)

The federal department responsible for formulating military policies and maintaining the armed U.S. armed forces.

détente

The term used to described U.S.-Soviet policy under President Richard Nixon and Secretary of State Henry Kissinger. Under détente, the U.S. had direct cooperative dealings with Cold War rivals without relaxing its ideological stand. The term is derived from the French word for the relaxation of tension.

diplomacy

Political relations among and between nations; settling conflicts among nations by peaceful means.

economic aid

A form of assistance to other nations; generally economic aid consists of grants, loans, or credits to buy the assisting nation's products.

executive agreement

A binding international agreement between chiefs of state. Unlike treaties, these do require the consent of the Senate.

foreign policy

A nation's goals in its interactions with other nations, and the techniques and strategies used to achieve them. These goals are decided and acted on in the "foreign policy process."

Foreign Relations Committee

A standing committee in the Senate charged with monitoring foreign relations.

intelligence community

The collection of government agencies that gather information about the desires, intentions, and capabilities of foreign governments or businesses, or work to further U.S. foreign policy aims.

interventionism

A broad term used to describe any foreign policy initiative in which the United States uses its power, in the form of sanctions, treaties, or even military force, to pursue its goals.

Iran-Contra affair (1987)

A series of events in which White House staff members sold sophisticated weapons to Iran in exchange for the release of American hostages. The funds from this transaction were placed in a secret Swiss bank account and used to support the Nicaraguan contra rebels in violation of the Boland Amendments.

Iron Curtain

The term used to describe the division of eastern and western Europe after World War II. Winston Churchill popularized the term in a speech about Europe's division between the West and the Soviet Union.

isolationist foreign policy

The policy of remaining uninvolved in international affairs and free from entangling alliances. This characterized U.S. foreign policy toward Europe during most of the 19th and part of the 20th centuries, though it has gradually declined since World War II.

Joint Chiefs of Staff

The principle military advisory group to the president, including the Chiefs of Staff of the Army and Airforce, the Chief of Naval Operations, and the Chief of Staff to the Secretary of Defense.

League of Nations

The first general international organization, established in 1919 to preserve peace and security and to promote cooperation among nations in economic and social fields. The League voted itself out of existence in 1946 and transferred its assets to the United Nations.

military-industrial complex

An informal alliance of key decision makers within the military, government, and defense industry that tries to implement policy that is beneficial for all three. See *iron triangle*.

Monroe Doctrine (1823)

An American foreign policy originally developed by President James Monroe in his annual message to Congress. The doctrine set out three principles: European nations were not to establish new colonies in the Western Hemisphere, they were not to interfere in the affairs of independent nations in the Western Hemisphere, and, in exchange, the United States would not become involved in the affairs of European nations. Monroe announced his doctrine to stop the Holy Alliance from helping Spain regain its former Latin American colonies, which had recently become independent. With the Monroe Doctrine, the U.S. claimed the Western Hemisphere as its own zone of influence.

National Security Advisor

The head of the NSC, who advises the president on immediate foreign policy and military problems.

National Security Council (NSC)

A staff agency in the Executive Office of the President that advises the president on matters relating to national security, both domestic and foreign. The NSC is made up of the president, vice president, Secretary of State, and Secretary of Defense. The director of the CIA and the Joint Chiefs of Staff are statutory advisors; others may serve at the president's request.

neutrality

The legal status of a nation that does not participate in a war between other states.

Non-Governmental Organizations (NGOs)

Groups with international interests and resources that may supplement or conflict with national interests. They might have interests in human rights, environmental protection, or humanitarian interests. Churches (and church organizations) and labor unions are NGOs.

NATO (North Atlantic Treaty Organization)

An organization established in 1949 to create a single, unified defense force to protect the North Atlantic area. Members include 16 Western European nations and the United States.

nuclear deterrence

A U.S. military policy that calls for hundreds and even thousands of nuclear missiles ready to be launched at a moment's notice with the intent of discouraging other nations (particularly the U.S.S.R during the Cold War) from using nuclear weapons on the U.S. or its allies.

Pentagon

The U.S. military establishment. The term comes from the shape of the military headquarters building.

power of the purse

The traditional power of democratic legislative bodies to control the finances of government.

rogue state

A government that does not abide by the norms of international diplomacy or international law.

Secretary of State

The leading Cabinet officer, who heads the Department of State and is responsible for formulating policies and conducting relations with foreign states.

State Department

The agency primarily responsible for making and executing U.S. foreign policy.

Strategic Arms Limitation Treaty (SALT I)

A treaty between the United States and the Soviet Union to reduce the nuclear arms competition between the two countries. The SALT I talks began in 1969 and were signed May 26, 1972.

treaty

A formal agreement entered into by two or more countries.

Truman Doctrine

The doctrine announced by President Harry Truman in 1947 to aid countries facing communist threats. The Truman Doctrine was formulated as a specific response to crises in Turkey and Greece, but applied to the world at large and marked the beginning of containment as the U.S. foreign policy regarding communist expansion.

United Nations

An international organization composed of most of the countries of the world. Founded in 1945 to promote peace, security, and economic development.

War Powers Resolution (1973)

A law specifying certain conditions the president must meet to commit U.S. troops without the approval of Congress. The Resolution attempted to close a loophole by which presidents were able to get around the constitutional requirement that only Congress can declare war.

Multiple-Choice Questions

1. American foreign policy since World War II has been based on all of the following except

   A. containment of communism.

   B. the Monroe Doctrine.

   C. détente with the Soviet Union.

   D. isolationism.

   E. support of Israel.

2. Which of the following does not explain why presidents tend to dominate Congress in the area of foreign policy?

   A. Few members of Congress are interested in foreign policy matters.

   B. The public is more likely to put pressure on Congress concerning domestic economic issues.

   C. The president's constitutional role as Commander-in-Chief gives him a lot of discretion regarding the use of the armed forces.

   D. Congress wants to present a unified appearance to leaders of other nations.

   E. The president is in a position to speak as a representative of the entire country.

3. The president's National Security Advisor (NSA) may have more control over U.S. foreign and military policy than the Secretaries of Defense and State because

   I. the NSA has no outside clientele or constituency while the Secretaries must contend with such private interests.

   II. the Secretaries have statutory authority for carrying out statutory policy while the NSA's only duty is to advise the president.

   III. the NSA is a less widely known individual than either department secretary.

   IV. the NSA is a trusted confidant of the president, while the two secretaries may be unknown to the president when he appoints them.

      A. I only

      B. II only

      C. I and III

      D. II and III

      E. I, II, and IV

4. Presidential powers to conduct foreign policy, using the military as necessary, may be limited by which of the following?

I. Congress' power to limit spending

II. the United Nations

III. restraints imposed by alliance allies

IV. the War Powers Resolution

    A. I and II

    B. I, II, and III

    C. II and III

    D. III and IV

    E. I, II, III, and IV

5. The failure of the United States to join the League of Nations indicates which of the following?

I. the advice and consent power of the Senate

II. a strong isolationist trend present in the country

III. disagreement among the allies over the terms of the peace treaty

IV. opposition from the War Department over the terms of the peace treaty

    A. I only

    B. I and II

    C. II only

    D. II, III, and IV

    E. III and IV

Essay Questions

1. Identify two private actors that play significant roles in the formulation of both domestic and foreign policy. Compare and contrast the differences and similarities in the roles these actors play in these two policy arenas.

2. Using one president from the following list, illustrate ideological forces that affected his administration's foreign policy. Explain how the president's ideology affected the formation of U.S. foreign policy.

* Harry Truman

* Dwight Eisenhower

* Lyndon Johnson

* Ronald Reagan

ANSWER KEY

Multiple-Choice Questions

1. D
2. A
3. E
4. E
5. B

Essay Questions

1. Actors involved in domestic and foreign policy formation might include the (1) automobile industry, (2) the pharmaceutical industry, (3) the clothing industry, or (4) the electronics industry. These industries most likely manufacture or sell consumer products to foreign and/or domestic markets. To effectively answer this question, your best bet would be to compare the various economic dimensions of each actor.

    The question asks you to compare and contrast the roles of these actors. Your answer will depend on the actors and industries you select. Is an actor involved in international marketing of products that are manufactured domestically, or rather, in the domestic sale of products that are manufactured abroad? There may well be a mixture of domestic and foreign production and marketing; a diagram might illustrate these relationships.

	Domestic Policy		Foreign Policy	
	Manufacturing	**Marketing**	**Manufacturing**	**Marketing**
Automobile Industry	Environment Workplace safety Labor Issues Product safety	Fair Trade Fraudulent advertising Anti-trust	Cheap labor Import restrictions	Exporting products Balance of payments Exchange rates
Electronic Industry	Similar to above	Similar to above	Similar to above	Similar to above

Make sure you systematically present your comparisons and contrasts. One of the most difficult features of this task is to keep the relationships between the industries and actors straight, and the chart might help in this regard.

Once these interests have been identified, comparisons can be made between an industry's domestic and foreign policy behavior. The question does not indicate how narrow the interests should be, so you are safe to assume it means two major industries. At this level of generality, there may be little difference between the two industries and their interests and actions.

2.   This question requires you to write about one of four presidents. Choose a president and the "times" that you feel confident writing about.

- Harry Truman: post-war era, economic revitalization of Europe, the containment of the spread of communism into Eastern Europe, and the Korean War

- Dwight Eisenhower: the Cold War and nuclear deterrence, the containment of Communism

- Lyndon Johnson: the Vietnam War

- Ronald Reagan: the decline of the Cold War and the "evil empire," the emergence of international terrorism

These historical items are not sufficient answers to the ideology part of the question. Rather, they were the underlying focal points and context that guided each president in foreign policy.

In order to illustrate the ideological forces that affected a president's foreign policy, you must assess first the president's ideology, and second, the ideology of the "times" with respect to foreign policy. Though these ideological dimensions are similar, a strong answer will differentiate between the two. It may be difficult to explain a presidents individual ideological predisposition, but you could address his role and the considerations he had to make in that role. For instance, you could argue that Americans' widespread concern for Communism in the 1940s, 1950s and even the 1960s colored the foreign policies of Truman, Eisenhower, and Johnson. The remnants of that concern drove some dimensions of foreign policy during the 1980s Reagan era as well.

UNIT EIGHT:

Practice Test

In this section is a full-length practice test. Tear out or photocopy the answer grid and use it to complete the test. You'll get the most benefit if you take this exam under test-like conditions.

Before taking this practice test, find a quiet room where you can work uninterrupted. Be sure to bring a watch so you can time yourself. Once you start this test, don't stop until you have finished. You'll have 45 minutes for Section I, and 100 minutes for Section II. Work on only one section at a time, and take a short break in between sections.

The format of the practice test in this book varies slightly from that of the actual AP exam since you will not be using separate booklets or answering questions about exam preparation.

Answer keys and detailed explanations for each question follow.

Good luck!

AP United States Government & Politics

ANSWER SHEET

1 Ⓐ Ⓑ Ⓒ Ⓓ Ⓔ   21 Ⓐ Ⓑ Ⓒ Ⓓ Ⓔ   41 Ⓐ Ⓑ Ⓒ Ⓓ Ⓔ

2 Ⓐ Ⓑ Ⓒ Ⓓ Ⓔ   22 Ⓐ Ⓑ Ⓒ Ⓓ Ⓔ   42 Ⓐ Ⓑ Ⓒ Ⓓ Ⓔ

3 Ⓐ Ⓑ Ⓒ Ⓓ Ⓔ   23 Ⓐ Ⓑ Ⓒ Ⓓ Ⓔ   43 Ⓐ Ⓑ Ⓒ Ⓓ Ⓔ

4 Ⓐ Ⓑ Ⓒ Ⓓ Ⓔ   24 Ⓐ Ⓑ Ⓒ Ⓓ Ⓔ   44 Ⓐ Ⓑ Ⓒ Ⓓ Ⓔ

5 Ⓐ Ⓑ Ⓒ Ⓓ Ⓔ   25 Ⓐ Ⓑ Ⓒ Ⓓ Ⓔ   45 Ⓐ Ⓑ Ⓒ Ⓓ Ⓔ

6 Ⓐ Ⓑ Ⓒ Ⓓ Ⓔ   26 Ⓐ Ⓑ Ⓒ Ⓓ Ⓔ   46 Ⓐ Ⓑ Ⓒ Ⓓ Ⓔ

7 Ⓐ Ⓑ Ⓒ Ⓓ Ⓔ   27 Ⓐ Ⓑ Ⓒ Ⓓ Ⓔ   47 Ⓐ Ⓑ Ⓒ Ⓓ Ⓔ

8 Ⓐ Ⓑ Ⓒ Ⓓ Ⓔ   28 Ⓐ Ⓑ Ⓒ Ⓓ Ⓔ   48 Ⓐ Ⓑ Ⓒ Ⓓ Ⓔ

9 Ⓐ Ⓑ Ⓒ Ⓓ Ⓔ   29 Ⓐ Ⓑ Ⓒ Ⓓ Ⓔ   49 Ⓐ Ⓑ Ⓒ Ⓓ Ⓔ

10 Ⓐ Ⓑ Ⓒ Ⓓ Ⓔ   30 Ⓐ Ⓑ Ⓒ Ⓓ Ⓔ   50 Ⓐ Ⓑ Ⓒ Ⓓ Ⓔ

11 Ⓐ Ⓑ Ⓒ Ⓓ Ⓔ   31 Ⓐ Ⓑ Ⓒ Ⓓ Ⓔ   51 Ⓐ Ⓑ Ⓒ Ⓓ Ⓔ

12 Ⓐ Ⓑ Ⓒ Ⓓ Ⓔ   32 Ⓐ Ⓑ Ⓒ Ⓓ Ⓔ   52 Ⓐ Ⓑ Ⓒ Ⓓ Ⓔ

13 Ⓐ Ⓑ Ⓒ Ⓓ Ⓔ   33 Ⓐ Ⓑ Ⓒ Ⓓ Ⓔ   53 Ⓐ Ⓑ Ⓒ Ⓓ Ⓔ

14 Ⓐ Ⓑ Ⓒ Ⓓ Ⓔ   34 Ⓐ Ⓑ Ⓒ Ⓓ Ⓔ   54 Ⓐ Ⓑ Ⓒ Ⓓ Ⓔ

15 Ⓐ Ⓑ Ⓒ Ⓓ Ⓔ   35 Ⓐ Ⓑ Ⓒ Ⓓ Ⓔ   55 Ⓐ Ⓑ Ⓒ Ⓓ Ⓔ

16 Ⓐ Ⓑ Ⓒ Ⓓ Ⓔ   36 Ⓐ Ⓑ Ⓒ Ⓓ Ⓔ   56 Ⓐ Ⓑ Ⓒ Ⓓ Ⓔ

17 Ⓐ Ⓑ Ⓒ Ⓓ Ⓔ   37 Ⓐ Ⓑ Ⓒ Ⓓ Ⓔ   57 Ⓐ Ⓑ Ⓒ Ⓓ Ⓔ

18 Ⓐ Ⓑ Ⓒ Ⓓ Ⓔ   38 Ⓐ Ⓑ Ⓒ Ⓓ Ⓔ   58 Ⓐ Ⓑ Ⓒ Ⓓ Ⓔ

19 Ⓐ Ⓑ Ⓒ Ⓓ Ⓔ   39 Ⓐ Ⓑ Ⓒ Ⓓ Ⓔ   59 Ⓐ Ⓑ Ⓒ Ⓓ Ⓔ

20 Ⓐ Ⓑ Ⓒ Ⓓ Ⓔ   40 Ⓐ Ⓑ Ⓒ Ⓓ Ⓔ   60 Ⓐ Ⓑ Ⓒ Ⓓ Ⓔ

AP United States Government & Politics

SECTION I

Directions: For the following questions, fill in the corresponding oval on the answer sheet. You have 45 minutes.

1. A policy entrepreneur
   I. is someone who may get media attention for a policy issue.
   II. is illustrated by Ralph Nader in his book *Unsafe at Any Speed*.
   III. may be a public official rather than a private citizen or interest group.
   IV. is a policy advocate who is successful in moving a policy issue to the next agenda level.
   A. I and II
   B. I, III, and IV
   C. II and III
   D. III and IV
   E. I, II, and III

2. Mancur Olson's theory of collective action suggests that:
   A. large groups are easier to form and maintain than are small groups.
   B. people join groups when they are offered selective incentives, like publications or inexpensive insurance.
   C. people join groups to help attain and benefit from a collective good.
   D. solidary incentives alone are enough to entice most people to join groups.
   E. small groups have more influence in government than do large ones.

3. Which of the following forms of expression are adviserprotected speechadviser under the 1st Amendment today as per the Supreme Court's decisions?
   I. Yelling at your neighbor over the back fence
   II. Burning an American flag in protest for government policy
   III. Burning a cross in the front yard of a residence
   IV. A soap-box speech that challenges people to riot and demonstrate
   A. I and II
   B. II and III
   C. I, II, and III
   D. II, III, and IV
   E. III and IV

4. Which of the following do(es) not require the advice and consent of the Senate?
   I. Executive Agreements
   II. Executive Orders
   III. Appointments of Federal Judges
   IV. Treaties
   A. I and III
   B. II and IV
   C. I, II, and III
   D. I, II, and IV
   E. I and II

GO ON TO THE NEXT PAGE ▶

5. Which stage of the policy cycle is described in the following example?

   The Department of Agriculture enforces rules governing how it will put the Freedom to Farm Act into effect.

   A. Agenda setting

   B. Policy formulation

   C. Policy implementation

   D. Policy adoption

   E. Policy evaluation

6. The formal structure and leadership of a political party, including its election committees, local, state, and national executives, and paid professional staff are known as the

   A. party-in-electorate.

   B. party organization.

   C. party-in-government.

   D. party leadership.

   E. party machine.

7. The federal bureaucracy derives it power from which of the following?

   I. general delegations of legislative authority to the agency that must fill in the gaps

   II. the permanent tenure of bureaucrats

   III. the number and the size of administrative agencies

   IV. the expertise that bureaucrats bring to policy development and administration

   A. I only

   B. I and II

   C. I and III

   D. I, II, and IV

   E. III and IV

8. The power of Congress to regulate interstate commerce is an example of a(n)

   A. concurrent power.

   B. delegated power.

   C. enumerated power.

   D. reserved power.

   E. implied power.

9. All of the following features of voting in America are true except

   A. about 40 percent of eligible voters vote regularly.

   B. about 25 percent of eligible voters are occasional voters.

   C. women are more likely to support Democratic candidates than men in elections today.

   D. citizens under 30 years vote in about the same proportion as those older than 30 years.

   E. Caucasians vote more regularly than do African Americans

10. Which of the following Cabinet departments are considered part of the "inner Cabinet"?

    I. State

    II. Commerce

    III. Treasury

    IV. Labor

    A. I and II

    B. II, III, and IV

    C. II and III

    D. I and III

    E. I and IV

GO ON TO THE NEXT PAGE ▶

11. The following constituencies are all of interest to a member of Congress except

    A. voters in the district.

    B. federal district judges in the district.

    C. party leaders in the chamber.

    D. lobbyists for interests connected with the district.

    E. fellow legislators who serve on the same committee.

12. If a Supreme Court justice agrees with the outcome of a decision but has a different rationale for reaching that decision, he will write a(n)

    A. petition for certiorari.

    B. appellate brief.

    C. dissenting opinion.

    D. concurring opinion.

    E. per curiam opinion.

13. Which of the following are true about the National Security Council in contrast to the State Department?

    I. It is staffed by military officers.

    II. It is completely loyal to the president.

    III. It carries out the president's foreign policy.

    IV. It selects the director of the CIA.

    V. It is staffed by career diplomats.

    A. I and II

    B. II only

    C. III only

    D. II, III, and IV

    E. III and V

14. Between 1964 and 1996, which of the following would have been most likely to vote for the Republican presidential candidate?

    A. A male high school dropout from Texas

    B. A female African American bus driver from New York City

    C. A female welfare recipient from Chicago

    D. A male Jewish college professor from Seattle

    E. A male fundamentalist Christian from Indiana

15. The differences between the legislative process in the House and the Senate include which of the following?

    I. the Senate Rules and Administration Committee

    II. the House Committee on Veterans

    III. the Senate Conference Committee

    IV. the Senate Filibuster

    V. the House Rules Committee

    A. I and II

    B. II and III

    C. III and V

    D. II and IV

    E. IV and V

GO ON TO THE NEXT PAGE ▶

16. The Americans with Disabilities Act, passed by Congress in 1990, requires all public buildings and services to be accessible to citizens with disabilities, and requires employers to make reasonable accommodations for workers with disabilities. This Act is an example of

    A. a categorical grant-in-aid.

    B. an unfunded federal mandate.

    C. affirmative action.

    D. judicial activism.

    E. dual federalism.

17. Because of state presidential primary elections, the role of the Democratic and Republican national conventions has been transformed into a(n)

    A. gathering where party dissidents make important decisions.

    B. gathering of interest group representatives.

    C. media showcase where newscasters influence the outcomes.

    D. place where delegates ratify decisions already made by voters.

    E. unimportant showcase that no one pays attention to.

18. Which of the following issues does not revolve around a constitutional right to privacy?

    A. Sexual harassment

    B. Doctor-assisted suicide

    C. Reproductive freedom

    D. The sale and use of contraceptives

    E. Restrictions on the use of wiretapping by law enforcement agencies

19. Redistricting of house seats is accomplished by what political body?

    A. legislatures in each state

    B. the Secretary of Commerce who appoints the director of the Census Bureau

    C. a majority of the voting members of the Federal Elections Commission

    D. a non-partisan commission created by the League of Women voters in each state

    E. the outgoing legislators from each state

20. The line-item veto, available to some governors and sought by several recent presidents, involves

    A. the executive selectively vetoing bills passed by Congress.

    B. the executive deleting salary lines from the Civil Service List of Occupations.

    C. a concurrent resolution on Congress.

    D. the executive deleting part of a spending bill.

    E. only revenue or taxing laws.

21. As written in 1787, the Constitution contained all the following provisions except

    I. legislative power to regulate the coinage of money

    II. a national bank

    III. the power of judicial review

    IV. the electoral college

    V. the direct election of Senators

    A. I, II, and V

    B. I, II, and III

    C. III, IV, and V

    D. II, III, and IV

    E. II, III, and V

GO ON TO THE NEXT PAGE ▶

22. Modern presidents rarely rely on the advice of cabinet members because

    A. cabinet members are strangers to the president.

    B. cabinet-level agencies often have loyalties and goals different from those of the president.

    C. cabinet members are adviseryesadviser people and are not permitted to disagree with the president.

    D. cabinet members belong to iron triangles.

    E. cabinet agencies get their funding from Congress.

23. The framers saw political parties as

    A. an important aspect of democracy.

    B. effective only in raising money for campaigns.

    C. appropriate for a direct democracy, but not for a republic.

    D. good for America as long as there were no more than two parties.

    E. factions motivated by ambition and self-interest.

Questions 24 and 25 refer to the following clause from the U.S. Constitution:

The Congress shall have Power . . . To regulate Commerce with foreign Nations, and among the several States, and with the Indiana Tribes.

24. Interpretations of this clause have been the basis for upholding the constitutionality of

    A. the Voting Rights Act of 1965.

    B. the Lend-Lease Program.

    C. the Civil Rights Act of 1964.

    D. the War Powers Resolution.

    E. the Vietnam War.

25. The practical effect of the development and the application of this clause has been to

    A. expand the power of states over intra-state activities.

    B. control the exercise of the power of judicial review.

    C. create the Federal Reserve Bank System.

    D. regulate the franchise.

    E. give Congress a national police power.

GO ON TO THE NEXT PAGE ▶

26. What most significantly influences a voter when selecting a candidate in an election campaign?

    A. the candidate's image

    B. the stand the candidate takes on issues

    C. Party platform

    D. Party identification

    E. the state of the relevant economy

27. All of the following rights and liberties contained in the Bill of Rights have been applied to the states as well as the federal government except

    A. the right to bear arms.

    B. the free exercise of religion.

    C. the just compensation for government taking private property.

    D. unreasonable search and seizure.

    E. freedom of speech.

28. An interest group is most likely to have influence in Congress when the issue at stake

    A. is part of the president's legislative package.

    B. has been dramatized by the media.

    C. engages legislators' deeply held convictions.

    D. is narrow in scope and low in public visibility.

    E. divides legislators along party lines.

29. The most important characteristic of Congress, as framed by the drafters of the Constitution, was that it would be

    A. cautious and deliberate.

    B. dominated by the president.

    C. controlled by majorities alone.

    D. representative of all interests.

    E. demographically representative.

30. All of the following are government corporations except

    A. AMTRAK.

    B. the Social Security Administration.

    C. the Federal Deposit Insurance Corporation.

    D. the U.S. Postal Service.

    E. the Smithsonian Institution.

31. A first-term member of the House of Representatives wishing to influence tax policy would most likely seek a seat on which of the following committees?

    A. Appropriations

    B. Rules

    C. Ways and Means

    D. Finance

    E. Education and Workforce

GO ON TO THE NEXT PAGE ▶

32. What is the purpose of the establishment clause in the Bill of Rights?

    A. It guarantees citizenship.

    B. It guarantees free speech against prior restraint.

    C. It protects the freedom of association.

    D. It guarantees the right to petition government.

    E. It prohibits the creation of a state religion.

33. The definition of political ideology is

    A. the belief that government is best that governs least.

    B. beliefs about which candidates to support in the general election.

    C. beliefs and attitudes about the functioning of the legislative and the executive branches of government.

    D. beliefs about the ideal political system, economic order, social goals, and moral values.

    E. attitudes and beliefs about government and the political process.

34. The Freedom of Information Act of 1967

    A. permitted agencies to award litigation costs and fees to parties in agency adjudications.

    B. gave citizens the right to inspect unprotected government documents.

    C. gave government corporations the ability to engage in industrial espionage.

    D. gave the executive branch access to information collected by Congress.

    E. gave courts reasonable access to the prior records of persons accused of crimes.

35. Which of the following explain why devolution has not been successful?

    I. The dependence of local governments on federal money

    II. The unwillingness of states to assume fiscal and substantive responsibility for policy areas

    III. The federal government's reluctance to give states policy responsibility

    IV. The Supreme Court's holding various devolution policies unconstitutional

    A. I and II

    B. II and III

    C. I, III, and IV

    D. I, II, and III

    E. IV

36. Independent regulatory agencies can be viewed or defined as

    A. independent of contact with interest groups.

    B. directly supervised by cabinet level departments.

    C. more independent of presidential control than cabinet departments.

    D. directly supplying a good or a service to the public.

    E. independent of the executive branch's budget.

GO ON TO THE NEXT PAGE ▶

37. Which of the following are likely to be active in the agenda-setting phase of the policy cycle?

   I. the media

   II. legislators

   III. lobbyists

   IV. the president

   V. Supreme Court justices

     A. II only

     B. II and III

     C. II and IV

     D. I, II, and III

     E. I, II, III, and IV

38. The existence of iron triangles or "subgovernments" calls for the president to play what role?

     A. An advocate for specialized interests

     B. An intermediary between the legislature and specialized interests

     C. An outsider or ineffective player

     D. An agenda setter

     E. An advocate for spending restraint

39. Which of the following does not explain why the media tends to report on the "horse race" nature of election campaigns?

     A. The media has to tell a story every day, so adviserwho's ahead nowadviser is a common theme.

     B. New media research indicates that most American want this type of coverage.

     C. The competition between news agencies engenders a preference for news that is quick and easy to report.

     D. adviserHorse raceadviser reporting tends to be cheap to produce, and the media has limited resources.

     E. The emphasis on conflict and competition tends to attract viewers and readers.

40. Which of the following provisions is contained in the War Powers Resolution?

     A. The president may unilaterally declare war in an emergency such as nuclear attack.

     B. Congress must declare war before American troops may be deployed abroad.

     C. The president must consult with the chairs of the Senate Armed Services Committee and the House National Security Committee.

     D. The Senate Armed Services Committee and the Military Deployment Commission must fund deployment of troops absent a declaration of war.

     E. Congress must extend the time that troops can be deployed beyond 60–90 days without a declaration of war.

GO ON TO THE NEXT PAGE ▶

41. Which of the following categories are considered to be part of an iron triangle?

   I. the House of Representatives

   II. A regulatory agency

   III. the U.S. Court of Appeals

   IV. interest groups

   V. the president

   A. II and IV

   B. II, and III

   C. II, IV, and V

   D. II, III, and IV

   E. III and IV

42. Which of the following constitutes an electoral plurality?

   A. an election with more than one candidate

   B. an election where the winner wins more votes than any other candidate

   C. an election where the winner wins a majority of the votes cast

   D. an election that elects electors who then vote for the candidates

   E. an election where the winner wins more votes than all the other candidates combined

43. An "unidentified source" is least likely to be which of the following?

   A. a U.S. Senator

   B. the president

   C. a mid-level official in the Defense Department

   D. a member of the staff for a House committee

   E. a member of the Council of Economic Advisors

44. Political institutions are an essential feature of any political system because

   A. they are a necessary element of structured policy making.

   B. they have the most political power in this country.

   C. they are the initial structure involved in the policy process.

   D. they are the most efficient methods of making public policy.

   E. they are the first elements in the sequence of policy making.

45. Which of the following are examples of checks and balances?

   I. Senate advice and consent on treaties and appointments

   II. the Congressional Budget Office

   III. cooperative Federalism

   IV. presidential veto power

   A. I and II

   B. II and III

   C. II, III, and IV

   D. I, II, and IV

   E. I, II, III, and IV

GO ON TO THE NEXT PAGE

46. The differences between executive agreements and treaties include all the following except

   I. Senate advice and consent is not required of agreements but is required of treaties.

   II. Presidents have used executive agreements with foreign governments more frequently than treaties since World War II.

   III. Treaties require a two-thirds vote by the Senate but executive agreements require only a majority vote.

   IV. Executive agreements are authorized by statute but treaties are provided for in the Constitution.

     A. I and II

     B. I and III

     C. II, III, and IV

     D. II and III

     E. III and IV

47. Compared to a restrained judge, a judicial activist believes

     A. the southern states to secede from the Union in 1860.

     B. courts should negate legislatively imposed affirmative action policies.

     C. the Constitution means exactly what the words in its provisions say.

     D. courts should be aggressive in exercising the power of judicial review.

     E. courts should not apply the bill of rights to the states through the 14th Amendment.

48. The Supreme Court decision in *Regents of the University of California v. Bakke* (1978) placed substantial limits on the policy of

     A. making low-interest student loans available.

     B. affirmative action.

     C. protecting intellectual property rights.

     D. academic freedom.

     E. allowing protests on the campuses of public colleges and universities.

49. In presidential-legislative relations, the president enjoys an advantage for which of the following reasons

   I. The president receives closer attention from the media than does Congress.

   II. The leadership of Congress almost always opposes any presidential policy proposal.

   III. Presidents are much better at parliamentary procedure than are legislators.

   IV. Congress must address many more policy interests and concerns than the president.

     A. I and II

     B. II and III

     C. III and IV

     D. I and IV

     E. II and IV

GO ON TO THE NEXT PAGE ▶

50. The power of Congress to prohibit racial discrimination in places of public accommodation was upheld in which case(s)?

   I. *United States v. Virginia* (1996))

   II. *Katzenbach v. McClung* (1964)

   III. *Heart of Atlanta Motel v. United States* (1964)

   IV. *Adarand Constructors v. Pena* (1965)

   V. *Johnson v. Transportation Agency, Santa Clara County* (1967)

   A. II and III

   B. I and II

   C. II, III, and IV

   D. III, IV, and V

   E. II, III, and V

51. The use of civil service examinations to hire and promote federal government employees is an example of

A. the patronage system.

B. the merit system.

C. a bureaucratic program designed by Max Weber.

D. a system used only in selected cases.

E. a system all presidents have opposed.

52. The 1965 Voting Rights Act

A. was also known as the Motor-Voter Bill.

B. confirmed the constitutionality of the grandfather clause.

C. increased African American voter registration in the South.

D. established a system of poll taxes.

E. was passed in spite of the opposition of President Johnson.

53. The number of justices sitting on the U.S. Supreme Court is set by

A. the Judicial Conference of the United States, by rule.

B. the Administrative Office of the U.S. Courts, by rule.

C. Article III of the U.S. Constitution.

D. Congress and the president, by law.

E. the Special Division of the Court of Appeals, by order.

54. Which approach to studying politics is the least democratic?

A. Political system

B. Pluralism

C. Structural-functionalism

D. Elitism

E. Hyperpluralism

GO ON TO THE NEXT PAGE ▶

55. From the following choices, how does the media influence or relate to public opinion?

    I. It may shape or alter the public's views on policy issues.

    II. It has significant access to people of higher education and income.

    III. It affects the issues that the public is concerned about or pays attention to.

    IV. It is most able to influence cable and satellite subscribers.

    A. I and II

    B. II and III

    C. III and IV

    D. I and III

    E. II and IV

56. What is the definition of a critical election?

    A. Groups of voters change their usual patterns of party loyalty.

    B. Significant numbers of voters vote for a third party candidate for president.

    C. Both houses of Congress and the presidency are controlled by the same party.

    D. Voter turnout declines sharply from previous elections.

    E. Racial minorities shift their voting allegiance.

57. Which of the following characterize the filibuster by members of Congress?

    I. It can occur in both houses of Congress.

    II. It can occur only in the Senate.

    III. It can be halted by a vote of cloture.

    IV. It can lead to a stoppage in the legislative process.

    V. It can only be initiated by a member of the majority party in the chamber.

    A. I, III, and IV

    B. II, III, and IV

    C. II, III, IV, and V

    D. III, IV. and V

    E. II, III, and V

58. Which type of policy best describes government price supports for farmers?

    A. Regulatory

    B. Entitlement

    C. Distributive

    D. Tax

    E. Redistributive

GO ON TO THE NEXT PAGE ▶

59. Which of the following are characteristic of U.S. political culture in the post-War period?

    I. People have become less trusting of government.

    II. People have become more supportive of school integration.

    III. More people have come to believe their actions affect government.

    IV. People have become more trusting of government institutions.

    A. I

    B. II

    C. I and II

    D. II and III

    E. II and IV

60. Which of the following illustrate checks and balances in our system of government?

    I. categorical grants-in-aid

    II. unfunded mandates

    III. Supreme Court invalidation of a federal statute

    IV. election of the president by the electoral college

    A. I and II

    B. III only

    C. II and III

    D. III and IV

    E. IV only

STOP!

SECTION II

Directions: Answer all four free-response questions. You have 100 minutes total. Your entire answer for each question must not exceed a page.

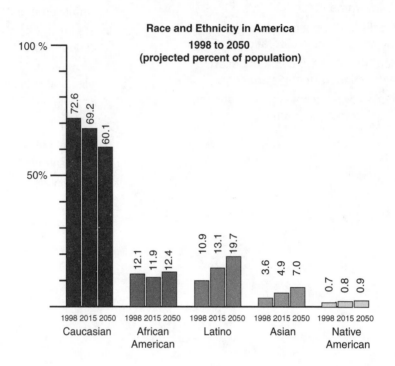

Race and Ethnicity in America
1998 to 2050
(projected percent of population)

1. Using the graph above, identify three trends that are likely to occur for racial and ethnic groups between 1998 and 2050. For each trend you identify, do the following:

   - Identify one electoral consequence of that trend in presidential politics.
   - Explain why you expect that trend to have the consequence you identified.

Apex Learning

2. After a policy speech to the American people, the White House often claims, sometimes within hours, that a high percentage of Americans approve of the president's actions or proposals.

- Identify two sources the White House may use to get these poll numbers.
  Explain why the White House would choose to select each source.

- Indicate the strengths and weaknesses (the level of reliability) of each source.

- Explain how the White House gets its numbers from each source.

3. Individual privacy has been recognized by many segments of our society as a fundamental right, now protected by the Constitution. Given the freedom of the press to investigate and publish its findings, there can be a great tension between public figures and the free press. Using one of the Supreme Court cases listed below, describe the facts in the case, state the Court's holding, and explain what that decision meant for the law in the area of privacy rights versus the media.

   - *New York Times v. Sullivan* (1964)
   - *New York Times v. United States* (1971)

Apex Learning

4. The relationship between Congress and the judiciary is somewhat more distant than it is between Congress and other institutions. However, Congress does have some control over the federal courts. Identify three such controls. For each one, do the following:

- Indicate the level of (1) partisanship and (2) policy differences on the part of the legislature that influences the control.

- Explain how effective the legislative control mechanism is in influencing or restraining the judiciary.

ANSWERS AND EXPLANATIONS TO PRACTICE TEST

Multiple-Choice Questions

1.   E   Only answer choice E is true of policy entrepreneurs. Policy entrepreneurs are not always successful in moving their agenda items to the next level of the policy process, so that eliminates statement IV. Statements I, II, and III are all true of policy entrepreneurs.

2.   B   Olson's theory focuses on the problem of free riders. It states that if groups can provide selective incentives and exclude free riders, they will be able to attract new members to join.

3.   C   The forms of expression contained in items I, II, and III have all been protected by Supreme Court decisions. Item IV, challenging people to riot, is not protected since it involves "fighting words" that might cause injury to those hearing the speech.

4.   E   This is a definitional question. Treaties and Appointments of Federal Judges must be approved by the Senate, but Executive Agreements and Executive Orders do not have that requirement.

5.   C   Implementing policy, choice C, involves a bureaucracy developing rules for administering the statute. Here, the administrative bureaucracy is the Agriculture Department, which is enforcing rules about how to implement the Freedom to Farm Act.

6.   B   The answer is party organization. The set of party members listed in the question stem includes more than party-in-government. This term refers to all the elected and appointed officials who identify with a particular party, so choice C is wrong. Choice A is wrong as well, since party-in-electorate is less than the given set, in that it refers to citizens who identify with a specific party. Party leadership and party machine, choices D and E, do not include "paid professional staff," so they can be ruled out as well.

7.   D   The only item that does not afford a bureau some power is the number or size of agencies in the government, item III. Small agencies with few employees may still exercise great power. All the other items provide an agency with some power or independence.

8.   C   This question involves the straightforward definition of the enumerated powers of Congress. Enumerated powers are powers specifically granted to the national government by the Constitution. Delegated powers relate to Congress' delegation of a power to a bureaucratic agency, so choice B is wrong.

9. D   All but answer choice D are empirically true about voting in this country. Voter turnout by age shows a very significant *drop* for those voters under 30 years.

10. D   The inner Cabinet includes the four "major" departments in the Executive Branch: State, Defense, Treasury, and Justice Departments. The Commerce and Labor departments are not part of this group.

11. B   Federal district judges have no influence over a legislator. All of the other answer choices can and do exert significant control or influence over legislators.

12. D   A concurring opinion would be written by a justice who agrees with the outcome of the decision, but disagrees with the reasoning or justification presented by the majority opinion.

13. B   The only correct statement is that the National Security Council is completely loyal to the president. Most staff members are neither military personnel nor career diplomats, so statements I and V are wrong. The NSC does not select the CIA Director; the president appointments that individual, so statement IV is wrong. Lastly, the NSC has no statutory duties to administer the laws of the country, so statement III is wrong as well.

14. E   A male fundamentalist Christian from Indiana would most likely have voted Republican at that time. All other answer choices would have been more likely to vote for a Democratic candidate.

15. E   The House Rules Committee is unique to the House, and. the Filibuster is unique to the Senate. The other items are not relevant or do not even exist in the Congress. The Senate Rules and Administration Committee is a minor, substantive committee and nothing more. The House has the Veterans Affairs Committee, but it is a substantive committee and there is an identical committee in the Senate. There is no such thing as a Senate Conference Committee. These are ad hoc and they are composed of both House and Senate members.

16. B   The Americans with Disabilities Act is an example of an unfunded federal mandate. The statute applies to public buildings, whether they are government buildings or buildings open to the public. A categorical grant-in-aid is a funded federal mandate, so choice A is wrong. Judicial activism, choice D, is totally off the topic, since it has to do with judges roles.

17. D   In the current political environment, delegates ratify decisions already made by voters at national party conventions. The other answer choices are non-essential features of national conventions.

18. A   Privacy is a component of all answer choices except A. Sexual harassment is not a privacy issue.

19. A   Redistricting of house seats is done by state legislatures. The Department of Commerce and the Census Bureau, the Federal Elections Commission, the League of Women voters, and outgoing legislators are not involved in the process of redistricting legislative seats.

20. D   The president's current veto power allows him to selectively veto bills adopted by Congress. Taxing or revenue bills are not affected by this procedure, only spending bills. The Civil Service Commission, choice B, is unrelated to the line-item veto. Choice C is out because a concurrent resolution by Congress would have no affect on instituting a line-item veto. The only method of instituting a line-item veto would be a constitutional amendment, as in *Clinton v. City of New York* (1998).

21. E   The only provisions that were contained in the original Constitution were the power to coin money (item I) and the electoral college (item IV). Items II, III, and V were not in the Constitution as initially ratified.

22. B   Answer choices A, C, and D all contain factual errors, so they can be eliminated. Choice E is factually correct but that does not pertain to the advice sought be the president. Choice B accounts for the fact that presidents often rely for advice more on people they trust than on cabinet secretaries.

23. E   The framers saw political parties as factions motivated by ambition and self-interest. Their beliefs were based on Madison's thesis about factions and their origins, as outlined in Federalist Paper No. 10. There was no consideration of raising money for campaigns at that time, so choice B is wrong.

24. C   The Civil Rights Act was based on the effect that racial segregation and discrimination had on interstate commerce. The other answer choices are all based on other Constitutional powers unrelated to interstate commerce.

25. E   The commerce clause has not expanded state powers over intra-state activities but rather has shrunk those powers. Judicial review has not been reduced by the commerce clause. The Federal Reserve System, choice C, is based on the necessary and proper clause of the Constitution. The franchise is the right to vote and unrelated to the commerce clause, so D is out as well.

26. D   Party identification remains the strongest predictor of how an individual will vote. No other factor contributes as much to a voter's selection.

27. A   The right to bear arms, choice A, is the only right listed that has not been incorporated by the Due Process Clause of the 14th Amendment and applied to the states. This means a state can regulate the possession and use of firearms in any way that is permitted by that state's law, without regard to the 2nd Amendment. The right to bear arms is in the 2nd Amendment.

28. D   An interest group will have more influence in Congress if its issue is narrow in scope and is being dealt with out of the public spotlight. The other answer choices raise factors that have more influence on legislators' voting decisions.

29. A   The framers intended the legislative body to be slow and deliberate rather than immediately reactive. Neither equal nor demographic representation was an objective of the framers in drafting Article I, so D and E can be ruled out. Dominance by the chief executive, choice B, was not intended. Majority rule was a principle, but the protection of minorities in the legislature was also intended, so choice C is incorrect as well.

30. B   The Social Security Administration is not a government corporation because it derives its authority and funding from annual authorizations and the payroll tax. This is contrary to the definition of a government corporation, which is a business enterprise whose activities are mainly commercial.

31. C   The Ways and Means Committee controls tax policy in the House. A representative who wants to influence that policy would be well served by being a member of that committee, so choice C is correct. The Appropriations Committee, choice A, recommends how much money to provide to federal agencies so that is wrong. There is no House Finance Committee, only a Senate Finance Committee, so D can be ruled out, and choice B, the Rules Committee, is the House's traffic cop for all bills, so it can be ruled out as well.

32. E   The establishment clause in the 1st Amendment protects against the state establishing an official church or religion.

33. D   Political ideology is the attitudes and fundamental beliefs about the ideal political system, economic order, social goals and moral values. The other answer choices address more short-term, or less comprehensive, beliefs.

34. B   The Freedom of Information Act was a crucial piece of legislation designed to open non-secret government records to the public.

35. A   This question focuses on devolution in the context of federalism. The failure of devolution has been due to statements I and II: the dependence of local governments on federal money and the unwillingness of states to assume fiscal responsibility for policy areas. Statement III is wrong because the federal government has not been reluctant to give policy responsibility to states and localities. Statement IV is wrong because the Supreme Court has not invalidated devolution policies.

36. C   Independent regulatory agencies tend to be free from presidential control, while cabinet departments receive close presidential attention. Regulatory agencies are designed to be less sensitive to presidential direction.

37. E   The only actors not active in the agenda-setting stage are Supreme Court justices. The media, legislators, lobbyists, and the president all have various levels of involvement.

38. C   Iron triangles do not directly include the president. The president is effectively outside the administration of such policies after they are enacted.

39. B   This question asks for the answer that does not explain the media's behavior. Choices A, C, D, and E are all correct. Answer choice B does not explain the media's behavior, since research does not indicate that most Americans want to watch "horse race" coverage. Therefore, B is the answer.

40. E   The Constitution requires that Congress declare war, so choice A is wrong. The president can deploy troops without a declaration of war, so B is wrong. C is wrong since the Resolution does not require the president to consult with the chairs; it requires the president to provide notification of the deployment. Funding involves Congress, and the Military Deployment Commission does not exist, so D is out as well.

41. A   Only two of the three corners of an iron triangle are listed among the answer choices. The correct choice involves the regulatory agency and interest groups, items II and IV. The other three items are considered to be outside any iron triangles. In this case, the third corner would likely be the relevent House and Senate committees.

42. B   A plurality occurs when the winner gets more votes than any other candidate. It need not be a majority, so choice C is out. It is most likely to result in an election where there are more than two candidates among whom the votes are split, so A is wrong as well. A plurality has nothing to do with an indirect elections, so D is wrong, as is E.

43. B   Given his visibility, the president would be the least likely source. Clearly he would be the hardest to hide; that is, a member of the media would likely identify him as an information source.

44. A   Here you must use the political system framework to analyze politics. Political institutions enable structured policy making to take place.

45. D   Only example III, cooperative Federalism, is not illustrative of checks and balances.

46. E   Items III and IV are not correct. Executive Agreements do not require any vote by the Senate (III), and Executive Agreements are not based on any statutory enactments (IV).

47. D   Judicial activism involves a court aggressively using the power of judicial review to scrutinize and invalidate legislation that does not coincide with the judge's interpretation of the Constitution. Choice A is a general definition of nullification. B focuses on a particular policy view of affirmative action programs. C refers to a literalist or original intent perspective on judicial interpretation. E is a definition of someone who opposes incorporation, and that is counter to judicial activism.

48. B   The *Bakke* case dealt with affirmative action admissions programs at the University of California's medical school. The case held invalid a state medical school admissions program based on a specific racial quota, but upheld the use of race as a factor in admissions decisions.

49. D   Reasons II and III are simply wrong. The president's programs are not always opposed by legislative leaders, particularly when the leadership is of the same party as the president. Even if the president is a great parliamentarian, he has virtually no opportunity to use such skill in the legislative process.

50. A   The cases that upheld Congress's power to enact the Civil Rights Act of 1964 were cases II and III. Case I, *United States v. Virginia*, dealt with gender restrictions on admission to state schools of higher education. Case IV, *Adarand*, dealt with affirmative action in hiring and contracting practices in the construction industry. Case V dealt with gender issues and the workplace.

51. B   This question stem is a definition of the merit system of bureaucratic recruitment. Choice E is wrong, since all presidents have not opposed this system. Choice A is wrong because the patronage (or spoils) system is one in which elected officials award government jobs to political supporters and friends. It has nothing to do with using civil service exams to hire government employees.

52. C   Choices A and D are clearly wrong. Choice E is wrong since President Johnson strongly supported and advocated the Voting Rights Act. The spirit and the substance of the law is directly contrary to choice B. The correct answer is C.

53. D   The number of justices sitting on the Supreme Court (as well as on lower federal courts) is set by statutory law, choice D. The number of justices is not set by rule or by order.

54. D   The least democratic approach would be Elitism. Elitism is least likely to consider or treat politics as "democratic."

55. D   Items I and III are correct. The media influences what issues reach the public agenda, through conveying information (or more information) about some issues over others. The media may also influence how people perceive issues. Items II and IV are not correct: There is no evidence that the media has more access to people with higher income or education, nor is there evidence that cable and satellite viewers are more susceptible to media influence than other segments of the population.

56. A   A critical election is generally seen when usual coalitions of voters shift their allegiance to a different party or set of party candidates. Choice B is wrong, since critical elections have nothing to do with third party candidates. C is a definition of undivided government and does not relate to critical elections. D focuses on voter turnout, not on critical elections. E focuses on racial minorities which may be involved in critical elections but are not necessary for a critical election to occur.

57. B   Options I and V are incorrect. A filibuster cannot occur in both houses; it can occur only in the Senate. Moreover, a filibuster can be initiated by a member of either party, not just the majority party. Therefore, choice B is correct.

58. C   Price supports are a type of policy that distributes monetary benefits to an identifiable set of recipients. Choice E is wrong because a redistributive policy is designed to shift benefits from one group to another. An entitlement policy, choice B, is one in which the government provides benefits to those who have a legally enforceable right, so that is wrong as well.

59. C   Characteristics I and II are correct, while III and IV are not: Fewer people believe they can affect government, and people have become more doubtful of government today.

60. B   Only item III, Supreme Court invalidation of a federal statute, deals with the relationship between two branches of the federal government. That is the core meaning of the principle of checks and balances. Items I and II have to do with federalism, while item IV involves only one branch of government—the president.

Essay Questions

1. This question asks for several items, based on a graph and on your knowledge of voting and elections. Your answer should clearly and numerically identify three trends.

    Since the figures in the graph indicate percentage of the population, not numbers, proportion changes must be a significant feature of the data. Also, since the graph displays population, not voters, your answer should include mention that these changing populations are mobilized to vote and become involved in elections. It would be helpful to calculate the population percentage changes so that you get a sense of the change from start to finish (1998–2050). That calculation would be the difference in percentage between 2050 and 1998, divided by the 1998 percentage.

    Possible trends:

    - A decline in the proportion of the Caucasian population (from 72% in 1998 to 60% in 2050)
    - A nearly stable African American population (about 12%)
    - A significant increase in the proportion of Latino population (11% to 20%)
    - A significant increase in the proportion of Asian population (3% to 7%)
    - No effective change in the proportion of Native Americans.

    The lack of change in the African American and Native American populations would be hard to explain, so you are better off selecting the other three trends. The greatest changes are in the Asian population, nearly a 95% increase, and in the Latino population, an 81% increase. The Caucasians in the population reflect a 17% decrease.

    For each ethnic or racial groups, clearly specify an electoral consequence of each trend in presidential politics. Only one consequence per group is necessary. Possible consequences might be:

    Caucasians:

    - This group remains the majority (but shrinking) proportion of the population. Therefore it will be difficult for candidates to overlook the broad interests of this category of voter.

    - The heterogeneity of this population will make it difficult to select specific policy issues for campaigning.

    - It is widely distributed geographically so candidates may not be able to single out and target this electoral population.

Latinos:

- The concentration of this population in specific regions of the country probably will make it a ripe target for candidates in the West Coast, South Western States, and Gulf Coast.

- Immigration may continue to be a significant policy issue for this group of people and may result in a campaign issue.

- Language instruction and education might also be salient policy issues for these voters.

Asians:

- This segment of the population is highly motivated and engaged in politics. Therefore, where there are identifiable concentrations, Asians may become a very significant feature of electoral politics.

- Education and business policy may be a significant policy issue for this group of voters.

2. This question is typical of AP essay questions that are fairly open-ended. The subject and perhaps the thesis, are provided, and it is your job to generate the connected factors or variables and to explain their relationships. Here, the subjects are the White House and spin control; public opinion and support for the president; and polling sources. You must first dissect these parts and then develop an essay that addresses their interconnectedness.

    This question focuses on White House use of public opinion to indicate widespread support for the president's proposals. You will need to cite different polling techniques or sources that the White House uses to generate specific impressions and images.

    Specifically, you must identify two sources for poll numbers. Once you have identified two polling sources, explain why the White House would select them, as well as the reliability of each. Last, explain how the White House gets its numbers from each source.

    A. List two polling sources: A brief sentence identifying each source will suffice. Do not address their strengths or weakness, or the nature of the data in this part of your answer. Possible sources are listed below.

        - Tabulating telephone calls made to the White House switchboard

        - Tabulating e-mail messages sent to the White House

        - Conducting an immediate phone survey of selected sources including known presidential supporters

- Talking to legislators know to favor the president's policies and then tabulating their reactions, and compiling the responses they have received from constituents, phone calls or e-mails

- Calling visible industry leaders who support the subject of the speech

- Relying on media polling conducted in the days after the speech

The White House might consider using these sources because they can be compiled quickly. That is, they do not take days to compile but rather minutes or hours. Instantaneous results and reaction allow the White House to quickly "spin" a favorable reaction to the speech, strengthening its "hand" in any policy debates that arise in response to the speech.

B. For second part of the question, you will address the accuracy of your selected sources. For each source, plan to write a separate paragraph each for strengths and for weaknesses. Use your own judgment on how many strengths and weaknesses to include, but three or four each is a good idea.

Some strengths and some weaknesses apply to more than one source, so if you use them more than once, rephrase them. You want each sentence to amplify your level of knowledge rather than minimize how much you know, so don't be redundant. If you use a strength or weakness more than once, think of another way to phrase it.

Possible strengths of a polling source:
- Information is speedily retrieved
- Source will be positive or favorable to speech
- Interpretation of responses can be controlled
- The poll might be representative of the population and therefore accurate (by random selection)

Possible weaknesses of a polling source:
- There may be a delay in getting results
- Results may be negative or unfavorable to president's position
- Interpretation of results might not be able to be controlled
- The poll might be unrepresentative of the population (an unrepresentative poll)

Some of these strengths and weaknesses are linked. For example, a randomly selected public opinion poll conducted by the media might be representative of the population, but it would be a relatively slow process, taking days at the very least. Nor might this type of poll favor the president's position. If you create a list of the pluses and minuses of various polling processes, you can attach the relevant ones to your selected sources.

C. The third segment of the question asks you to explain how the White House gets its results. Some responses are voluntary, within the random responses, such as phone calls or e-mails. Other responses might have to be sought out by White House staff. They might have to initiate calls to supportive legislators or industry leaders. Still other responses are reactive, as in waiting for the results of a media poll conducted completely beyond the reach of the White House.

3. This question is a long one to read, but it is designed to get you on the right track from the outset. You are provided with the subject and a clear outline of what you are to do. Here, the topic is individual privacy versus freedom of the press.

You are not asked to write a general essay about free press or the history of its development. You are asked to discuss one of two cases in the context of privacy. This level of detailed knowledge is commonly expected on the AP test.

First, in one sentence, indicate which case you will discuss. Select the one that is most familiar. Then, write a short paragraph—two or three sentences—about the facts of the case. Identify what parties were involved and what they had done. Explain the Court's holding in the case, but do not elaborate on the facts that gave rise to the holding. This may be pretty difficult unless you are entirely familiar with the case. However, both from the perspective of civil rights and liberties and of the relationship between government and the press, these two cases are essential, core elements today.

A full explanation should follow: This asks for the significance of the case. Make a connection between the case and the principle of privacy or secrecy. This part of your answer should be a maximum of one full paragraph, but a minimum of three or four detailed sentences.

Case 1: *New York Times v. Sullivan* (1964)

Facts: Sullivan, a County Commissioner in Alabama, sued the New York Times for publication of an advertisement that criticized the local handling of civil rights demonstrations in Montgomery, Alabama. He sued on the grounds that the advertisement contained factual errors about the conduct of the police. The *New York Times* argued that this did not constitute libel of a public official.

Holding: For a public official to prove libel against a newspaper that has published a critical advertisement, the official has to prove the errors were made knowingly or with reckless disregard for the truth. The reasonable mistakes in this advertisement indicated no reckless disregard for the truth.

Explanation: The significance of this case is that it protects the press at a higher level from libel actions when (1) a public official is the target and (2) there are some unintended factual errors in the coverage. This expands the right of the press to criticize public officials. Since public officials have chosen to hold public office, they thereby can expose themselves to rigorous public scrutiny and criticism. Later cases expanded this press protection to public figures not just public officials.

Case 2: *New York Times v. United States* (1971)

Facts: The government sought to block (enjoin) the publication of the Pentagon Papers which had been stolen from the Pentagon by a former employee (Daniel Elsberg). The government argued that its publication would prolong the Vietnam War and embarrass the country and the government. The government also argued that its release would violate national security because it contained embarrassing disclosures about the country's involvement in the Vietnam War. The *New York Times* countered with the argument that this constituted prior restraint or censorship of the press.

Holding: The government could not prevent the publication of the (revealing and controversial) Pentagon Papers by the *New York Times* without proving immediate, inevitable, and irreparable injury.

Explanation: This case involved the principle of prior restraint which has long been rejected under the Freedom of the Press Doctrine (see *Near v. Minnesota* (1931)). While the facts in this case might have truly involved matters of national security that would have warranted prior restraint for publication, the government failed to make the case for that restraint. The burden of proof on the government is a very heavy one. This decision enhanced the power of the press to explore and publish material that is critical of or revealing of government mistakes.

4. This question asks you to discuss features of the institutional relationship between the judiciary and the legislature. Do not write a general essay about this relationship. The question asks for three forms of control that Congress has over the federal courts.

    Controls:
    - Budget (operating budget for the Court)

    - Judicial salaries (only to increase salaries, not to lower them)

    - Appellate jurisdiction of the Court (removing existing appellate jurisdiction and not providing appellate jurisdiction in new statutes)

    - Control of the number of Justices on the Court (not even threatened these days)

    - Senate advice and consent (approving or rejecting) of presidential nominations to the Court

    - Revising a statute that the Court has declared unconstitutional

    First, you must identify three controls that Congress has over the judiciary. Rather than write out a description of each, compile a succinct list with bullets or with numbers. Each one should be no longer than one sentence. The itemized list is the heart of the question.

    Then you must assess partisan and policy differences between the two branches of government, and how that may shape the legislature's use of control. You must be able to recognize the political and policy dimensions of each control mechanism. How might each one influence the use and the effectiveness of your identified controls?

Specific cases are not necessary to answer this question. They may enhance your discussion, but they are not essential.

- Budget controls are generally less partisan and more policy oriented. That means the opposition of southern legislators to the Court's decisions from *Brown* regarding racial integration led to opposition to operating budget increases to salary increases. The opposition included both Democrats and Republicans. Salary and operating budget control generally is a broad-gauged (rough) tool for control since individual justices cannot be sanctioned or singled out using this mechanism.

- Judicial salaries cannot be lowered or cut, only frozen. Congress has repeatedly failed to allow even cost of living adjustments to judicial salaries, and some federal judges. Salaries are more often used to convey disapproval with court decisions.

- Appellate jurisdiction efforts have generally been unsuccessful although proposed usually by individual senators or Representatives on the grounds that the Court should not be deciding issues of school prayer or busing to achieve racial integration of schools. These are almost always unsuccessful, probably because there is widely recognized need among legislators for a single, final interpreter or Court decision, and because many, including those who oppose particular court decisions, who do not think it wise to tinker with a co-equal institution.

- Controlling the number of justices on the Court is possible. There are only two examples of policy efforts in this regard. This technique, based on historical precedent, is not a partisan feature of legislative control but rather a matter of policy differences.

  The first example was in the Reconstruction era when the Court, with ten members, was reduced to nine in order to preclude the president (Andrew Johnson) from appointing a replacement when the next vacancy occurred.

  The second example was FDR's court-packing plan in 1937 which was proposed but not adopted by either house of the Congress. This was made (by the president) on policy disagreement grounds.

- The Senate has some significant role over Supreme Court appointments through its advice and consent power. It has been used successfully in the past three decades to block the confirmation of three Supreme Court nominees. This is an exceptionally high effectiveness rate given the history of our country on this matter. How successful this mechanism of control is certainly an open question.

- Revising a statute relates to modifying a statute that the Court has declared unconstitutional, in order to get the same policy in place, but without the constitutional flaw. This is usually a direct legislative effort to circumvent a policy problem with the first law. This is rarely a partisan issue although it can be if the majority party is coalesced around the issue and seeks to re-insure the policy by pushing a bill through. It is usually a policy difference between a coalition of congress members and is the result of a strong believe among these members that the policy should be adopted, even if their first effort was constitutionally infirm.

The second task in this question is to explain how effective this mechanism is. This requires some discussion of each of the selected methods, and can probably be focused on how often and with what success the method has been employed. It is not always clear that the mechanism has been effective or ineffective, so this calls for some argument on your part. Illustrations or examples might support your assessment.

Budget control. This is often used in connection with denying salary increases, even cost-of-living adjustments given automatically to all other government employees. That has caused judicial salaries to lag behind those of most of the legal profession in private practice, and perhaps discourages some possible appointees from accepting an appointment. Cutting operating budgets for courts is done in much the same way that other agencies may face fixed percentage cuts during recessions or budget-cutting episodes.

Appellate jurisdiction. There have also been a few times when denying the Court appellate jurisdiction in newly proposed legislation has been seriously considered. This effort is usually proposed by a few legislators who think lower courts would decide cases about this statute more favorably to their policy positions. Again this has been an unsuccessful mechanism, though the mere threat by Congress may produce some modification in the Court's decisions.

Control of the number of Justices. This technique has been used with some effect, but rarely in the history of the country. It is not often even considered a possibility, and many opposed it in 1937 only because it was tinkering with an equal branch of government in a way that the public and some officials thought inappropriate.

Senate advice and consent to nominees. This has been used successfully several times in the past few decades to clock a presidential nominee. The effect on the existing court members is certainly unclear and it would be at best indirect.

Statutory revisions. This method if control is usually unsuccessful. That is because a policy coalition is difficult to maintain or reconstruct, even if only months after the first enactment. Usually the bill would be considered years later, after the issue has been litigated to the Supreme Court, so the original legislators may no longer be in the Congress that is reconsidering the proposal.

Scoring Your Practice Test

Scoring information for the AP U.S. Government & Politics Test is detailed in Unit One: The Basics. Here's a quick recap.

You can earn a maximum score of 120 points on the test:

Section I:	**60 Multiple-Choice Questions**	**60 points for the section**
Section II:	**Four Essay Questions**	**60 points for the section**

The multiple-choice section is scored by computer. The essay answers are scored by AP teachers and college professors. Both raw scores are added to form a *composite score*.

Your composite score is translated into an AP grade. There is no fixed composite score range that is consistent from year to year, or even from AP subject to subject. These score ranges change yearly. To get an idea, though, look at the score range used in 1999.

Composite Score	**AP Grade**	**Comment**
86–120	5	Extremely well qualified*
70–85	4	Well qualified*
49–69	3	Qualified*
27–48	2	Possibly qualified*
0–26	1	No recommendation

*Qualified here means qualified to receive college credit or advanced placement.

There is no way for you to accurately score your practice test since the essay answers have no set point value. If you would like, find your raw score out of 60 points on the multiple-choice section. Remember, you are not penalized for answers left blank.

$$\boxed{\text{Number right}} - \left(0.25 \times \boxed{\text{Number wrong}}\right) = \boxed{\text{Raw score (rounded)}}$$

The point of this practice test is to give you a chance to work through a realistic test, not to identify you at a specific assessment level. That will depend not only on how well you do, but on how many applicants there are taking the test and how well they do. Learn as much as you can from your performance on this test and then go back and review sections of this book and your class textbook as needed.

As you practice, don't be demoralized just because you don't know how to answer all the questions. Just do your best and learn from your mistakes.

APPENDIXES

APPENDIXES

Appendix A   *The U.S. Constitution*

WE THE PEOPLE of the United States, in Order to form a more perfect Union, establish justice, insure domestic Tranquility, provide for the common defence, promote the general Welfare, and secure the Blessings of Liberty to ourselves and our Posterity, do ordain and establish this Constitution for the United States of America.

ARTICLE I

Section 1.   All legislative Powers herein granted shall be vested in a Congress of the United States, which shall consist of a Senate and House of Representatives.

Section 2.   The House of Representatives shall be composed of Members chosen every second Year by the People of the several States, and the Electors in each State shall have the Qualifications requisite for Electors of the most numerous Branch of the State Legislature.

No Person shall be a Representative who shall not have attained to the Age of twenty five Years, and been seven Years a Citizen of the United States, and who shall not, when elected, be an Inhabitant of that State in which he shall be chosen.

[Representatives and [direct Taxes] shall be apportioned among the several States [which may be included within this Union,] according to their respective Numbers, which shall be determined by adding to the whole Number of free Persons, in-cluding those bound to Service for a Term of Years, and excluding Indians not taxed, three fifths of all other Persons. (This clause was changed by section 2 of the Fourteenth Amendment.)] The actual Enumeration shall be made within three Years after the first Meet-ing of the Congress of the United States, and within every sub-sequent Term of ten Years, in such Manner as they shall by Law direct. The Number of Representatives shall not exceed one for every thirty Thousand, but each State shall have at Least one Representative; and until such enumeration shall be made, the State of New Hampshire shall be entitled to chuse three, Massachusetts eight, Rhode Island and Providence Plantations one, Connecticut five, New York six, New Jersey four, Pennsylvania eight, Delaware one, Maryland six, Virginia ten, North Carolina five, South Carolina five, and Georgia three.

When vacancies happen in the Representation from any State, the Executive Authority thereof shall issue Writs of Election to fill such Vacancies.

The House of Representatives shall chuse their Speaker and other Officers; and shall have the sole Power of Impeachment.

Section 3.   The Senate of the United States shall be composed of two Senators from each State, [chosen by the Legislature thereof, (This provision was changed by section 1 of the Seventeenth Amendment.)] for six Years; and each Senator shall have one Vote.

Immediately after they shall be assembled in Consequence of the first Election, they shall be divided as equally as may be into three Classes. The Seats of the Senators of the first Class shall be vacated at the Expiration of the second Year, of the second Class at the Expiration of the fourth Year, and of the third Class at the Expiration of the sixth Year, so that one third may be chosen every second Year; [and if Vacancies happen by Resignation, or otherwise, during the Recess of the Legislature of any State, the Executive thereof may make temporary Appointments until the next Meeting of the Legislature, which shall then fill such Vacancies. (This clause was changed by section 2 of the Seventeenth Amendment.)]

No Person shall be a Senator who shall not have attained to the Age of thirty Years, and been nine Years a Citizen of the United States, and who shall not, when elected, be an Inhabitant of that State for which he shall be chosen.

The Vice President of the United States shall be President of the Senate, but shall have no Vote, unless they be equally divided.

The Senate shall chuse their other Officers, and also a President pro tempore, in the Absence of the Vice President, or when he shall exercise the Office of President of the United States.

The Senate shall have the sole Power to try all Impeachments. When sitting for that Purpose, they shall be on Oath or Affirmation. When the President of the United States is tried, the Chief justice shall preside: And no Person shall be convicted without the Concurrence of two thirds of the Members present.

Judgment in Cases of Impeachment shall not extend further than to removal from Office, and disqualification to hold and enjoy any Office of honor, Trust or Profit under the United States: but the Party convicted shall nevertheless be liable and subject to Indictment, Trial, Judgment and Punishment, according to Law.

Section 4.   The Times, Places and Manner of holding Elections for Senators and Representatives, shall be prescribed in each State by the Legislature thereof; but the Congress may at any time by Law make or alter such Regulations, except as to the Places of chusing Senators.

The Congress shall assemble at least once in every Year, and such Meeting shall be [on the first Monday in December, (This provision was changed by section 2 of the Twentieth Amendment.)] unless they shall by Law appoint a different Day.

Section 5.   Each House shall be the judge of the Elections, Returns and Qualifications of its own Members, and a Majority of each shall constitute a Quorum to do Business; but a smaller Number may adjourn from day to day, and may be authorized to compel the Attendance of absent Members, in such Manner, and under such Penalties as each House may provide.

Each House may determine the Rules of its Proceedings, punish its Members for disorderly Behaviour, and, with the Concurrence of two thirds, expel a Member.

Each House shall keep a journal of its Proceedings, and from time to time publish the same, excepting such Parts as may in their judgment require Secrecy; and the Yeas and Nays of the Members of either House on any question shall, at the Desire of one fifth of those Present, be entered on the journal.

Neither House, during the Session of Congress, shall, without the Consent of the other, adjourn for more than three days, nor to any other Place than that in which the two Houses shall be sitting.

Section 6.   The Senators and Representatives shall receive a Compensation for their Services, to be ascertained by Law, and paid out of the Treasury of the United States. They shall in all Cases, except Treason, Felony and Breach of the Peace, be privileged from Arrest during their Attendance at the Session of their respective Houses, and in going to and returning from the same; and for any Speech or Debate in either House, they shall not be questioned in any other Place.

No Senator or Representative shall, during the Time for which he was elected, be appointed to any civil Office under the Au-thority of the United States, which shall have been created, or the Emoluments whereof shall have been encreased during such time; and no Person holding any Office under the United States, shall be a Member of either House during his Continuance in Office.

Section 7.   All Bills for raising Revenue shall originate in the House of Representatives; but the Senate may propose or concur with Amendments as on other Bills.

Every Bill which shall have passed the House of Representatives and the Senate, shall, before it become a Law, be presented to the President of the United States; If he approve he shall sign it, but if not he shall return it, with his Objections to that House in which it shall have originated, who shall enter the Objections at large on their

Journal, and proceed to reconsider it. If after such Reconsideration two thirds of that House shall agree to pass the Bill, it shall be sent, together with the Objections, to the other House, by which it shall likewise be reconsidered, and if approved by two thirds of that House, it shall become a Law. But in all such Cases the Votes of both Houses shall be determined by yeas and Nays, and the Names of the Persons voting for and against the Bill shall be entered on the journal of each House respectively. If any bill shall not be returned by the President within ten Days (Sundays excepted) after it shall have been presented to him, the Same shall be a Law, in like Manner as if he had signed it, unless the Congress by their Adjournment prevent its Return, in which Case it shall not be a Law.

Every Order, Resolution, or Vote to which the Concurrence of the Senate and House of Representatives may be necessary (ex-cept on a question of Adjournment) shall be presented to the President of the United States; and before the Same shall take Effect, shall be approved by him, or being disapproved by him, shall be repassed by two thirds of the Senate and House of Representatives, according to the Rules and Limitations prescribed in the Case of a Bill.

Section 8.   The Congress shall have Power To lay and collect Taxes, Duties, Imposts and Excises, to pay the Debts and provide for the common Defence and general Welfare of the United States; but all Duties, Imposts and Excises shall be uniform throughout the United States;

To borrow Money on the credit of the United States;

To regulate Commerce with Foreign Nations, and among the several States, and with the Indian tribes;

To establish an uniform Rule of Naturalization, and uniform Laws on the subject of Bankruptcies throughout the United States;

To coin Money, regulate the Value thereof, and of foreign Coin, and fix the Standard of Weights and Measures;

To provide for the Punishment of counterfeiting the Securities and current Coin of the United States;

To establish Post Offices and post Roads;

To promote the Progress of Science and useful Arts, by securing for limited Times to Authors and Inventors the exclusive Right to their respective Writings and Discoveries; ˋ

To constitute Tribunals inferior to the supreme Court;

To define and punish Piracies and Felonies committed on the high Seas, and Offences against the Law of Nations;

To declare War, grant Letters of Marque and Reprisal, and make Rules concerning Captures on Land and Water;

To raise and support Armies, but no Appropriation of Money to that Use shall be for a longer Term than two Years;

To provide and maintain a Navy;

To make Rules for the Government and Regulation of the land and naval Forces;

To provide for calling forth the Militia to execute the Laws of the Union, suppress Insurrections and repel Invasions;

To provide for organizing, arming, and disciplining, the Militia and for governing such Part of them as may be employed in the Service of the United States, reserving to the States respectively, the Appointment of the Officers, and the Authority of training the Militia according to the discipline prescribed by Congress;

To exercise exclusive Legislation in all Cases whatsoever, over such District (not exceeding ten Miles square) as may, by Cession of particular States, and the Acceptance of Congress, become the Seat of the Government of the United States, and to exercise like Authority over all Places purchased by the Consent of the Legislature of the State in which the Same shall be, for the Erection of Forts, Magazines, Arsenals, dock-Yards, and other needful Buildings; -And

To make all Laws which shall be necessary and proper for carrying into Execution the foregoing Powers, and all other Powers vested by this Constitution in the Government of the United States, or in any Department or Officer thereof.

Section 9.   The Migration or Importation of such Persons any of the States now existing shall think proper to admit, shall not be prohibited by the Congress prior to the Year one thousand eight hundred and eight, but a Tax or duty may be imposed on such Importation, not exceeding ten dollars for each Person.

The Privilege of the Writ of Habeas Corpus shall not be suspended, unless when in Cases of Rebellion or Invasion the public Safety may require it.

No Bill of Attainder or ex post facto Law shall be passed.

No Capitation, or other direct, Tax shall be laid, unless in Pro-portion to the Census or Enumeration herein before directed to be taken.

No Tax or Duty shall be laid on Articles exported from any State.

No Preference shall be given by any Regulation of Commerce or Revenue to the Ports of one State over those of another: nor shall Vessels bound to, or from, one State, be obliged to enter, clear, or pay Duties in another.

No Money shall be drawn from the Treasury, but in Conse-quence of Appropriations made by Law; and a regular Statement and Account of the Receipts and Expenditures of all public Money shall be published from time to time.

No Title of Nobility shall be granted by the United States: And no Person holding any Office of Profit or Trust under them, shall, without the Consent of the Congress, accept of any present, Emol-ument, Office, or Tide, of any kind whatever, from any King, Prince, or foreign State.

Section 10. No State shall enter into any Treaty, Alliance, or Confederation; grant Letters of Marque and Reprisal; coin Money; emit Bills of Credit; make any Thing but gold and silver Coin a Tender in Payment of Debts; pass any Bill of Attainder, ex post facto Law, or Law impairing the Obligation of Contracts, or grant any Title of Nobility.

No State shall, without the Consent of the Congress, lay any Imposts or Duties on Imports or Exports, except what may be absolutely necessary for executing it's inspec-tion Laws: and the net Produce of all Duties and Imposts, laid by any State on Im-ports or Exports, shall be for the Use of the Treasury of the United States; and all such Laws shall be subject to the Revision and Controul of the Congress.

No State shall, without the Consent of Congress, lay any Duty of Tonnage, keep Troops, or Ships of War in time of Peace, enter into any Agreement or Compact with another State, or with a foreign Power, or engage in War, unless actually invaded, or in such imminent Danger as will not admit of delay.

ARTICLE II

Section 1. The executive Power shall be vested in a President of the United States of America. He shall hold his Office during the Term of four Years, and, together with the Vice President, chosen for the same Term, be elected, as follows

Each State shall appoint, in such Manner as the Legislature thereof may direct, a Number of Electors, equal to the whole Number of Senators and Representatives to which the State may be entitled in the Congress: but no Senator or Representative, or Person holding an Office of Trust or Profit under the United States, shall be appointed an Elector.

[The Electors shall meet in their respective States, and vote by Ballot for two Persons, of whom one at least shall not be an inhabitant of the same State with themselves. And they shall make a List of all the Persons voted for, and of the Number of Votes for each; which List they shall sign and certify, and transmit sealed to the Seat of the Government of the United States, directed to the President of the Senate. The President of the Senate shall, in the Presence of the Senate and House of Representatives, open all the Certificates, and the Votes shall then be counted. The Person having the greatest Number of Votes shall be the President, if such Number be a Majority of the whole

Number of Electors appointed; and if there be more than one who have such Majority, and have an equal Number of Votes, then the House of Representatives shall immediately chuse by Ballot one of them for President; and if no Person have a Majority, then from the five highest on the List the said House shall in like Manner chuse the President. But in chusing the President, the Votes shall be taken by States, the Representation from each State having one Vote; A quorum for this purpose shall consist of a Member or Members from two thirds of the States, and a Majority of all the States shall be necessary to a Choice. In every Case, after the Choice of the President, the Person having the greatest Number of Votes of the Electors shall be the Vice President. But if there should remain two or more who have equal Votes, the Senate shall chuse from them by Ballot the Vice President. (This clause was superseded by the Twelfth Amendment.)]

The Congress may determine the Time of chusing the Electors, and the Day on which they shall give their Votes; which Day shall be the same throughout the United States.

No Person except a natural born Citizen, or a Citizen of the United States, at the time of the Adoption of this Constitution, shall be eligible to the Office of President; neither shall any Person be eligible to that Office who shall not have attained to the Age of thirty five Years, and been fourteen Years a Resident within the United States.

[In Case of the Removal of the President from Office, or of his Death, Resignation, or Inability to discharge the Powers and Duties of the said Office, the Same shall devolve on the Vice President, and the Congress may by Law provide for the Case of Removal, Death, Resignation or Inability, both of the President and Vice President, declaring what Officer shall then act as President, and such Officer shall act accordingly, until the Disability be removed, or a President shall be elected. (This clause was modified by the Twenty-Fifth Amendment.)]

The President shall, at stated Times, receive for his Services, a Compensation, which shall neither be increased nor diminished during the Period for which he shall have been elected, and he shall not receive within that Period any other Emolument from the United States, or any of them.

Before he enter on the Execution of his Office, he shall take the following Oath or Affirmation:-"I do solemnly swear (or affirm) that I will faithfully execute the Office of President of the United States, and will to the best of my Ability, preserve, protect and defend the Constitution of the United States."

Section 2.   The President shall be Commander in Chief of the Army and Navy of the United States, and of the Militia of the several States, when called into the actual Service of the United States; he may require the Opinion, in writing, of the principal Officer in each of the executive Departments, upon any Subject relating to the Duties of their respective Offices, and he shall have Power to grant Reprieves and Pardons for Offences against the United States, except in Cases of Impeachment.

He shall have Power, by and with the Advice and Consent of the Senate, to make Treaties, provided two thirds of the Senators present concur; and he shall nominate, and by and with the Advice and Consent of the Senate, shall appoint Ambassadors, other public Ministers and Consuls, judges of the supreme Court, and all other Officers of the United States, whose Appointments are not herein otherwise provided for, and which shall be established by Law: but the Congress may by Law vest the Appointment of such inferior Officers, as they think proper, in the President alone, in the Courts of Law, or in the Heads of Departments.

The President shall have Power to fill up all Vacancies that may happen during the Recess of the Senate, by granting Commissions which shall expire at the End of their next Session.

Section 3.   He shall from time to time give to the Congress Information of the State of the Union, and recommend to their Consideration such Measures as he shall judge necessary and expedient; he may, on extraordinary Occasions, convene both Houses, or either of them, and in Case of Disagreement between them, with Respect to the Time of Adjournment, he may adjourn them to such Time as he shall think proper; he shall receive Ambassadors and other public Ministers; he shall take Care that the Laws be faithfully executed, and shall Commission all the Officers of the United States.

Section 4.   The President, Vice President and all civil Officers of the United States, shall be removed from Office on Impeachment for, and Conviction of, Treason, Bribery, or other high Crimes and Misdemeanors.

ARTICLE III

Section 1.   The judicial Power of the United States, shall be vested in one supreme Court, and in such inferior Courts as the Congress may from time to time ordain and establish. The judges, both of the supreme and inferior Courts, shall hold their Offices during good Behaviour, and shall, at stated Times receive for their Services, a Compensation, which shall not be diminished during their Continuance in Office.

Section 2.   The judicial Power shall extend to all Cases, in Law and Equity, arising under this Constitution, the Laws of the United States, and Treaties made, or which shall be made, under their Authority; to all Cases affecting Ambassadors, other public Ministers and Consuls; to all Cases of admiralty and maritime jurisdiction; to Controversies to which the United States shall be a Party; to Controversies between two or more States; between a State and Citizens of another State; between Citizens of different States, between Citizens of the same State claiming Lands under Grants of different States, and between a State, or the Citizens thereof, and foreign States, Citizens or Subjects.

In all Cases affecting Ambassadors, other public Ministers and Consuls, and those in which a State shall be Party, the supreme Court shall have original jurisdiction. In all the other Cases before mentioned, the supreme Court shall have appellate jurisdiction, both as to Law and Fact, with such Exceptions, and under such Regulations as the Congress shall make.

The Trial of all Crimes, except in Cases of Impeachment, shall be by jury; and such Trial shall be held in the State where the said Crimes shall have been committed; but when not committed within any State, the Trial shall be at such Place or Places as the Congress may by Law have directed.

Section 3.   Treason against the United States, shall consist only in levying War against them, or in adhering to their Enemies, giving them Aid and Comfort. No Person shall be convicted of Treason unless on the Testimony of two Witnesses to the same overt Act, or on Confession in open Court.

The Congress shall have Power to declare the Punishment of Treason, but no Attainder of Treason shall work Corruption of Blood, or Forfeiture except during the Life of the Person attainted.

ARTICLE IV

Section 1.   Full Faith and Credit shall be given in each State to the public Acts, Records, and judicial Proceedings of every other State; And the Congress may by general Laws prescribe the Man-ner in which such Acts, Records and Proceedings shall be proved, and the Effect thereof.

Section 2.   The Citizens of each State shall be entitled to all Privileges and Immunities of Citizens in the several States.

A Person charged in any State with Treason, Felony, or other Crime, who shall flee from justice, and be found in another State, shall on Demand of the executive Authority of the State from which he fled, be delivered up, to be removed to the State having jurisdiction of the Crime.

[No Person held to Service or Labour in one State, under the Laws thereof, escaping into another, shall, in Consequence of any Law or Regulation therein, be discharged from such Service or Labour, but shall be delivered up on Claim of the Party to whom such Service or Labour may be due. (This clause was superseded by the Thirteenth Amendment.)]

Section 3.   New States may be admitted by the Congress into this Union; but no new State shall be formed or erected within the jurisdiction of any other State; nor any State be formed by the junction of two or more States, or Parts of States, without the Consent of the Legislatures of the States concerned as well as of the Congress.

The Congress shall have Power to dispose of and make all need-ful Rules and Regulations respecting the Territory or other Property belonging to the United States; and nothing in this Constitution shall be so construed as to Prejudice any Claims of the United States, or of any particular State.

Section 4.   The United States shall guarantee to every State in this Union a Republican Form of Government, and shall protect each of them against Invasion; and on Application of the Legislature, or of the Executive (when the Legislature cannot be convened) against domestic Violence.

ARTICLE V

The Congress, whenever two thirds of both Houses shall deem it necessary, shall propose Amendments to this Constitution, or, on the Application of the Legislatures of two thirds of the several States, shall call a Convention for proposing Amendments, which, in either Case, shall be valid to all Intents and Purposes, as Part of this Constitution, when ratified by the legislatures of three fourths of the several States, or by Conventions in three fourths thereof, as the one or the other Mode of Ratification may be proposed by the Congress; Provided that no Amendment which may be made prior to the Year One thousand eight hundred and eight shall in any Manner affect the first and fourth Clauses in the Ninth Section of the first Article; and that no State, without its Consent, shall be deprived of its equal Suffrage in the Senate.

ARTICLE VI

All Debts contracted and Engagements entered into, before the Adoption of this Constitution, shall be as valid against the United States under this Constitution, as under the Confederation.

This Constitution, and the Laws of the United States which shall be made in Pursuance thereof; and all Treaties made, or which shall be made, under the Authority of the United States, shall be the supreme Law of the Land; and the judges in every State shall be bound thereby, any Thing in the Constitution or Laws of any State to the Contrary notwithstanding.

The Senators and Representatives before mentioned, and the Members of the several State Legislatures, and all executive and judicial Officers, both of the United States and of the several States, shall be bound by Oath or Affirmation, to support this Constitution; but no religious Test shall ever be required as a Qualification to any Office or public Trust under the United States.

ARTICLE VII

The Ratification of the Conventions of nine States, shall be sufficient for the Establishment of this Constitution between the States so ratifying the Same.

DONE in Convention by the Unanimous Consent of the States present the Seventeenth Day of September in the Year of our Lord one thousand seven hundred and Eighty seven and of the Independance of the United States of America the Twelfth.

IN WITNESS whereof We have hereunto subscribed our Names.

The first ten amendments (the Bill of Rights) were ratified December 15, 1791.

AMENDMENT I

Congress shall make no law respecting an establishment of re-ligion, or prohibiting the free exercise thereof; or abridging the freedom of speech, or of the press, or the right of the people peaceably to assemble, and to petition the Government for a re-dress of grievances.

AMENDMENT II

A well regulated Militia, being necessary to the security of a free State, the right of the people to keep and bear Arms, shall not be infringed.

AMENDMENT III

No Soldier shall, in time of peace be quartered in any house, without the consent of the Owner, nor in time of war, but in a manner to be prescribed by law.

AMENDMENT IV

The right of the people to be secure in their persons, houses, papers, and effects, against unreasonable searches and seizures, shall not be violated, and no Warrants shall issue, but upon prob-able cause, supported by Oath or affirmation, and particularly describing the place to be searched, and the persons or things to be seized.

AMENDMENT V

No person shall be held to answer for a capital, or otherwise infamous crime, unless on a presentment or indictment of a Grand jury, except in cases arising in the land or naval forces, or in the Militia, when in actual service in time of War or public danger; nor shall any person be subject for the same offence to be twice put in jeopardy of life or limb, nor shall be compelled in any criminal case to be a witness against himself, nor be de-prived of life, liberty, or property, without due process of law; nor shall private property be taken for public use, without just compensation.

AMENDMENT VI

In all criminal prosecutions, the accused shall enjoy the right to a speedy and public trial, by an impartial jury of the State and district wherein the crime shall have been committed; which dis-trict shall have been previously ascertained by law, and to be in-formed of the nature and cause of the accusation; to be confronted with the witnesses against him; to have compulsory process for obtaining Witnesses in his favor, and to have the as-sistance of counsel for his defence.

AMENDMENT VII

In Suits at common law, where the value in controversy shall exceed twenty dollars, the right of trial by jury shall be preserved, and no fact tried by a jury, shall be otherwise reex-amined in any Court of the United States, than according to the rules of the common law.

AMENDMENT VIII

Excessive bail shall not be required, nor excessive fines im-posed, nor cruel and unusual punishments inflicted.

AMENDMENT IX

The enumeration in the Constitution, of certain rights, shall not be construed to deny or disparage others retained by the people.

AMENDMENT X

The powers not delegated to the United States by the Constitution, nor prohibited by it to the States, are reserved to the States respectively, or to the people.

AMENDMENT XI (Ratified February 7, 1795)

The judicial power of the United States shall not be construed to extend to any suit in law or equity, commenced or prosecuted against one of the United States by Citizens of another State, or by Citizens or Subjects of any Foreign State.

AMENDMENT XII (Ratified June 15, 1804)

The Electors shall meet in their respective states, and vote by ballot for President and Vice President, one of whom, at least, shall not be an inhabitant of the same state with themselves; they shall name in their ballots the person voted for as President, and in distinct ballots the person voted for as Vice President, and they shall make distinct lists of all persons voted for as President, and of all persons voted for as Vice President, and of the number of votes for each, which lists they shall sign and certify, and transmit sealed to the seat of the government of the United States, directed to the President of the Senate;-The President of the Senate shall, in the presence of the Senate and House of Representatives, open all the certificates and the votes shall then be counted;-The person having the greatest number of votes for President, shall be the President, if such number be a majority of the whole number of Electors appointed; and if no person have such majority, then from the persons having the highest numbers not exceeding three on the list of those voted for as President, the House of Representatives shall choose immediately, by ballot, the President. But in choosing the President, the votes shall be taken by states, the representation from each state having one vote; a quorum for this purpose shall consist of a member or members from two-thirds of the states, and a majority of all the states shall be necessary to a choice. [And if the House of Representatives shall not choose a President whenever the right of choice shall devolve upon them, before the fourth day of March next following, then the Vice-President shall act as President, as in the case of the death or other constitutional disability of the President(This clause was superseded by section 3 of the Twentieth Amendment.)]. The person having the greatest number of votes as Vice-President, shall be the Vice-President, if such number be a majority of the whole number of Electors appointed, and if no person have a majority, then from the two highest numbers on the list, the Senate shall choose the Vice-President; a quorum for the purpose shall consist of two-thirds of the whole number of Senators, and a majority of the whole number shall be necessary to a choice. But no person constitutionally ineligible to the office of President shall be eligible to that of Vice President of the United States.

AMENDMENT XIII (Ratified December 6, 1865)

Section 1.　Neither slavery nor involuntary servitude, except as a punishment for crime whereof the parry shall have been duly convicted, shall exist within the United States, or any place subject to their jurisdiction.

Section 2.　Congress shall have power to enforce this article by appropriate legislation.

AMENDMENT XIV (Ratified July 9, 1868)

Section 1.　All persons born or naturalized in the United States, and subject to the jurisdiction thereof, are citizens of the United States and of the State wherein they reside. No State shall make or enforce any law which shall abridge the privileges or immunities of citizens of the United States; nor shall any State deprive any person of life, liberty, or property, without due process of law; nor deny to any person within its jurisdiction the equal protection of the laws.

Section 2.　Representatives shall be apportioned among the several States according to their respective numbers, counting the whole number of persons in each State, excluding Indians not taxed. But when the right to vote at any election for the choice of electors for President and Vice President of the United States, Representatives in Congress, the Executive and judicial officers of a State, or the members of the Legislature thereof, is denied to any of the male inhabitants of such State, being twenty-one years of age, and citizens of the United States, or in any way abridged, except for participation in rebellion, or other crime, the basis of representation therein shall be reduced in the proportion which the number of such male citizens shall bear to the whole number of male citizens twenty-one years of age in such State.

Section 3.　No person shall be a Senator or Representative in Congress, or elector of President and Vice President, or hold any office, civil or military, under the United States, or under any State, who, having previously taken an oath, as a member of Congress, or as an officer of the United States, or as a member of any State legislature, or as an executive or judicial officer of any State, to support the Constitution of the United States, shall have engaged in insurrection or rebellion against the same, or given aid or comfort to the enemies thereof. But Congress may by a vote of two-thirds of each House, remove such disability.

Section 4.　The validity of the public debt of the United States, authorized by law, including debts incurred for payment of pensions and bounties for services in suppressing insurrection or rebellion, shall not be questioned. But neither the United States nor any State shall assume or pay any debt or obligation incurred in aid of insurrection or rebellion against the United States, or any claim for the loss of emancipation of any slave; but all such debts, obligations and claims shall be held illegal and void.

Section 5.   The Congress shall have power to enforce, by appropriate legislation, the provisions of this article.

AMENDMENT XV (Ratified February 3, 1870)

Section 1.   The right of citizens of the United States to vote shall not be denied or abridged by the United States or by any State on account of race, color, or previous condition of servitude.

Section 2.   The Congress shall have power to enforce this article by appropriate legislation.

AMENDMENT XVI (Ratified February 3, 1913)

The Congress shall have power to lay and collect taxes on incomes, from whatever source derived, without apportionment among the several States, and without regard to any census or enumeration.

AMENDMENT XVII (Ratified April 8, 1913)

The Senate of the United States shall be composed of two Senators from each State, elected by the people thereof, for six years; and each Senator shall have one vote. The electors in each State shall have the qualifications requisite for electors of the most numerous branch of the State legislatures.

When vacancies happen in the representation of any State in the Senate, the executive authority of such State shall issue writs of election to fill such vacancies: Provided, That the legislature of any State may empower the executive thereof to make temporary appointments until the people fill the vacancies by election as the legislature may direct.

This amendment shall not be so construed as to affect the election or term of any Senator chosen before it becomes valid as part of the Constitution.

AMENDMENT XVIII (Ratified January 16, 1919.)

Section 1.   After one year from the ratification of this article the manufacture, sale, or transportation of intoxicating liquors within, the importation thereof into, or the exportation thereof from the United States and all territory subject to the jurisdiction thereof for beverage purposes is hereby prohibited.

Section 2.   The Congress and the several States shall have concurrent power to enforce this article by appropriate legislation.

Section 3.   This article shall be inoperative unless it shall have been ratified as an amendment to the Constitution by the legislatures of the several States, as provided in the Constitution, within seven years from the date of the submission hereof to the States by the Congress.

AMENDMENT XIX (Ratified August 18, 1920)

The right of citizens of the United States to vote shall not be denied or abridged by the United States or by any State on account of sex.

Congress shall have power to enforce this article by appropriate legislation.

AMENDMENT XX (Ratified January 23, 1933)

Section 1.   The terms of the President and Vice President shall end at noon on the 20th day of January, and the terms of Senators and Representatives at noon on the 3d day of January, of the years in which such terms would have ended if this article had not been ratified; and the terms of their successors shall then begin.

Section 2.   The Congress shall assemble at least once in every year, and such meeting shall begin at noon on the 3d day of January, unless they shall by law appoint a different day.

Section 3.   If, at the time fixed for the beginning of the term of the President, the President elect shall have died, the Vice President elect shall become President. If a President shall not have been chosen before the time fixed for the beginning of his term, or if the President elect shall have failed to qualify, then the Vice President elect shall act as President until a President shall have qualified; and the Congress may by law provide for the case wherein neither a President elect nor a Vice President elect shall have qualified, declaring who shall then act as President, or the manner in which one who is to act shall be selected, and such person shall act accordingly until a President or Vice President shall have qualified.

Section 4.   The Congress may by law provide for the case of the death of any of the persons from whom the House of Representatives may choose a President whenever the right of choice shall have devolved upon them, and for the case of the death of any of the persons from whom the Senate may choose a Vice President whenever the right of choice shall have devolved upon them.

Section 5.   Sections 1 and 2 shall take effect on the 15th day of October following the ratification of this article.

Section 6.   This article shall be inoperative unless it shall have been ratified as an amendment to the Constitution by the legislatures of three-fourths of the several States within seven years from the date of its submission.

AMENDMENT XXI (Ratified December 3, 1933)

Section 1.   The eighteenth article of amendment to the Constitution of the United States is hereby repealed.

Section 2. The transportation or importation into any State, Territory, or possession of the United States for delivery or use therein of intoxicating liquors, in violation of the laws thereof, is hereby prohibited.

Section 3. This article shall be inoperative unless it shall have been ratified as an amendment to the Constitution by conventions in the several States, as provided in the Constitution, within seven years from the date of the submission hereof to the States by the Congress.

AMENDMENT XXII (Ratified February 27, 1951)

Section 1. No person shall be elected to the office of the President more than twice, and no person who has held the office of President, or acted as President, for more than two years of a term to which some other person was elected President shall be elected to the office of the President more than once. But this Article shall not apply to any person holding the office of President when this Article was proposed by the Congress, and shall not prevent any person who may be holding the office of President, or acting as President, during the term within which this Article becomes operative from holding the office of President or acting as President during the remainder of such term.

Section 2. This article shall be inoperative unless it shall have been ratified as an amendment to the Constitution by the legislatures of three-fourths of the several States within seven years from the date of its submission to the States by the Congress.

AMENDMENT XXIII (Ratified March 29, 1961)

Section 1. The District constituting the seat of Government of the United States shall appoint in such manner as the Congress may direct:

A number of electors of President and Vice President equal to the whole number of Senators and Representatives in Congress to which the District would be entitled if it were a State, but in no event more than the least populous State; they shall be in addition to those appointed by the States, but they shall be considered, for the purposes of the election of President and Vice President, to be electors appointed by a State; and they shall meet in the District and perform such duties as provided by the twelfth article of amendment.

Section 2. The Congress shall have power to enforce this article by appropriate legislation.

AMENDMENT XXIV (Ratified January 23, 1964)

Section 1. The right of citizens of the United States to vote in any primary or other election for President or Vice President, for electors for President or Vice President, or for Senator or Representatives in Congress, shall not be denied or abridged by the United States or any State by reason of failure to pay any poll tax or other tax.

Section 2.   The Congress shall have power to enforce this article by appropriate legislation.

AMENDMENT XXV (Ratified February 10, 1967)

Section 1.   In case of the removal of the President from office or of his death or resignation, the Vice President shall become President.

Section 2.   Whenever there is a vacancy in the office of the Vice President, the President shall nominate a Vice President who shall take office upon confirmation by a majority vote of both Houses of Congress.

Section 3.   Whenever the President transmits to the President pro tempore of the Senate and the Speaker of the House of Representatives his written declaration that he is unable to discharge the powers and duties of his office, and until he transmits to them a written declaration to the contrary, such powers and duties shall be discharged by the Vice President as Acting President.

Section 4.   Whenever the Vice President and a majority of either the principal officers of the executive departments or of such other body as Congress may by law provide, transmit to the President pro tempore of the Senate and the Speaker of the House of Representatives their written declaration that the President is unable to discharge the powers and duties of his office, the Vice President shall immediately assume the powers and duties of the office as Acting President.

Thereafter, when the President transmits to the President pro tempore of the Senate and the Speaker of the House of Representatives his written declaration that no inability exists, he shall resume the powers and duties of his office unless the Vice President and a majority of either the principal officers of the executive department or of such other body as Congress may by law provide, transmit within four days to the President pro tempore of the Senate and the Speaker of the House of Representatives their written declaration that the President is unable to discharge the powers and duties of his office. Thereupon Congress shall decide the issue, assembling within forty-eight hours for that purpose if not in session. If the Congress, within twenty-one days after receipt of the latter written declaration, or, if Congress is not in session, within twenty-one days after Congress is required to assemble, determines by two-thirds vote of both Houses that the President is unable to discharge the powers and duties of his office, the Vice President shall continue to discharge the same as Acting President; otherwise, the President shall resume the powers and duties of his office.

AMENDMENT XXVI (Ratified July 1, 1971)

Section 1.   The right of citizens of the United States, who are eighteen years of age or older, to vote shall not be denied or abridged by the United States or by any State on account of age.

Section 2.   The Congress shall have power to enforce this article by appropriate legislation.

AMENDMENT XXVII (Ratified May 7, 1992)

No law varying the compensation for the services of Senators and Representatives shall take effect until an election of Representatives shall have intervened.

Appendix B *Federalist Paper No. 10*

by James Madison

Read this essay and use it to enhance your knowledge and understanding of Constitutional Foundations (chapter 2), Campaigns and Elections (chapter 7), Interest Groups (chapter 8), and the Congress (chapter 10). You should recognize that the concepts and the arguments presented here reflect the Federalist views. The essay may assist your understanding of these modern day matters.

▲ What is Madison's thesis?

▲ What does he mean by "factions"?

▲ What causes factions?

▲ Are factions good or bad? Why?

▲ Are they inevitable?

▲ Can factions be eliminated?

■ How?

■ How does Madison suggest the "new constitution" will deal with factions and their problems?

▲ How does the reasoning here by Madison balance the principle of majority rule and minority rights?

To the People of the State of New York: Among the numerous advantages promised by a well-constructed union, none deserves to be more accurately developed than its tendency to break and control the violence of faction. The friend of popular governments, never finds himself so much alarmed for their character and fate, as when he contemplates their propensity of this dangerous vice. He will not fail, therefore, to set a due value on any plan which, without violating the principles to which he is attached, provides a proper cure for it. The instability, injustice, and confusion introduced into the public councils, have, in truth, been the mortal diseases under which popular governments have everywhere perished; as they continue to be the favorite and fruitful topics from which the adversaries to liberty derive their most specious declamations. The valuable improvements made by the American constitutions on the popular models, both ancient and modern, cannot certainly be too much admired; but it would be an unwarrantable partiality, to contend that they have as effectually obviated the danger on this side, as was wished and expected. Complaints are everywhere heard from our most considerate and virtuous citizens, equally the friends of public and private faith, and of public and personal liberty that our governments are too unstable; that the public good is disregarded in the conflicts of rival parties; and that measures are too often decided, not according to the rules of justice, and the rights of the minor party but by the superior force of an interested and overbearing majority. However anxiously we may wish that these complaints had no foundation, the evidence of known facts will not permit us to deny that they are in some degree true. It will be found, indeed, on a candid review of our situation, that some of the distresses under which we labor have been erroneously charged on the operations of our governments; but it will be found, at the same time, that other causes will not alone account for many of our heaviest misfortunes; and, particularly, for that prevailing and increasing distrust of public engagements, and alarm for private rights, which are echoed from one end of the continent to the other. These must be chiefly, if not wholly, effects of the unsteadiness and injustice, with which a factious spirit has tainted our public administrations.

By a faction, I understand a number of citizens, whether amounting to a majority of the whole, who are united and actuated by some common impulse of passion, or of interest, adverse to the rights of other citizens, or to the permanent and aggregate interests of the community.

There are two methods of curing the mischiefs of faction: the one, by removing its causes; the other, by controlling its effects.

There are again two methods of removing the causes of faction: the one, by destroying the liberty which is essential to its existence; the other, by giving to every citizen the same opinions, the same passions, and the same interests.

It could never be more truly said, than of the first remedy, that it was worse than the disease. Liberty is to faction what air is to fire, an aliment without which it instantly expires. But it could not be a less folly to abolish liberty which is essential to political life, because it nourishes faction, than it would be to wish the annihilation of air, which is essential to animal life, because it imparts to fire its destructive agency.

The second expedient is as impracticable, as the first would be unwise. As long as the reason of man continues fallible, and he is at liberty to exercise it, different opinions will be formed. As long as the connection subsists between his reason and his self-love, his opinions and his passions will have a reciprocal influence on each other; and the former will be objects to which the latter will attach themselves. The diversity in the faculties of men, from which the rights of property originate, is not less an insuperable obstacle to an uniformity of interests. The protection of these faculties is the first object of government. From the protection of different and unequal faculties of acquiring property, the possession of different degrees and kinds of property immediately results; and from the influence of these on the sentiments and views of the respective proprietors, ensues a division of the society into different interests and parties.

The latent causes of faction are thus sown in the nature of man; and we see them everywhere brought into different degrees of activity according to the different circumstances of civil society. A zeal for different opinions concerning religion, concerning government, and many other points, as well of speculation as of practice; an attachment to different leaders ambitiously contending for preeminence and power; or to persons of other descriptions whose fortunes have been interesting to the human passions, have, in turn, divided mankind into parties, inflamed them with mutual animosity, and rendered them much more disposed to vex and oppress each other, than to cooperate for their common good. So strong is this propensity of mankind, to fall into mutual animosities, that where no substantial occasion presents itself, the most frivolous and fanciful distinctions have been sufficient to kindle their unfriendly passions and excite their most violent conflicts. But the most common and durable source of factions, has been the various and unequal distribution of property. Those who hold, and those who are without property, have ever formed distinct interests in society. Those who are creditors, and those who are debtors, fall under a like discrimination. A landed interest, a manufacturing interest, a mercantile interest, a moneyed interest, with many lesser interests, grow up of necessity in civilized nations, and divide them into different classes, actuated by different sentiments and views. The regulation of these various and interfering interests forms the principal task of modern legislation, and involves the spirit of the party and faction in the necessary and ordinary operations of the government.

No man is allowed to be a judge in his own cause; because his interest will certainly bias his judgment, and, not improbably, corrupt his integrity. With equal, nay, with greater reason, a body of men are unfit to be both judges and parties at the same time; yet what are many of the most important acts of legislation, but so many judicial determinations, not indeed concerning the right of single persons, but concerning the rights of large bodies of citizens? And what are the different classes of legislators, but advocates and parties to the causes which they determine? Is a law proposed concerning private debts? It is a question to which the creditors are parties on one side, and the debtors on the other. Justice ought to hold the balance between them. Yet the parties are, and must be, themselves the judges; and the most numerous party, or, in other words, the most powerful faction, must be expected to prevail. Shall domestic manufacturers be encouraged, and in what degree, by restrictions on foreign manufacturers? Are questions which would be differently decided by the landed and the manufacturing classes; and probably by neither with a sole regard to justice and the public good. The apportionment of taxes, on the various descriptions of property, is an act which seems to require the most exact impartiality; yet there is, perhaps, no legislative act, in which greater opportunity and temptation are given to a predominant party to trample on the rules of justice. Every shilling, with which they overburden the inferior number, is a shilling saved to their own pockets.

It is in vain to say, that enlightened statesmen will be able to adjust these clashing interests, and render them all subservient to the public good. Enlightened statesmen will not always be at the helm, nor, in many cases, can such an adjustment be made at all, without taking into view indirect and remote considerations, which will rarely prevail over the immediate interest which one party may find in disregarding the rights of another, or the good of the whole.

The inference to which we are brought is, that the causes of faction cannot be removed; and that relief is only to be sought in the means of controlling its effects.

If a faction consists of less than a majority, relief is supplied by the republican principle, which enables the majority to defeat its sinister views, by regular vote. It may clog the administration, it may convulse the society; but it will be unable to execute and mask its violence under the forms of the Constitution. When a majority is included in a faction, the form of popular government, on the other hand, enables it to sacrifice to its ruling passion or interest, both the public good and the rights of other citizens. To secure the public good, and private rights, against the danger of such a faction, and at the same time to preserve the spirit and the form of popular government, is then the great object to which our inquiries are directed. Let me add, that it is the great desideratum, by which alone this form of government can be rescued from the opprobrium under which it has so long laboured, and be recommended to the esteem and adoption of mankind.

By what means is this object attainable? Evidently by one of two only. Either the existence of the same passion or interest in a majority, at the same time, must be prevented; or the majority, having such coexistent passion or interest, must be rendered, by their number and local situation, unable to concert and carry into effect schemes of oppression. If the impulse and the opportunity be suffered to coincide, we well know that neither moral nor religious motives can be relied on as an adequate control. They are not found to be such on the injustice and violence of individuals, and lose their efficacy in proportion to the number combined together; that is, in proportion as their efficacy becomes needful.

From this view of the subject, it may be concluded, that a pure democracy, by which I mean a society consisting of a small number of citizens, who assemble and administer the government in person, can admit of no cure for the mischiefs of faction. A common passion or interest will, in almost every case, be felt by a majority of the whole; a communication and concert, results from the form of government itself; and there is nothing to check the inducements to sacrifice the weaker party, or an obnoxious individual. Hence, it is, that such democracies have ever been spectacles of turbulence and contention; have ever been found incompatible with personal security, or the rights of property; and have in general been as short in their lives, as they have been violent in their deaths. Theoretic politicians, who have patronized this species of government, have erroneously supposed, that by reducing mankind to a perfect equality in their political rights, they would, at the same time be perfectly equalized and assimilated in their possessions, their opinions, and their passions.

A republic, by which I mean a government in which the scheme of representation takes place, opens a different prospect, and promises the cure for which we are seeking. Let us examine the points in which it varies from pure democracy, and we shall comprehend both the nature of the cure and the efficacy which it must derive from the union.

The two great points of difference, between a democracy and a republic, are, first, the delegation of the government, in the latter, to a small number of citizens, elected by the rest; secondly, the greater number of citizens, and greater sphere of country, over which the latter may be extended.

The effect of the first difference is, on the one hand, to refine and enlarge the public views, by passing them through the medium of a chosen body of citizens, whose wisdom may best discern the true interest of their country, and whose patriotism and love of justice, will be least likely to sacrifice it to temporary or partial considerations. Under such a regulation, it may well happen, that the public voice, pronounced by the representatives of the people, will be more consonant to the public good, than if pronounced by the people themselves, convened for the purpose. On the other hand the effect may be inverted. Men of factious tempers, of local prejudices, or of sinister designs, may by intrigue, by corruption, or by other means, first obtain the suffrages, and then betray the interest of the people. The question resulting is, whether small or extensive republics are most favourable to the election of proper guardians of the public weal; and it is clearly decided in favour of the latter by two obvious considerations.

In the first place, it is to be remarked that, however small the republic may be, the representatives must be raised to a certain number, in order to guard against the cabals of a few; and that however large it may be, they must be limited to a certain number, in order to guard against the confusion of a multitude. Hence, the number of representatives in the two cases not being in proportion to that of the constituents, and being proportionally greatest in the small republic, it follows, that if the proportion of fit characters be not less in the large than in the small republic, the former will present a greater option, and consequently a greater probability of a fit choice.

In the next place, as each representative will be chosen by a greater number of citizens in the large than in the small republic, it will be more difficult for unworthy candidates to practice with success the vicious arts, by which elections are too often carried; and the suffrages of the people being more free, will be more likely to centre in men who possess the most attractive merit, and the most diffusive and established characters.

It must be confessed, that in this, as in most other cases, there is a mean, on both sides of which inconveniences will be found to lie. By enlarging too much the number of electors, you render the representatives too little acquainted with all their local circumstances and lesser interests; as by reducing it too much, you render him unduly attached to these, and too little fit to comprehend and pursue great and national objects. The federal constitution forms a happy combination in this respect; the great and aggregate interests being referred to the national, the local and particular to the state legislatures.

The other point of difference is, the greater number of citizens, and extent of territory, which may be brought within the compass of republican, than of democratic government; and it is this circumstance principally which renders factious combinations less to be dreaded in the former, than in the latter. The smaller the society, the fewer probably will be the distinct parties and interests composing it; the fewer the distinct parties and interests, the more frequently will a majority be found of the same party; and the smaller the number of individuals composing a majority, and the smaller the compass within which they are placed, the more easily will they concert and execute their plans of oppression. Extend the sphere, and you take in a greater variety of parties and interests; you make it less probable that a majority of the whole will have a common motive to invade the rights of other citizens; or if such a common motive exists, it will be more difficult for all who feel it to discover their own strength, and to act in unison with each other. Besides other impediments, it may be remarked, that where there is a consciousness of unjust or dishonourable purposes, communication is always checked by distrust, in proportion to the number whose concurrence is necessary.

Hence, it clearly appears, that the same advantage, which a republic has over a democracy, in controlling the effects of faction, is enjoyed by a large over a small republic – enjoyed by the union over the states composing it. Does this advantage consist in the substitution of representatives, whose enlightened views and virtuous sentiments render them superior to local prejudices, and to schemes of injustice? It will not be denied that the representation of the union will be most likely to possess these requisite endowments. Does it consist in the greater security afforded by a greater variety of parties, against the event of any one party being able to outnumber and oppress the rest? In an equal degree does the increased variety of parties, comprised within the union, increase the security? Does it, in fine, consist in the greater obstacles opposed to the concert and accomplishment of the secret wishes of an unjust and interested majority? Here, again, the extent of the union gives it the most palpable advantage.

The influence of factious leaders may kindle a flame within their particular states, but will be unable to spread a general conflagration through the other states; a religious sect may, degenerate into a political faction in a part of the confederacy ; but the variety of sects dispersed over the entire face of it, must secure the national councils against any, danger from that source: a rage for paper money, for an abolition of debts, for an equal division of property, or for any other improper or wicked project, will be less apt to pervade the whole body of the union than a particular member of it; in the same proportion as such a malady is more likely to taint a particular county or district. than an entire state.

In the extent and proper structure of the union, therefore, we behold a republican remedy for the diseases most incident to republican government. And according to the degree of pleasure and pride we feel in being republicans, ought to be our zeal in cherishing the spirit, and supporting the character of federalists.

Appendix C   *Federalist Paper No. 51*

by James Madison

This Federalist essay should be read in conjunction with the chapter on the Constitution (chapter 2), Federalism (chapter 3), and the chapters on the institutions of Government (chapters 10, 11, 12, and 13).

▲ What is the particular "evil" that Madison deals with in this Paper?

▲ What does Madison say about the selection process of government officials?

▲ What does Madison believe is the most important fundamental, constitutional arrangement of the government that will protect against this evil?

▲ How does Madison differentiate between federalism and the separation of powers?

- Do they have the same or different constitutional purposes?

- Does Madison consider one more important than the other?

▲ What does Madison add here to the debate about majority rule and minority rights?

To what expedient, then, shall we finally resort, for maintaining in practice the necessary partition of power among the several departments as laid down in the Constitution? The only answer that can be given is that as all these exterior provisions are found to be inadequate the defect must be supplied, by so contriving the interior structure of the government as that its several constituent parts may, by their mutual relations, be the means of keeping each other in their proper places. Without presuming to undertake a full development of this important idea I will hazard a few general observations which may perhaps place it in a clearer light, and enable us to form a more correct judgment of the principles and structure of the government planned by the convention.

In order to lay a due foundation for that separate and distinct exercise of the different powers of government, which to a certain extent is admitted on all hands to be essential to the preservation of liberty, it is evident that each department should have a will of its own; and consequently should be so constituted that the members of each should have as little agency as possible in the appointment of the members of the others. Were this principle rigorously adhered to, it would require that all the appointments for the supreme executive, legislative, and judiciary magistracies should be drawn from the same fountain of authority, the people, through channels having no communication whatever with one another. Perhaps such a plan of constructing the several departments would be less difficult in practice than it may in contemplation appear. Some difficulties, however, and some additional expense would attend the execution of it. Some deviations, therefore, from the principle must be admitted. In the constitution of the judiciary department in particular, it might be inexpedient to insist rigorously on the principle: first, because peculiar qualifications being essential in the members, the primary consideration ought to be to select that mode of choice which best secures these qualifications; second, because the permanent tenure by which the appointments are held in that department must soon destroy all sense of dependence on the authority conferring them.

It is equally evident that the members of each department should be as little dependent as possible on those of the others for the emoluments annexed to their offices. Were the executive magistrate, or the judges, not independent of the legislature in this particular, their independence in every other would be merely nominal.

But the great security against a gradual concentration of the several powers in the same department consists in giving to those who administer each department the necessary constitutional means and personal motives to resist encroachments of the others. The provision for defense must in this, as in all other cases, be made commensurate to the danger of attack. Ambition must be made to counteract ambition. The interest of the man must be connected with the constitutional rights of the place. It may be a reflection on human nature that such devices should be necessary to control the abuses of government. But what is government itself but the greatest of all reflections on human nature? If men were angels, no government would be necessary. If angels were to govern men, neither external nor internal controls on government would be necessary. In framing a government which is to be administered by men over men, the great difficulty lies in this: you must first enable the government to control the governed; and in the next place oblige it to control itself. A dependence on the people is, no doubt, the primary control on the government; but experience has taught mankind the necessity of auxiliary precautions.

This policy of supplying, by opposite and rival interests, the defect of better motives, might be traced through the whole system of human affairs, private as well as public. We see it particularly displayed in all the subordinate distributions of power, where the constant aim is to divide and arrange the several offices in such a manner as that each may be a check on the other – that the private interest of every individual may be a sentinel over the public rights. These inventions of prudence cannot be less requisite in the distribution of the supreme powers of the State.

But it is not possible to give to each department an equal power of self-defense. In republican government, the legislative authority necessarily predominates. The remedy for this inconveniency is to divide the legislature into different branches; and to render them, by modes of election and different principles of action, as little connected with each other as the nature of their common functions and their common dependence on the society will admit. It may even be necessary to guard against dangerous encroachments by still further precautions. As the weight of the legislative authority requires that it should be thus divided, the weakness of the executive may require, on the other hand, that it should be fortified. An absolute negative on the legislature appears, at first view, to be the natural defense with which the executive magistrate should be armed. But perhaps it would be neither altogether safe nor alone sufficient. On ordinary occasions it might not be exerted with the requisite firmness, and on extraordinary occasions it might be perfidiously abused. May not this defect of an absolute negative be supplied by some qualified connection between this weaker department and the weaker branch of the stronger department, by which the latter may be led to support the constitutional rights of the former, without being too much detached from the rights of its own department?

If the principles on which these observations are founded be just, as I persuade myself they are, and they be applied as a criterion to the several State constitutions, and to the federal Constitution, it will be found that if the latter does not perfectly correspond with them, the former are infinitely less able to bear such a test.

There are, moreover, two considerations particularly applicable to the federal system of America, which place that system in a very interesting point of view.

First. In a single republic, all the power surrendered by the people is submitted to the administration of a single government; and the usurpations are guarded against by a division of the government into distinct and separate departments. In the compound republic of America, the power surrendered by the people is first divided between two distinct governments, and then the portion allotted to each subdivided among distinct and separate departments. Hence a double security arises to the rights of the people. The different governments will control each other, at the same time that each will be controlled by itself.

Second. It is of great importance in a republic not only to guard the society against the oppression of its rulers, but to guard one part of the society against the injustice of the other part. Different interests necessarily exist in different classes of citizens. If a majority be united by a common interest, the rights of the minority will be insecure. There are but two methods of providing against this evil: the one by creating a will in the community independent of the majority – that is, of the society itself; the other, by comprehending in the society so many separate descriptions of citizens as will render an unjust combination of a majority of the whole very improbable, if not impracticable. The first method prevails in all governments possessing an hereditary or self-appointed authority. This, at best, is but a precarious security; because a power independent of the society may as well espouse the unjust views of the major as the rightful interests of the minor party, and may possibly be turned against both parties. The second method will be exemplified in the federal republic of the United States. Whilst all authority in it will be derived from and dependent on the society, the society itself will be broken into so many parts, interests and classes of citizens, that the rights of individuals, or of the minority, will be in little danger from interested combinations of the majority. In a free government the security for civil rights must be the same as that for religious rights. It consists in the one case in the multiplicity of interests, and in the other in the multiplicity of sects. The degree of security in both cases will depend on the number of interests and sects; and this may be presumed to depend on the extent of country and number of people comprehended under the same government. This view of the subject must particularly recommend a proper federal system to all the sincere and considerate friends of republican government, since it shows that in exact proportion as the territory of the Union may be formed into more circumscribed Confederacies, or States, oppressive combinations of a majority will be facilitated; the best security, under the republican forms, for the rights of every class of citizen, will be diminished; and consequently the stability and independence of some member of the government, the only other security, must be proportionally increased. justice is the end of government. It is the end of civil society. It ever has been and ever will be pursued until it be obtained, or until liberty be lost in the pursuit. In a society under the forms of which the stronger faction can readily unite and oppress the weaker, anarchy may as truly be said to reign as in a state of nature, where the weaker individual is not secured against the violence of the stronger; and as, in the latter state, even the stronger individuals are prompted, by the uncertainty of their condition, to submit to a government which may protect the weak as well as themselves; so, in the former state, will the more powerful factions or parties be gradually induced, by a like motive, to wish for a government which will protect all parties, the weaker as well as the more powerful. It can be little doubted that if the State of Rhode Island was separated from the Confederacy and left to itself, the insecurity of rights under the popular form of government within such narrow limits would be displayed by such reiterated oppressions of factious majorities that some power altogether independent of the people would soon be called for by the voice of the very factions whose misrule had proved the necessity to it. In the extended republic of the United States, and among the great variety of interests, parties, and sects which it embraces, a coalition of a majority of the whole society could seldom take place on any other principles than those of justice and the general good; whilst there being thus less danger to a minor from the will of a major party, there must be less pretext, also, to provide for the security of the former, by introducing into the government a will not dependent on the latter, or, in other words, a will independent of the society itself. It is no less certain that it is important, notwithstanding the contrary opinions which have been entertained that the larger the society, provided it lie within a practicable sphere, the more duly capable it will be of self-government. And happily for the republican cause, the practicable sphere may be carried to a very great extent by a judicious modification and mixture of the federal principle.

Appendix D   *Federalist Paper No. 78*

by Alexander Hamilton

Read this essay before exploring the chapters related to the judiciary. That would be chapters 2, 13, 15, and 16.

▲ What institutions of government are discussed in this Federalist Paper?

▲ How does Hamilton characterize this branch of government? In terms of its powers? Its role in the political system?

▲ What reason(s) does Hamilton give for the method of selecting judges in the Constitution?

▲ What does Hamilton "say" about the power of Judicial Review?

▲ What reasons does Hamilton give to support judicial independence (separation) from the legislative branch?

▲ What does Hamilton add to the debate about majority rule and minority rights?

WE PROCEED now to an examination of the judiciary department of the proposed government.

In unfolding the defects of the existing Confederation, the utility and necessity of a federal judicature have been clearly pointed out. It is the less necessary to recapitulate the considerations there urged, as the propriety of the institution in the abstract is not disputed; the only questions which have been raised being relative to the manner of constituting it, and to its extent. To these points, therefore, our observations shall be confined.

The manner of constituting it seems to embrace these several objects: 1st. The mode of appointing the judges. 2d. The tenure by which they are to hold their places. 3d. The partition of the judiciary authority between different courts, and their relations to each other.

First. As to the mode of appointing the judges; this is the same with that of appointing the officers of the Union in general, and has been so fully discussed in the last two numbers, that nothing can be said here which would not be useless repetition.

Second. As to the tenure by which the judges are to hold their places; this chiefly concerns their duration in office; the provisions for their support; the precautions for their responsibility.

According to the plan of the convention, all judges who may be appointed by the United States are to hold their offices during good behavior; which is conformable to the legislative or executive powers, most approved of the State constitutions and among the rest, to that of this State. Its propriety having been drawn into question by the adversaries of that plan, is no light symptom of the rage for objection, which disorders their imaginations and judgments. The standard of good behavior for the continuance in office of the judicial magistracy, is certainly one of the most valuable of the modern improvements in the practice of government. In a monarchy it is an excellent barrier to the despotism of the prince; in a republic it is a no less excellent barrier to the encroachments and oppressions of the representative body. And it is the best expedient which can be devised in any government, to secure a steady, upright, and impartial administration of the laws.

Whoever attentively considers the different departments of power must perceive, that, in a government in which they are separated from each other, the judiciary, from the nature of its functions, will always be the least dangerous to the political rights of the Constitution; because it will be least in a capacity to annoy or injure them. The Executive not only dispenses the honors, but holds the sword of the community. The legislature not only commands the purse, but prescribes the rules by which the duties and rights of every citizen are to be regulated. The judiciary, on the contrary, has no influence over either the sword or the purse; no direction either of the strength or of the wealth of the society; and can take no active resolution whatever. It may truly be said to have neither force nor will, but merely judgment; and must ultimately depend upon the aid of the executive arm even for the efficacy of its judgments.

This simple view of the matter suggests several important consequences. It proves incontestably, that the judiciary is beyond comparison the weakest of the three departments of power; that it can never attack with success either of the other two; and that all possible care is requisite to enable it to defend itself against their attacks. It equally proves, that though individual oppression may now and then proceed from the courts of justice, the general liberty of the people can never be endangered from that quarter; I mean so long as the judiciary remains truly distinct from both the legislature and the Executive. For I agree, that "there is no liberty, if the power of judging is not separated from the legislative and executive powers." And it proves, in the last place, that as liberty can have nothing to fear from the judiciary alone, but would have everything to fear from its union with either of the other departments; that as all the effects of such a union must ensue from a dependence of the former on the latter, notwithstanding a nominal and apparent separation; that as, from the natural feebleness of the judiciary, it is in continual jeopardy of being overpowered, awed, or influenced by its co-ordinate branches; and that as nothing can contribute so much to its firmness and independence as permanency in office, this quality may therefore be justly regarded as an indispensable ingredient in its constitution, and, in a great measure, as the citadel of the public justice and the public security.

The complete independence of the courts of justice is peculiarly essential in a limited Constitution. By a limited Constitution, I understand one which contains certain specified exceptions to the legislative authority; such, for instance, as that it shall pass no bills of attainder, no ex-post-facto laws, and the like. Limitations of this kind can be preserved in practice no other way than through the medium of courts of justice, whose duty it must be to declare all acts contrary to the manifest tenor of the Constitution void. Without this, all the reservations of particular rights or privileges would amount to nothing. Some perplexity respecting the rights of the courts to pronounce legislative acts void, because contrary to the Constitution, has arisen from an imagination that the doctrine would imply a superiority of the judiciary to the legislative power. It is urged that the authority which can declare the acts of another void, must necessarily be superior to the one whose acts may be declared void. As this doctrine is of great importance in all the American constitutions, a brief discussion of the ground on which it rests cannot be unacceptable.

There is no position which depends on clearer principles, than that every act of a delegated authority, contrary to the tenor of the commission under which it is exercised, is void. No legislative act, therefore, contrary to the Constitution, can be valid. To deny this, would be to affirm, that the deputy is greater than his principal; that the servant is above his master; that the representatives of the people are superior to the people themselves; that men acting by virtue of powers, may do not only what their powers do not authorize, but what they forbid.

If it be said that the legislative body are themselves the constitutional judges of their own powers, and that the construction they put upon them is conclusive upon the other departments, it may be answered, that this cannot be the natural presumption, where it is not to be collected from any particular provisions in the Constitution. It is not otherwise to be supposed, that the Constitution could intend to enable the representatives of the people to substitute their will to that of their constituents. It is far more rational to suppose, that the courts were designed to be an intermediate body between the people and the legislature, in order, among other things, to keep the latter within the limits assigned to their authority. The interpretation of the laws is the proper and peculiar province of the courts. A constitution is, in fact, and must be regarded by the judges, as a fundamental law. It therefore belongs to them to ascertain its meaning, as well as the meaning of any particular act proceeding from the legislative body. If there should happen to be an irreconcilable variance between the two, that which has the superior obligation and validity ought, of course, to be preferred; or, in other words, the Constitution ought to be preferred to the statute, the intention of the people to the intention of their agents.

Nor does this conclusion by any means suppose a superiority of the judicial to the legislative power. It only supposes that the power of the people is superior to both; and that where the will of the legislature, declared in its statutes, stands in opposition to that of the people, declared in the Constitution, the judges ought to be governed by the latter rather than the former. They ought to regulate their decisions by the fundamental laws, rather than by those which are not fundamental.

This exercise of judicial discretion, in determining between two contradictory laws, is exemplified in a familiar instance. It not uncommonly happens, that there are two statutes existing at one time, clashing in whole or in part with each other, and neither of them containing any repealing clause or expression. In such a case, it is the province of the courts to liquidate and fix their meaning and operation. So far as they can, by any fair construction, be reconciled to each other, reason and law conspire to dictate that this should be done; where this is impractable, it becomes a matter of necessity to give effect to one, in exclusion of the other. The rule which has obtained in the courts for determining their relative validity is, that the last in order of time shall be preferred to the first. But this is a mere rule of construction, not derived from any positive law, but from the nature and reason of the thing. It is a rule not enjoined upon the courts by legislative provision, but adopted by themselves, as consonant to truth the propriety, for the direction of their conduct as interpreters of the law. They thought it reasonable, that between the interfering acts of an equal authority, that which was the last indication of its will should have the preference.

But in regard to the interfering acts of a superior and subordinate authority, of an original and derivative power, the nature and reason of the thing indicate the converse of that rule as proper to be followed. They teach us that the prior act of a superior ought to be preferred to the subsequent act of an inferior and subordinate authority; and that accordingly, whenever a particular statute contravenes the Constitution, it will be the duty of the judicial tribunals to adhere to the latter and disregard the former.

It can be of no weight to say that the courts, on the pretense of a repugnancy, may substitute their own pleasure to the constitutional intentions of the legislature. This might as well happen in the case of two contradictory statutes; or it might as well happen in every adjudication upon any single statute. The courts must declare the sense of the law; and if they should be disposed to exercise will instead of judgment, the consequence would equally be the substitution of their pleasure to that of the legislative body. The observation, if it prove anything, would prove that there ought to be no judges distinct from that body.

If, then, the courts of justice are to be considered as the bulwarks of a limited Constitution against legislative encroachments, this consideration will afford a strong argument for the permanent tenure of judicial offices, since nothing will contribute so much as this to that independent spirit in the judges which must be essential to the faithful performance of so arduous a duty.

The independence of the judges is equally requisite to guard the Constitution and the rights of individuals from the effects of those ill humors, which the arts of designing men, or the influence of particular conjunctures, sometimes disseminate among the people themselves, and which, though they speedily give place to better information, and more deliberate reflection, have a tendency, in the meantime, to occasion danger-ous innovations in the government, and serious oppressions of the minor party in the community. Though I trust the friends of the proposed Constitution will never concur with its enemies, in questioning that fundamental principle of republican government, which admits the right of the people to alter or abolish the established Constitution, whenever they find it inconsistent with their happiness, yet it is not to be inferred from this principle, that the representatives of the people, whenever a momentary inclination happens to lay hold of a majority of their constituents, incompatible with the provisions of the existing Constitution, would, on that account, be justifiable in a violation of those provisions; or that the courts would be under a greater obligation to connive at infractions in this shape, than when they had proceeded wholly from the cabals of the representative body. Until the people have, by some solemn and authoritative act, annulled or changed the established form, it is binding upon themselves collectively, as well as individually; and no presumption, or even knowledge, of their sentiments, can warrant their representatives in a departure from it, prior to such an act. But it is easy to see, that it would require an uncommon portion of fortitude in the judges to do their duty as faithful guardians of the Constitution, where legislative invasions of it had been instigated by the major voice of the community.

But it is not with a view to infractions of the Constitution only, that the independence of the judges may be an essential safeguard against the effects of occasional ill humors in the society. These sometimes extend no farther than to the injury of the private rights of particular classes of citizens, by unjust and partial laws. Here also the firmness of the judicial magistracy is of vast importance in mitigating the severity and confining the operation of such laws. It not only serves to moderate the immediate mischiefs of those which may have been passed, but it operates as a check upon the legislative body in passing them; who, perceiving that obstacles to the success of iniquitous intention are to be expected from the scruples of the courts, are in a manner compelled, by the very motives of the injustice they meditate, to qualify their attempts. This is a circumstance calculated to have more influence upon the character of our governments, than but few may be aware of. The benefits of the integrity and moderation of the judiciary have already been felt in more States than one; and though they may have displeased those whose sinister expectations they may have disappointed, they must have commanded the esteem and applause of all the virtuous and disinterested. Considerate men, of every description, ought to prize whatever will tend to beget or fortify that temper in the courts; as no man can be sure that he may not be tomorrow the victim of a spirit of injustice, by which he may be a gainer to-day. Any every man must now feel, that the inevitable tendency of such a spirit is to sap the foundations of public and private confidence, and to introduce in its stead universal distrust and distress.

That inflexible and uniform adherence to the rights of the Constitution, and of individuals, which we perceive to be indispensable in the courts of justice, can certainly not be expected from judges who hold their offices by a temporary commission. Periodical appointments, however regulated, or by whomsoever made, would, in some way or other, be fatal to their necessary independence. If the power of making them was committed either to the Executive or legislature, there would be danger of an improper complaisance to the branch which possessed it; if to both, there would be an unwillingness to hazard the displeasure of either; if to the people, or to persons chosen by them for the special purpose, there would be too great a disposition to consult popularity, to justify a reliance that nothing would be consulted but the Constitution and the laws.

There is yet a further and a weightier reason for the permanency of the judicial offices, which is deducible from the nature of the qualifications they require. It has been frequently remarked, with great propriety, that a voluminous code of laws is one of the inconveniences necessarily connected with the advantages of a free government. To avoid an arbitrary discretion in the courts, it is indispensable that they should be bound down by strict rules and precedents, which serve to define and point out their duty in every particular case that comes before them; and it will readily be conceived from the variety of controversies which grow out of the folly and wickedness of mankind, that the records of those precedents must unavoidably swell to a very considerable bulk, and must demand long and laborious study to acquire a competent knowledge of them. Hence it is, that there can be but few men in the society who will have sufficient skill in the laws to qualify them for the stations of judges. And making the proper deductions for the ordinary depravity of human nature, the number must be still smaller of those who unite the requisite integrity with the requisite knowledge. These considerations apprise us, that the government can have no great option between fit character; and that a temporary duration in office, which would naturally discourage such characters from quitting a lucrative line of practice to accept a seat on the bench, would have a tendency to throw the administration of justice into hands less able, and less well qualified, to conduct it with utility and dignity. In the present circumstances of this country, and in those in which it is likely to be for a long time to come, the disadvantages on this score would be greater than they may at first sight appear; but it must be confessed, that they are far inferior to those which present themselves under other aspects of the subject.

Upon the whole, there can be no room to doubt that the convention acted wisely in copying from the models of those constitutions which have established good behavior as the tenure of their judicial offices, in point of duration; and that so far from being blamable on this account, their plan would have been inexcusably defective, if it had wanted this important feature of good government. The experience of Great Britain affords an illustrious comment on the excellence of the institution.